JÜRGEN MOLTMANN

JÜRGEN MOLTMANN

COLLECTED READINGS

MARGARET KOHL, EDITOR

Fortress Press
Minneapolis

JURGEN MOLTMANN
Collected Readings

Unless otherwise noted, scripture quotations are from the New Revised Standard Version Bible, copyright © 1989 by the Division of Christian Education of the National Council of Churches of Christ in the USA, and are used with permission.

Cover design: Tory Herman

Cover image © iStockphoto / Aptyp_koK

Library of Congress Cataloging-in-Publication Data is available

Print ISBN: 978-0-8006-9989-5

The paper used in this publication meets the minimum requirements of American National Standard for Information Sciences—Permanence of Paper for Printed Library Materials, ANSI Z329.48-1984.

Manufactured in the U.S.A.

This book was produced using PressBooks.com, and PDF rendering was done by PrinceXML.

CONTENTS

Introduction

Richard Bauckham

In publications spanning fifty years, Jürgen Moltmann has pursued what he calls an adventure in theological discovery. It all began in prisoner-of-war camps in the late 1940s. As a young German soldier faced with the newly revealed horrors of the Nazi regime, he found God in the gift of unexpected hope and in the companionship of the Christ who suffers with us. Over the years he has written frequently of this deep experiential root of his theology, but when, in the 1960s, his first major book, *Theology of Hope*, became a theological phenomenon (even on the front page of the *New York Times*), what drew so much attention was the way it seemed to chime with the mood of that remarkable decade. In western Europe and North America, it was a time when unlimited possibilities of radical change for the better seemed within reach. But Christian churches focused on individual salvation beyond this world lacked the theological resources for positive engagement with the secular hopes of the time. Moltmann's work sought to restore the full dimensions of Christian hope. Sweeping aside the aversion to future eschatology in the German theological tradition, Moltmann showed how the biblical history of promise projects a new future for this world and its history. Within the horizon of God's coming renewal of God's whole creation there was plenty of room for proximate hopes of social and political transformation, awakened and sustained by ultimate hope. This was a programmatic reorientation of theology that, in a single move, turned the church toward both the future and the world. Of course, it was far from the only way in which Christians worldwide were recovering an impetus to seek transformation in all dimensions of human life, but it would be hard to exaggerate its influence.

I first read *Theology of Hope* when it was still Moltmann's only major work. No doubt I was not immune to the optimistic mood of the time, but what impressed and excited me was that Moltmann was not giving theological support to some general notion of hope, still less to optimism. The center of his theology was (and has always remained) the biblical history of Jesus Christ, crucified and risen. Against the background of the Old Testament history of God's promises, Moltmann read the history of Jesus as messianic history, full of promise for the all-embracing kingdom of God. Christian eschatology speaks

1

of Jesus Christ and his future, which is the world's future only because it is first of all the future of the world's Messiah. This not only inspires Christians to join with others in pursuing present possibilities of change that correspond to the coming kingdom. It also gives Christian hope a critical potential, especially when it is remembered that the resurrection gave new life to the *crucified* Christ, the one who in his abandoned death was identified with the most wretched and the most hopeless. Christian hope has nothing in common with the complacent optimism of the successful. Solidarity with the victims—including the victims of "progress"—alone gives it Christian authenticity. While those who saw in *Theology of Hope* little more than a theological gloss on the progressivist optimism of the modern age were surprised, even shocked, by the turn Moltmann's theology took in his next major book; those attuned to the christological heart of his early work were somewhat less taken off-guard. Whereas *Theology of Hope* found God-given hope in the resurrection of the crucified Christ, *The Crucified God* found the suffering love of God in the cross of the risen Christ. A dialectic of cross and resurrection was at work in both.

There is continuity and coherence between the two books, but not even Moltmann had anticipated where he would be led by his attempt to retrieve the "profane horror and godlessness" of the cross from interpretations that disguise its offensiveness. It required a "revolution" in the concept of God that then took a good part of several more books to be developed fully. In effect, Moltmann put Jesus' dying cry, "My God, my God, why have you abandoned me," at the center of his understanding of God. Taking this cry seriously requires both that God must be understood to suffer, with consequences for the traditional understanding of divine impassibility, and also that the cross as an event of divine suffering be understood as anevent "between God and God," a trinitarian event. At the cross, Jesus, the divine Son incarnate, identified with the world in all its godlessness and godforsakenness so as to take it within the love between the Son and the Father. In their love for the world, the Father abandoned his Son to death, suffering his loss, and the Son voluntarily suffered abandonment by his Father. Their mutual love, the Holy Spirit, united them at this point of agonizing separation, such that the whole of the world's pain was taken up into a trinitarian history in hope of the overcoming of all evil. This was "revolutionary" because it made the cross an event internal to God's own trinitarian relationships and an event that affects not only the world, but also God. From this beginning, Moltmann was to develop a trinitarian understanding of the world in God and God in the world.

Theology of Hope and *The Crucified God* are undoubtedly classics of twentieth-century theology. One could approach them by locating them in the history of German theology. Moltmann was one of several theologians who in the 1960s took up the theme of eschatological hope as a way of opening up theology to the world and the future. *The Crucified God* was one of the first books to take up the task of Christian theology "after Auschwitz"—that is, in the light of what the Holocaust has made theologically unthinkable. Moltmann's radical probing of the meaning of the cross for our understanding of God has much in common with the work of his Tübingen colleague Eberhard Jüngel, while the trinitarian theologies of both belong to a wider renaissance of trinitarian theology in the later part of the twentieth century. Yet classics are classics because they transcend their own time. If these two books seem less remarkable now than they did in their time, it is precisely because of the huge influence they have had. Yet such is the passion and the vigor of their argument, that new readers continue to find them profoundly inspiring in ways which are certainly not available through merely secondhand acquaintance.

Theology of Hope and *The Crucified God* were programmatic works or, one might say, "orienting" works, which serve to give to the whole of theology a particular kind of orientation. Eschatological hope has remained a decisive characteristic of all of Moltmann's theology and the cross has remained for him a decisive criterion of an adequately Christian theology. *The Church in the Power of the Spirit* completed this early trilogy, and performs a similar role, not so much through its understanding of the church as through its development of *The Crucified God*'s rather rudimentary account of the Spirit, making more fully viable the notion of a trinitarian history of God with the world. Then Moltmann's work took a new turn. He embarked on what became a series of seven planned volumes, five on classic Christian doctrines (Trinity, creation, Christology, pneumatology, eschatology), one on theological method (*Experiences in Theology*, not represented in this volume), and one on theological ethics. They have something like the traditional shape of a dogmatics or systematic theology, but he preferred to call them "contributions to theology," characteristically stressing their open and dialogical character as one theologian's contribution to the ongoing task. Early in his career, Moltmann had thought Karl Barth's achievement was something that left nothing more to be said, and he had not been able to write creative theology until he saw that Barth's treatment of future eschatology was seriously reductive. In his own work, he has no ambition to say the last word.

Moreover, while his early works created a fundamental structure of thought that has supported all his later work, Moltmann's thinking has proved constantly able to integrate new insights and to develop in fresh directions. Throughout his career, he has traveled frequently and extensively, and wherever he goes he has attempted to engage with the churches, the theology, and the politics. As a result, it would be hard to think of a theologian whose work has benefited from such a wide and diverse range of ecumenical influences. In his trinitarian theology, he engaged with Orthodox theology, and in his pneumatology, with Pentecostalism. In his emphasis on the discipleship ethics of the Sermon on the Mount, he came close to the churches of the Radical Reformation. From feminist theology, especially through his wife Elisabeth Moltmann-Wendel, herself a leading feminist theologian, came an affirmation of bodily experience and, in some of his latest work, a turn from professorial objectivity to a more personal form of expression. A dialogue with Jewish theology has been important throughout his working life. At the same time, he has constantly returned to the theological tradition, retrieving its insights, learning from its mistakes, and continuing its debates.

This is not the place for a descriptive account or analysis of Moltmann's mature theology. Instead, by way of inviting readers into the rich experience of engaging with his work, I would like to highlight three key themes or characteristics:

1. *Passion.* This word, in its multiple meanings and dimensions, is a helpful clue to Moltmann's understanding of God. In his work, God's love is not the dispassionate benevolence of the God of traditional theism, who is impassible in the sense that he not only cannot suffer but cannot be affected by the world he loves, whether in suffering or in joy. Rather, for Moltmann, God's love is his passionate concern, his committed and costly involvement with the world. In the passion of Christ (in the traditional sense of his suffering), we find the com-passion of God, God's fellow suffering with all who suffer. The apathetic God (where "apathetic" is the Greek term for impassible, unmoved by anything outside himself) has his counterpart in apathetic humanity, people who hold back from life and love, commitment and involvement, for fear of suffering. The contemporary world respects competitiveness and success, not vulnerability. But in the company of the passionate and compassionate God, apathetic humans become open for love, suffering, and joy.

2. *Mutuality* and *Perichoresis.* For Moltmann, God is love because the three persons who are God constitute their unity in an intimate reciprocity of loving relationships. In the terminology of the Greek Fathers, *perichoresis* means that the three persons are "in" one another. Moltmann abandons the traditional idea of a fixed "order" of the persons in favor of a dynamic of changing relationships, in which the divine persons engage with each other in the course of engaging with the world. For the Trinity is not a closed circle of love, but an open and inviting unity. In God's history with the world, the world is

drawn into the loving relationships of the Trinity. Moltmann here extends the application of *perichoresis*, using it to describe the relationship between God and the world. God is in the world and the world is in God. As in the Trinity, this mutual indwelling does not obliterate difference, but constitutes relationship-in-difference or difference-in-relationship. The parallel is not complete, however, because in the Trinity God is in unity with God, like with like, whereas in God's relationship with the world God is united with what is not God, God's other. God's creation participates in the divine life, but does not become God.

In discarding the traditional idea of an "order" within the Trinity, in which the Father has a certain sort of priority, Moltmann grounds in God his rejection of hierarchical relationships in favor of relationships of mutuality. While hierarchy expresses dominance and suppresses freedom, relationships of loving mutuality are liberating. In the "kingdom" of God, the lordship of God is a provisional image and friendship with God the more adequate one. In Moltmann's political thought, the nondominating relationships within the Trinity ground democratic freedoms in society, while in his ecclesiology, hierarchy gives way to the reciprocity of different gifts exercised by equal participants. Moltmann's preferred model of the church is the image of open friendship, which does not form a closed circle of familiarity among those who are like each other, but is open in love for the outsider and the unlike.

The notion of mutuality, opposed to hierarchy and domination, also comes into its own in Moltmann's ecological understanding of the world. He sees the creation, humans included, as a community of God's creatures who share the earth in mutual interdependence. Creation itself is a perichoretic community constituted by relationships of mutuality. In the face of ecological catastrophe, humans need to move away from the exploitative domination that is destroying the natural world on which they are inescapably dependent. They also need to modify the purely objectifying form of knowledge that has accompanied domination of nature, a form of knowledge in which the knowing subject masters its object by isolating and analyzing it. An ecological theology requires instead a participatory form of knowledge, in which things are perceived in the totality of their relationships and the human subject perceives itself as a participant in the interdependence of all things.

3. *Life.* Moltmann's book on the Spirit, not initially part of his plan for the series, testifies to the growing importance of life as a unifying or embracing term in his theology. It is entitled *The Spirit of Life: A Universal Affirmation.* He understands the Spirit as "the divine wellspring of life"—source of all life, continually renewing all life, as well as ultimately source of eternal life for all

creation. This makes it possible for the whole of life to be experience of God and for God to be experienced in all things. The Spirit of life is God experienced in the profundity and vitality of life lived in God. In an important move to overcome the persistent duality of the "spiritual" and the "material," Moltmann insists that, as the Spirit of *life*, the Spirit of God is not related to the "spiritual" as opposed to the "material," nor to the human as opposed to the rest of creation. Life in the Spirit is not a life of withdrawal from the bodily, social, and natural world, but is characterized by a love of life and an affirmation of all life. This is a fresh form of Moltmann's characteristic concern for a theology of positive involvement in God's world. In the face of accumulating threats to life in our time, Moltmann gives an "ethics of life" an important place in his final work, *Ethics of Hope.*

Of course, the title of this concluding study of theological ethics reaffirms Moltmann's starting point. It is an *Ethics of Hope* that finally fulfills the ethical promise of his *Theology of Hope.* Moltmann's fifty years of theological exploration have taken him through times in which it has become much harder to hope than it seemed in the 1960s. He has come to see the contemporary world as an increasingly perilous experiment. So it has become even more important that Christian hope means resisting and anticipating—resisting the normative force of what dominates the present and anticipating the new and liberating future that comes from God.

1

Theology of Hope

On its publication in 1964, during the postwar years of ferment and change, Jürgen Moltmann's Theology of Hope *made an immediate and astonishing impact. It was to some extent a critical response to the Marxist philosopher Ernst Bloch's* Principle of Hope,[1] *which had deeply impressed him. But Moltmann took up Bloch's "hopes for a world without God" so as to link them with "the God of hope" (Rom. 15:13) of Jewish and Christian tradition. The church had always seen eschatology (the doctrine of the last things) as an appendix, something that clocks in once hope for the world has nothing more to offer. But Moltmann sees the Christian faith not only as hope for the end but as hope and promise from the beginning, a hope and promise based on the resurrection of Jesus. The future hope remains "this-worldly," because expectation leads to a new setting forth and a transformation of the present, and therefore takes in history. In his autobiography,* A Broad Place,[2] *he later wrote:*

> *I believe that three key concepts are essential for every Christian theology of hope:*
>> *1. the concept of the divine promise in the Old Testament;*
>> *2. the concept of the raising of the crucified Christ as God's future for the world, in the New Testament;*
>> *3. an understanding of human history as the mission of the kingdom of God today.*

INTRODUCTION: MEDITATION ON HOPE

Source: Moltmann 1964; ET 1967/1993:15–36.

1. WHAT IS THE LOGOS OF CHRISTIAN ESCHATOLOGY?

Eschatology was long called "the doctrine of the last things" or "the doctrine of the end." By these last things were meant events which will one day break upon man, history, and the world at the end of time. They included the return of Christ in universal glory, the judgment of the world and the consummation of the kingdom, the general resurrection of the dead and the new creation of all things. These end events were to break into this world from somewhere beyond history, and to put an end to the history in which all things here live and move. But the relegating of these events to the "last day" robbed them of their directive, uplifting, and critical significance for all the days which are spent here, this side of the end, in history. Thus these teachings about the end led a peculiarly barren existence at the end of Christian dogmatics. They were like a loosely attached appendix that wandered off into obscure irrelevancies. They bore no relation to the doctrine of the cross and resurrection, the exaltation and sovereignty of Christ, and did not derive from these by any logical necessity. They were as far removed from them as All Souls' Day sermons are from Easter. The more Christianity became an organization for discipleship under the auspices of the Roman state religion, the more eschatology and its mobilizing, revolutionizing, and critical effects upon history as it has now to be lived were left to fanatical sects and revolutionary groups. Owing to the fact that Christian faith banished from its life the future hope by which it is upheld, and relegated the future to a beyond, or to eternity, whereas the biblical testimonies which it handed on are yet full to the brim with future hope of a messianic kind for the world—owing to this, hope emigrated as it were from the church and turned in one distorted form or another against the church.

In actual fact, however, eschatology means the doctrine of the Christian hope, which embraces both the object hoped for and also the hope inspired by it. From first to last, and not merely in the epilogue, Christianity is eschatology, is hope, forward looking and forward moving, and therefore also revolutionizing and transforming the present. The eschatological is not one element *of* Christianity, but it is the medium of Christian faith as such, the key in which everything in it is set, the glow that suffuses everything here in the dawn of an expected new day. For Christian faith lives from the raising of the crucified Christ, and strains after the promise of the universal future of Christ. Eschatology is the passionate suffering and passionate longing kindled by the Messiah. Hence eschatology cannot really be only a part of Christian doctrine.

Rather, the eschatological outlook is characteristic of all Christian proclamation, of every Christian existence, and of the whole church. There is therefore only one real problem in Christian theology, which its own object forces upon it and which it in turn forces on mankind and on human thought: the problem of the future. For the element of otherness that encounters us in the hope of the Old and the New Testaments—the thing we cannot already think out and picture for ourselves on the basis of the given world and of the experiences we already have with the world—is one that confronts us with a promise of something new and with the hope of a future given by God. The God spoken of here is no intra-worldly or extra-worldly God, but the "God of hope" (Rom. 15:13), a God with "future as his essential nature" (as [Ernst] Bloch puts it), as made known in Exodus and in Israelite prophecy, the God whom we therefore cannot have either in us or over us but always only before us, who encounters us in his promises for the future, and whom we therefore cannot have either, but can only await in active hope. A proper theology would therefore have to be constructed in the light of its future goal. Eschatology should not be its end, but its beginning.

But how can anyone speak of the future, which is not yet here, and of coming events in which one has not as yet had any part? Are these not dreams, speculations, longings, and fears, which must all remain vague and indefinite because no one can verify them? The term "eschato-*logy*" is wrong. There can be no "doctrine" of the last things, if by "doctrine" we mean a collection of theses which can be understood on the basis of experiences that constantly recur and are open to anyone. The Greek term *logos* refers to a reality which is there, now and always, and is given true expression in the word appropriate to it. In this sense there can be no *logos* of the future, unless the future is the continuation or regular recurrence of the present. If, however, the future were to bring something startlingly new, we have nothing to say of that, and nothing meaningful can be said of it either, for it is not in what is new and accidental, but only in things of an abiding and regularly recurring character that there can be log-ical truth. Aristotle, it is true, can call hope a "waking dream," but for the Greeks it is nevertheless an evil out of Pandora's box.

But how, then, can Christian eschatology give expression to the future? Christian eschatology does not speak of the future as such. It sets out from a definite reality in history and announces the future of that reality, its future possibilities, and its power over the future. Christian eschatology speaks of Jesus Christ and *his* future. It recognizes the reality of the raising of Jesus and proclaims the future of the risen Lord. Hence the question whether all statements about the future are grounded in the person and history of Jesus

Christ provides it with the touchstone by which to distinguish the spirit of eschatology from that of utopia.

If, however, the crucified Christ has a future because of his resurrection, then that means on the other hand that all statements and judgments about him must at once imply something about the future which is to be expected from him. Hence the form in which Christian theology speaks of Christ cannot be the form of the Greek *logos* or of doctrinal statements based on experience, but only the form of statements of hope and of promises for the future. All predicates of Christ not only say who he was and is, but imply statements as to who he will be and what is to be expected from him. They all say: "He is our hope" (Col. 1:27). In thus announcing his future in the world in terms of promise, they point believers in him towards the hope of his still outstanding future. Hope's statements of promise anticipate the future. In the promises, the hidden future already announces itself and exerts its influence on the present through the hope it awakens.

The truth of doctrinal statements is found in the fact that they can be shown to agree with the existing reality which we can all experience. Hope's statements of promise, however, must stand in contradiction to the reality which can at present be experienced. They do not result from experiences, but are the condition for the possibility of new experiences. They do not seek to illuminate the reality which exists, but the reality which is coming. They do not seek to make a mental picture of existing reality, but to lead existing reality towards the promised and hoped-for transformation. They do not seek to bear the train of reality, but to carry the torch before it. In so doing they give reality a historical character. But if reality is perceived in terms of history, then we have to ask with J. G. Hamann: "Who would form proper concepts of the present without knowing the future?"

Present and future, experience and hope, stand in contradiction to each other in Christian eschatology, with the result that man is not brought into harmony and agreement with the given situation, but is drawn into the conflict between hope and experience. "We are saved by hope. But hope that is seen is not hope; for what a man seeth, why doth he yet hope for? But if we hope for that we see not, then do we with patience wait for it" (Rom. 8:24, 25). Everywhere in the New Testament the Christian hope is directed towards what is not yet visible; it is consequently a "hoping against hope" and thereby brands the visible realm of present experience as a godforsaken, transient reality that is to be left behind. The contradiction to the existing reality of himself and his world in which man is placed by hope is the very contradiction out of which this hope itself is born—it is the contradiction between the resurrection and the cross. Christian hope is resurrection hope, and it proves its truth in the contradiction of the future prospects thereby offered and guaranteed for righteousness as opposed to sin, life as opposed to death, glory as opposed to suffering, peace as opposed to dissension. Calvin perceived very plainly the discrepancy involved in the resurrection hope: "To us is given the promise of eternal life—but to us, the dead. A blessed resurrection is proclaimed to us—meantime we are surrounded by decay. We are called righteous—and yet sin lives in us. We hear of ineffable blessedness—but meantime we are here oppressed by infinite misery. We are promised abundance of all good things—yet we are rich only in hunger and thirst. What would become of us if we did not take our stand on hope, and if our heart did not hasten beyond this world through the midst of darkness upon the path illumined by the word and Spirit of God!" (on Heb. 11:1).

It is in this contradiction that hope must prove its power. Hence eschatology, too, is forbidden to ramble, and must formulate its statements of hope in contradiction to our present experience of suffering, evil, and death. For that reason it will hardly ever be possible to develop an eschatology on its own. It is much more important to present hope as the foundation and the mainspring of theological thinking as such, and to introduce the eschatological perspective into our statements on divine revelation, on the resurrection of Christ, on the mission of faith, and on history.

2. THE BELIEVING HOPE

In the contradiction between the word of promise and the experiential reality of suffering and death, faith takes its stand on hope and "hastens beyond this world," said Calvin. He did not mean by this that Christian faith flees the world, but he did mean that it strains after the future. To believe does in fact mean to cross and transcend bounds, to be engaged in an exodus. Yet this happens in a way that does not suppress or skip the unpleasant realities. Death is real death, and decay is putrefying decay. Guilt remains guilt and suffering remains, even for the believer, a cry to which there is no ready-made answer. Faith does not overstep these realities into a heavenly utopia, does not dream itself into a reality of a different kind. It can overstep the bounds of life, with their closed wall of suffering, guilt, and death, only at the point where they have in actual fact been broken through. It is only in following the Christ who was raised from suffering, from a godforsaken death and from the grave that it gains an open prospect in which there is nothing more to oppress us, a view of the realm of freedom and of joy. Where the bounds that mark the end of all human hopes are broken through in the raising of the crucified one, there faith can and must expand into hope. There it becomes παρρησία and μακροθυμία. There its hope becomes a "passion for what is possible" (Kierkegaard), because it can be a passion for what has been made possible. There the *extensio animi ad magna* [the reaching out of the soul toward the great], as it was called in the Middle Ages, takes place in hope. Faith recognizes the dawning of this future of openness and freedom in the Christ event. The hope thereby kindled spans the horizons which then open over a closed existence. Faith binds man to Christ. Hope sets this faith open to the comprehensive future of Christ. Hope is therefore the "inseparable companion of faith. "When this hope is taken away, however eloquently or elegantly we discourse concerning faith, we are convicted of having none. . . . Hope is nothing else than the expectation of those things which faith has believed to have been truly promised by God. Thus, faith believes God to be true, hope awaits the time when this truth shall be manifested; faith believes that he is our Father, hope anticipates that he will ever show himself to be a Father towards us; faith believes that eternal life has been given to us, hope anticipates that it will some time be revealed; faith is the foundation upon which hope rests, hope nourishes and sustains faith. For as no one except him who already believes His promises can look for anything from God, so again the weakness of our faith must be sustained and nourished by patient hope and expectation, lest it fail and grow faint. . . . By unremitting renewing and restoring, it [hope] invigorates faith again and again with perseverance."[3] Thus in the Christian life faith has the priority, but hope the primacy. Without faith's knowledge of Christ, hope becomes a utopia and remains hanging in the air. But without hope, faith falls to pieces, becomes a fainthearted and ultimately a dead faith. It is through faith that man finds the path of true life, but it is only hope that keeps him on that path. Thus it is that faith in Christ gives hope its assurance. Thus it is that hope gives faith in Christ its breadth and leads it into life.

To believe means to cross in hope and anticipation the bounds that have been penetrated by the raising of the crucified. If we bear that in mind, then this faith can have nothing to do with fleeing the world, with resignation, and with escapism. In this hope the soul does not soar above our vale of tears to some imagined heavenly bliss, nor does it sever itself from the earth. For, in the words of Ludwig Feuerbach, it puts "in place of the beyond that lies above our grave in heaven the beyond that lies above our grave on earth, the historic *future*, the future of mankind."[4] It sees in the resurrection of Christ not the eternity of heaven, but the future of the very earth on which his cross stands. It sees in him the future of the very humanity for which he died. That is why it finds the cross the hope of the earth. This hope struggles for the obedience of the body, because it awaits the quickening of the body. It espouses in all meekness the cause of the devastated earth and of harassed humanity, because it is promised possession of the earth. *Ave crux!—unica spes!* [Hail cross, the only hope].

But on the other hand, all this must inevitably mean that the man who thus hopes will never be able to reconcile himself with the laws and constraints of this earth, neither with the inevitability of death nor with the evil that constantly bears further evil. The raising of Christ is not merely a consolation to him in a life that is full of distress and doomed to die, but it is also God's contradiction of suffering and death, of humiliation and offense, and of the wickedness of evil. Hope finds in Christ not only a consolation *in* suffering, but also the protest of the divine promise *against* suffering. If Paul calls death the "last enemy" (1 Cor. 15:26), then the opposite is also true: that the risen Christ, and with him the resurrection hope, must be declared to be the enemy of death and of a world that puts up with death. Faith takes up the contradiction and thus becomes itself a contradiction to the world of death. That is why faith, wherever it develops into hope, causes not rest but unrest, not patience but impatience. It does not calm the unquiet heart, but is itself this unquiet heart in man. Those who hope in Christ can no longer put up with reality as it is, but begin to suffer under it, to contradict it. Peace with God means conflict with the world, for the goad of the promised future stabs inexorably into the flesh of every unfulfilled present. If we had before our eyes only what we see, then we should cheerfully or reluctantly reconcile ourselves with things as they happen to be. That we do not reconcile ourselves, that there is no pleasant harmony between us and reality, is due to our unquenchable hope. This hope keeps man unreconciled until the great day of the fulfillment of all the promises of God. It keeps him *in statu viatoris* [in the position of the wanderer], in that unresolved openness to world questions which has its origin in the promise of God in the resurrection of Christ and can therefore be resolved only when the same God fulfills his promise. This hope makes the Christian church a constant disturbance in human society, seeking as the latter does to stabilize itself into a "continuing city." It makes the church the source of continual new impulses towards the realization of righteousness, freedom, and humanity here in the light of the promised future that is to come. This church is committed to "answer for the hope" that is in it (1 Peter 3:15). It is called in question "on account of the hope and resurrection of the dead" (Acts 23:6). Wherever that happens, Christianity embraces its true nature and becomes a witness of the future of Christ.

3. THE SIN OF DESPAIR

If faith thus depends on hope for its life, then the sin of unbelief is manifestly grounded in hopelessness. To be sure, it is usually said that sin in its original form is man's wanting to be as God. But that is only the one side of sin. The other side of such pride is hopelessness, resignation, inertia, and melancholy. From this arise the *tristesse* and frustration which fill all living things with the seeds of a sweet decay. Among the sinners whose future is eternal death in Rev. 21:8, the "fearful" are mentioned before unbelievers, idolaters, murderers, and the rest. For the Epistle to the Hebrews, falling away from the living hope, in the sense of being disobedient to the promise in time of oppression, or of being carried away from God's pilgrim people as by a flood, is the great sin which threatens the hopeful on their way. Temptation then consists not so much in the titanic desire to be as God, but in weakness, timidity, weariness, not wanting to be what God requires of us.

God has exalted man and given him the prospect of a life that is wide and free, but man hangs back and lets himself down. God promises a new creation of all things in righteousness and peace, but man acts as if everything were as before and remained as before. God honors him with his promises, but man does not believe himself capable of what is required of him. That is the sin which most profoundly threatens the believer. It is not the evil he does, but the good he does not do, not his misdeeds but his omissions, that accuse him. They accuse him of lack of hope. For these so-called sins of omission all have their ground in hopelessness and weakness of faith. "It is not so much sin that plunges us into disaster, as rather despair," said Chrysostom. That is why the Middle Ages reckoned *acedia* [listlessness or sloth] or *tristitia* [melancholy] among the sins against the Holy Spirit which lead to death.

Josef Pieper in his treatise *Über die Hoffnung* (1949) has very neatly shown how this hopelessness can assume two forms. It can be presumption, *praesumptio*, and it can be despair, *desperatio*. Both are forms of the sin against hope. Presumption is a premature, self-willed anticipation of the fulfillment of what we hope for from God. Despair is the premature, arbitrary anticipation of the non-fulfillment of what we hope for from God. Both forms of hopelessness, by anticipating the fulfillment or by giving up hope, cancel the wayfaring character of hope. They rebel against the patience in which hope trusts in the God of the promise. They demand impatiently either fulfillment "now already" or "absolutely no" hope. "In despair and presumption alike we have the rigidifying and freezing of the truly human element, which hope alone can keep flowing and free" (p. 51).

Thus despair, too, presupposes hope. "What we do not long for, can be the object neither of our hope nor of our despair" (Augustine). The pain of despair surely lies in the fact that a hope is there, but no way opens up towards its fulfillment. Thus the kindled hope turns against the one who hopes and consumes him. "Living means burying hopes," says [Theodor] Fontane in one of his novels, and it is these "dead hopes" that he portrays in it. Our hopes are bereft of faith and confidence. Hence despair would seek to preserve the soul from disappointments. "Hope as a rule makes many a fool." Hence we try to remain on the solid ground of reality, "to think clearly and not hope any more" ([Albert] Camus), and yet in adopting this so-called realism dictated by the facts we fall victim to the worst of all utopias—the utopia of the status quo, as [Robert] Musil called this kind of realism.

The despairing surrender of hope does not even need to have a desperate appearance. It can also be the mere tacit absence of meaning, prospects, future, and purpose. It can wear the face of smiling resignation: *bonjour tristesse!* All that remains is a certain smile on the part of those who have tried out the full range of their possibilities and found nothing in them that could give cause for hope. All that remains is a *taedium vitae*, a life that has little further interest in itself. Of all the attitudes produced by the decay of non-eschatological, bourgeois Christianity, and then consequently found in a no longer Christian world, there is hardly any which is so general as *acedia*, *tristesse*, the cultivation and dandling manipulation of faded hopes. But where hope does not find its way to the source of new, unknown possibilities, there the trifling, ironical play with the existing possibilities ends in boredom, or in outbreaks of absurdity.

At the beginning of the nineteenth century the figure of presumption is found at many points in German idealism. For [Johann Wolfgang] Goethe, [Friedrich] Schiller, [Leopold von] Ranke, Karl Marx, and many others, Prometheus became the great saint of the modern age. Prometheus, who stole fire from the gods, stood in contrast to the figure of the obedient servant of God. It was possible to transform even Christ into a Promethean figure. Along with that there frequently went a philosophical, revolutionary millenarianism which set itself to build at last that realm of freedom and human dignity which had been hoped for in vain from the God of the divine servant.

In the middle of the twentieth century we find in the literary writings of the existentialists the other form of apostasy from hope. Thus the patron saint that was Prometheus now assumes the form of Sisyphus, who certainly knows the pilgrim way, and is fully acquainted with struggle and decision and with patient toil, yet without any prospect of fulfillment. Here the obedient servant of God can be transformed into the figure of the honest failure. There is no hope and no God any more. There is only Camus's "thinking clearly and hoping no more," and the honest love and fellow-feeling exemplified in Jesus. As if thinking could gain clarity without hope! As if there could be love without hope for the beloved!

Neither in presumption nor in despair does there lie the power to renew life, but only in the hope that is enduring and sure. Presumption and despair live off this hope and regale themselves at its expense. "He who does not hope for the unexpected, will not find it," runs a saying of Heraclitus. The uniform of the day is patience and its only decoration the pale star of hope over its heart" ([Ingeborg] Bachmann).

Hope alone is to be called "realistic," because it alone takes seriously the possibilities with which all reality is fraught. It does not take things as they happen to stand or to lie, but as progressing, moving things with possibilities of change. Only as long as the world and the people in it are in a fragmented and experimental state which is not yet resolved, is there any sense in earthly hopes. The latter anticipate what is possible to reality, historic and moving as it is, and use their influence to decide the processes of history. Thus hopes and anticipations of the future are not a transfiguring glow superimposed upon a darkened existence, but are realistic ways of perceiving the scope of our real possibilities, and as such they set everything in motion and keep it in a state of change. Hope and the kind of thinking that goes with it consequently cannot submit to the reproach of being utopian, for they do not strive after things that have "no place," but after things that have "no place *as yet*" but can acquire one. On the other hand, the celebrated realism of the stark facts, of established objects and laws, the attitude that despairs of its possibilities and clings to reality as it is, is inevitably much more open to the charge of being utopian, for in its eyes there is "no place" for possibilities, for future novelty, and consequently for the historic character of reality. Thus the despair which imagines it has reached the end of its tether proves to be illusory, as long as nothing has yet come to an end but everything is still full of possibilities. Thus positivistic realism also proves to be illusory, so long as the world is not a fixed body of facts but a network of paths and processes, so long as the world does not only run according to laws but these laws themselves are also flexible, so long as it is a realm in which necessity means the possible, but not the unalterable.

Statements of hope in Christian eschatology must also assert themselves against the rigidified utopia of realism, if they would keep faith alive and would guide obedience in love on to the path towards earthly, corporeal, social reality. In its eyes the world is full of all kinds of possibilities, namely all the possibilities of the God of hope. It sees reality and mankind in the hand of him whose voice calls into history from its end, saying, "Behold, I make all things new," and from hearing this word of promise it acquires the freedom to renew life here and to change the face of the world.

4. DOES HOPE CHEAT MAN OF THE HAPPINESS OF THE PRESENT?

The most serious objection to a theology of hope springs not from presumption or despair, for these two basic attitudes of human existence presuppose hope, but the objection to hope arises from the religion of humble acquiescence in the present. Is it not always in the present alone that man is truly existent, real, contemporary with himself, acquiescent, and certain? Memory binds him to the past that no longer is. Hope casts him upon the future that is not yet. He remembers having lived, but he does not live. He remembers having loved, but he does not love. He remembers the thoughts of others, but he does not think. It seems to be much the same with him in hope. He hopes to live, but he does not live. He expects to be happy one day, and this expectation causes him to pass over the happiness of the present. He is never, in memory and hope, wholly himself and wholly in his present. Always he either limps behind it or hastens ahead of it. Memories and hopes appear to cheat him of the happiness of being undividedly present. They rob him of his present and drag him into times that no longer exist or do not yet exist. They surrender him to the non-existent and abandon him to vanity. For these times subject him to the stream of transience—the stream that sweeps him to annihilation.

Pascal lamented this deceitful aspect of hope: "We do not rest satisfied with the present. We anticipate the future as too slow in coming, as if in order to hasten its course; or we recall the past, to stop its too rapid flight. So imprudent are we that we wander in times which are not ours, and do not think of the only one which belongs to us; and so idle are we that we dream of those times which are no more, and thoughtlessly overlook that which alone exists. . . . We scarcely ever think of the present; and if we think of it, it is only to take light from it to arrange the future. The present is never our end. The past and the present are our means; the future alone is our end. So we never live, but we hope to live; and, as we are always preparing to be happy, it is inevitable we should never be so."[5] Always the protest against the Christian hope and against the transcendent consciousness resulting from it has stubbornly insisted on the rights of the present, on the good that surely lies always to hand, and on the eternal truth in every moment. Is the "present" not the only time in which man wholly exists, which belongs wholly to him, and to which he wholly belongs? Is the "present" not time and yet at once also more than time in the sense of coming and going—namely, a *nunc stans* [an existing "now"] and to that extent also a *nunc aeternum* [an eternal "now"]? Only of the present can it be said that it "is," and only present being is constantly with us. If we are wholly present—*tota simul*—then in the midst of time we are snatched from the transient and annihilating workings of time.

Thus Goethe, too, could say: "All these passing things we put up with; if only the eternal remains present to us every moment, then we do not suffer from the transience of time." He had found this eternally resting present in "nature" itself, because he understood "nature" as the *physis* that exists out of itself: "All is always present in it. Past and future it does not know. The present is its eternity." Should not man, too, therefore become present like nature?

> Why go chasing distant fancies?
> Lo, the good is ever near!
> Only learn to grasp your chances!
> Happiness is always here.

Thus the true present is nothing else but the eternity that is immanent in time, and what matters is to perceive in the outward form of temporality and transience the substance that is immanent and the eternal that is present—so said the early Hegel. Likewise Nietzsche endeavored to get rid of the burden and deceit of the Christian hope by seeking "the eternal Yea of existence" in the present and finding the love of eternity in "loyalty to the earth." It is always only in the present, the moment, the *kairos*, the "now" that being itself is present in time. It is like noon, when the sun stands high and nothing casts a shadow any more, nor does anything stand in the shadow.

But now, it is not merely the *happiness of the present*, but it is more, it is the *God of the present*, the eternally present God, and it is not merely the present being of man, but still more the eternal presence of being, that the Christian hope appears to cheat us of. Not merely man is cheated, but still more God himself is cheated, where hope does not allow man to discover an eternal present. It is only here that the objection to our future hopes on the ground of the "present" attains to its full magnitude. Not merely does life protest against the torture of the hope that is imposed upon it, but we are also accused of godlessness in the name of the God whose essential attribute is *numen praesentiae* [present being]. Yet what God is this in whose name the "present" is insisted upon as against the hope of what is not yet?

It is at bottom ever and again the god of Parmenides, of whom it is said in Fragment 8 (Diels): "The unity that is being never was, never will be, for now it Is all at once as a whole" (νῦν ἔστιν ὁμοῦ πᾶν). This "being" does not exist "always," as it was still said to do in Homer and Hesiod, but it "is," and is "now." It has no extension in time, its truth stands on the "now," its eternity is present, it "is" all at once and in one (*tota simul*). In face of the epiphany of the eternal presence of being, the times in which life rises and passes fade away to mere phenomena in which we have a mixture of being and non-being, day and night, abiding and passing away. In the contemplation of the eternal present, however, "origin is obliterated and decay is vanished." In the present of being, in the eternal Today, man is immortal, invulnerable, and inviolable ([Georg] Picht). If, as Plutarch reports, the divine name over the portal of the Delphic temple of Apollo was given as *EI*, then this, too, could mean "Thou art" in the sense of the eternal present. It is in the eternal nearness and presence of the god that we come to knowledge of man's nature and to joy in it.

The god of Parmenides is "thinkable," because he is the eternal, single fullness of being. The non-existent, the past, and the future, however, are not "thinkable." In the contemplation of the present eternity of this god, non-existence, movement and change, history and future become unthinkable, because they "are" not. The contemplation of this god does not make a meaningful experience of history possible, but only the meaningful negation of history. The *logos* of this being liberates and raises us out of the power of history into the eternal present.

In the struggle against the seeming deceit of the Christian hope, Parmendides's concept of God has thrust its way deeply indeed into Christian theology. When in the celebrated third chapter of Kierkegaard's treatise on *The Concept of Dread* the promised "fullness of time" is taken out of the realm of expectation that attaches to promise and history, and the "fullness of time" is called the "moment" in the sense of the eternal, then we find ourselves in the field of Greek thinking rather than of the Christian knowledge of God. It is true that Kierkegaard modified the Greek understanding of temporality in the light of the Christian insight into our radical sinfulness, and that he intensifies the Greek difference between *logos* and *doxa* into a paradox, but does that really imply any more than a modification of the "epiphany of the eternal present"? "The present is not a concept of time. The eternal conceived as the present is arrested temporal succession. The moment characterizes the present as a thing that has no past and no future. The moment is an atom of eternity. It is the first reflection of eternity in time, its first attempt as it were to halt time." It is understandable that then the believer, too, must be described in parallel terms to the Parmenidean and Platonic contemplator. The believer is the man who is entirely present. He is in the supreme sense contemporaneous with himself and one with himself. "And to be with the eternal's help utterly and completely contemporaneous with oneself today, is to gain eternity. The believer turns his back on the eternal, so to speak, precisely in order to have it by him in the one day that is today. The Christian believes, and thus he is quit of tomorrow."

Much the same is to be found in Ferdinand Ebner, whose personalist thinking and pneumatology of language has had such an influence on modern theology: "Eternal life is so to speak life in the absolute present and is in actual fact the life of man in his consciousness of the presence of God." For it is of the essence of God to be absolute spiritual presence. Hence man's "present" is nothing else but the presence of God. He steps out of time and lives in the present. Thus it is that he lives "in God." Faith and love are timeless acts which remove us out of time, because they make us wholly "present."

Christian faith then means tuning in to the nearness of God in which Jesus lived and worked, for living amid the simple everyday things of today is of course living in the fullness of time and living in the nearness of God. To grasp the never-returning moment, to be wholly one with oneself, wholly self-possessed and on the mark, is what is meant by "God." The concepts of God which are constructed in remoteness from God and in his absence fall to pieces in his nearness, so that to be wholly present means that "God" happens, for the "happening" of the uncurtailed present is the happening of God.

This mysticism of being, with its emphasis on the living of the present moment, presupposes an immediacy to God which the faith that believes in God on the ground of Christ cannot adopt without putting an end to the historic mediation and reconciliation of God and man in the Christ event, and so also, as a result of this, putting an end to the observation of history under the category of hope. This is not the "God of hope," for the latter is present in promising the future—his own and man's and the world's future—and in sending men into the history that is not yet. The God of the exodus and of the resurrection "is" not eternal presence, but he promises his presence and nearness to him who follows the path on which he is sent into the future. YHWH, as the name of the God who first of all promises his presence and his kingdom and makes them prospects for the future, is a God "with future as his essential nature," a God of promise and of leaving the present to face the future, a God whose freedom is the source of new things that are to come. His name is not a cipher for the "eternal present," nor can it be rendered by the word *EI*, "thou art." His name is a wayfaring name, a name of promise that discloses a new future, a name whose truth is experienced in history inasmuch as his promise discloses its future possibilities. He is therefore, as Paul says, the God who raises the dead and calls into being the things that are not (Rom. 4:17). This God is present where we wait upon his promises in hope and transformation. When we have a God who calls into being the things that are not, then the things that are not yet, that are future, also become "thinkable" because they can be hoped for.

The "now" and "today" of the New Testament is a different thing from the "now" of the eternal presence of being in Parmenides, for it is a "now" and an "all of a sudden" in which the newness of the promised future is lit up and seen in a flash. Only in this sense is it to be called an "eschatological" today. "Parousia" for the Greeks was the epitome of the presence of God, the epitome of the presence of being. The parousia of Christ, however, is conceived in the New Testament only in categories of expectation, so that it means not *praesentia Christi* but *adventus Christi*, and is not his eternal presence bringing time to a standstill, but his "coming," as our Advent hymns say, opening the road to life in time, for the life of time is hope. The believer is not set at the high noon of life, but at the dawn of a new day at the point where night and day, things passing and things to come, grapple with each other. Hence the believer does not simply take the day as it comes, but looks beyond the day to the things which according to the promise of him who is the *creator ex nihilo* and raiser of the dead are still to come. The present of the coming parousia of God and of Christ in the promises of the gospel of the crucified does not translate us out of time, nor does it bring time to a standstill, but it opens the way for time and sets history in motion, for it does not tone down the pain caused us by the non-existent, but means the adoption and acceptance of the non-existent in memory and hope. Can there be any such thing as an "eternal Yea of being" without a Yea to what no longer is and to what is not yet? Can there be such a thing as harmony and contemporaneity on man's part in the moment of today, unless hope reconciles him with what is non-contemporaneous and disharmonious? Love does not snatch us from the pain of time, but takes the pain of the temporal upon itself. Hope makes us ready to bear the "cross of the present." It can hold to what is dead, and hope for the unexpected. It can approve of movement and be glad of history. For its God is not he who "never was nor will be, because he now Is all at once as a whole," but God is he "who maketh the dead alive and calleth into being the things that are not." The spell of the dogma of hopelessness—*ex nihilo nihil fit*—is broken where he who raises the dead is recognized to be God. Where in faith and hope we begin to live in the light of the possibilities and promises of this God, the whole fullness of life discloses itself as a life of history and therefore a life to be loved. Only in the perspective of this God can there possibly be a love that is more than *philia*, love to the existent and the like—namely, *agape*, love to the non-existent, love to the unlike, the unworthy, the worthless, to the lost, the transient, and the dead; a love that can take upon it the annihilating effects of pain and renunciation because it receives its power from hope of a *creatio ex nihilo*. Love does not shut its eyes to the non-existent and say it is nothing, but becomes itself the magic power that brings it into being. In its hope, love surveys the open possibilities of history. In love, hope brings all things into the light of the promises of God.

Does this hope cheat man of the happiness of the present? How could it do so! For it is itself the happiness of the present. It pronounces the poor blessed, receives the weary and heavy laden, the humbled and wronged, the hungry and the dying, because it perceives the parousia of the kingdom for them. Expectation makes life good, for in expectation man can accept his whole present and find joy not only in its joy but also in its sorrow, happiness not only in its happiness but also in its pain. Thus hope goes on its way through the midst of happiness and pain, because in the promises of God it can see a future also for the transient, the dying, and the dead. That is why it can be said that living without hope is like no longer living. Hell is hopelessness, and it is not for nothing that at the entrance to Dante's hell there stand the words: "Abandon hope, all ye who enter here."

An acceptance of the present which cannot and will not see the dying of the present is an illusion and a frivolity—and one which cannot be grounded on eternity either. The hope that is staked on the *creator ex nihilo* becomes the happiness of the present when it loyally embraces all things in love, abandoning nothing to annihilation but bringing to light how open all things are to the possibilities in which they can live and shall live. Presumption and despair have a paralyzing effect on this, while the dream of the eternal present ignores it.

5. HOPING AND THINKING

But now, all that we have so far said of hope might be no more than a hymn in praise of a noble quality of heart. And Christian eschatology could regain its leading role in theology as a whole, yet still remain a piece of sterile theologizing if we fail to attain to the new thought and action that are consequently necessary in our dealings with the things and conditions of this world. As long as hope does not embrace and transform the thought and action of men, it remains topsy-turvy and ineffective. Hence Christian eschatology must make the attempt to introduce hope into worldly thinking, and thought into the believing hope.

In the Middle Ages, Anselm of Canterbury set up what has since been the standard basic principle of theology: *fides quaerens intellectum—credo, ut intelligam* [faith that seeks understanding—I believe in order to understand]. This principle holds also for eschatology, and it could well be that it is of decisive importance for Christian theology today to follow the basic principle: *spes quaerens intellectum—spero, ut intelligam* [hope that seeks understanding—I hope in order to understand]. If it is hope that maintains and upholds faith and keeps it moving on, if it is hope that draws the believer into the life of love, then it will also be hope that is the mobilizing and driving force of faith's thinking, of its knowledge of, and reflections on, human nature, history, and society. Faith hopes in order to know what it believes. Hence all its knowledge will be an anticipatory, fragmentary knowledge forming a prelude to the promised future, and as such is committed to hope. Hence also *vice versa* the hope which arises from faith in God's promise will become the ferment in our thinking, its mainspring, the source of its restlessness and torment. The hope that is continually led on further by the promise of God reveals all thinking in history to be eschatologically oriented and eschatologically stamped as provisional. If hope draws faith into the realm of thought and of life, then it can no longer consider itself to be an eschatological hope as distinct from the minor hopes that are directed towards attainable goals and visible changes in human life, neither can it as a result dissociate itself from such hopes by relegating them to a different sphere while considering its own future to be supra-worldly and purely spiritual in character. The Christian hope is directed towards a *novum ultimum*, towards a new creation of all things by the God of the resurrection of Jesus Christ. It thereby opens a future outlook that embraces all things, including also death, and into this it can and must also take the limited hopes of a renewal of life, stimulating them, relativizing them, giving them direction. It will destroy the *presumption* in these hopes of better human freedom, of successful life, of justice and dignity for our fellow men, of control of the possibilities of nature, because it does not find in these movements the salvation it awaits, because it refuses to let the entertaining and realizing of utopian ideas of this kind reconcile it with existence. It will thus outstrip these future visions of a better, more humane, more peaceable world—because of its own "better promises" (Heb. 8:6), because it knows that nothing can be "very good" until "all things are become new." But it will not be in the name of "calm despair" that it seeks to destroy the presumption in these movements of hope, for such kinds of presumption still contain more of true hope than does skeptical realism, and more truth as well. There is no help against presumption to be found in the despair that says, "It will always be the same in the end," but only in a persevering rectifying hope that finds articulated expression in thought and action. Realism, still less cynicism, was never a good ally of Christian faith. But if the Christian hope destroys the presumption in futuristic movements, then it does so not for its own sake, but in order to destroy in these hopes the *seeds of resignation*, which emerge at latest with the ideological reign of terror in the utopias in which the hoped-for reconciliation with existence becomes an enforced resignation. This, however, brings the movements of historic change within the range of the *novum ultimum* of hope. They are taken up into the Christian hope and carried further. They become precursory, and therewith provisional, movements. Their goals lose the utopian fixity and become provisional, penultimate, and hence flexible goals. Over against the impulses of this kind that seek to give direction to the history of mankind, Christian hope cannot cling rigidly to the past and the given and ally itself with the utopia of the *status quo*. Rather, it is itself summoned and empowered to creative transformation of reality, for it has hope for the whole of reality. Finally, the believing hope will itself provide *inexhaustible resources* for the creative, inventive imagination of love. It constantly provokes and produces thinking of an anticipatory kind in love to man and the world, in order to give shape to the newly dawning possibilities in the light of the promised future, in order as far as possible to create here the best that is possible, because what is promised is within the bounds of possibility. Thus it will constantly arouse the "passion for the possible," inventiveness and elasticity in self-transformation, in breaking with the old and coming to terms with the new. Always the Christian hope has had a revolutionary effect in this sense on the intellectual history of the society affected by it. Only it was often not in church Christianity that its impulses were at work, but in the Christianity of the fanatics. This has had a detrimental result for both.

But how can knowledge of reality and reflection upon it be pursued from the standpoint of eschatological hope? Luther once had a flash of inspiration at this point, although it was not realized either by himself or by Protestant philosophy. In 1516 he writes of the "earnest expectation of the creature" of which Paul speaks in Rom. 8:19: "The apostle philosophizes and thinks about things in a different way from the philosophers and metaphysicians. For the philosophers fix their eyes on the presence of things and reflect only on their qualities and quiddities. But the apostle drags our gaze away from contemplating the present state of things, away from their essence and attributes, and directs it towards their future. He does not speak of the essence or the workings of the creature, of *actio*, *passio*, or movement, but employs a new, strange, theological term and speaks of the expectation of the creature (*expectatio creaturae*)." The important thing in our present context is, that on the basis of theological view of the "expectation of the creature" and its anticipation he demands a new kind of thinking about the world, an expectation-thinking that corresponds to the Christian hope. Hence in the light of the prospects for the whole creation that are promised in the raising of Christ, theology will have to attain to its own, new way of reflecting on the history of men and things. In the field of the world, of history and of reality as a whole, Christian eschatology cannot renounce the *intellectus fidei et spei* [the understanding of faith and hope]. Creative action springing from faith is impossible without new thinking and planning that springs from hope.

For our knowledge and comprehension of reality, and our reflections on it, that means at least this: that in the medium of hope our theological concepts become not judgments which nail reality down to what it is, but anticipations which show reality its prospects and its future possibilities. Theological concepts do not give a fixed form to reality, but they are expanded by hope and anticipate future being. They do not limp after reality and gaze on it with the night eyes of Minerva's owl, but they illuminate reality by displaying its future. Their knowledge is grounded not in the will to dominate, but in love to the future of things. *Tantum cognoscitur, quantum diligitur* (Augustine). They are thus concepts which are engaged in a process of movement, and which call forth practical movement and change.

"Spes quaerens intellectum" [hope seeking knowledge] is the first step towards eschatology, and where it is successful it becomes *docta spes* [educated hope].

Promise and History

Source: Moltmann 1964; ET 1967/1993:102–106.

The Word of Promise

If in the word promise we have before us a key-word of Israel's "religion of expectation," then it must now by explained what we have to understand by "promise" and more specifically by the "promise of (the guide-) God.[6]

(a) A promise is a declaration which announces the coming of a reality that does not yet exist. Thus promise sets man's heart on a future history in which the fulfilling of the promise is to be expected. If it is a case of a divine promise, then that indicates that the expected future does not have to develop within the framework of the possibilities inherent in the present, but arises from that which is possible to the God of the promise. This can also be something which by the standard of present experience appears impossible.[7]

(b) The promise binds man to the future and gives him a sense for history. It does not give him a sense for world history in general, nor yet for the historic character of human existence as such, but it binds him to its own peculiar history. Its future is not the vague goal of possible change, nor the hope aroused by the idea of possible change; it is not openness towards coming events as such. The future which it discloses is made possible and determined by the promised fulfillment. It is in the first instance always a question here of [Martin] Buber's "hopes of history." The promise takes man up into its own history in hope and obedience, and in so doing stamps his existence with a historic character of a specific kind.

(c) The history which is initiated and determined by promise does not consist in cyclic recurrence, but has a definite turn towards the promised and outstanding fulfillment. This irreversible direction is not determined by the urge of vague forces or by the emergence of laws of its own, but by the word of direction that points us to the free power and the faithfulness of God. It is not evolution, progress, and advance that separate time into yesterday and tomorrow, but the word of promise cuts into events and divides reality into one reality which is passing and can be left behind, and another which must be expected and sought. The meaning of past and the meaning of future comes to light in the word of promise.

(d) If the word is a word of promise, then that means that this word has not yet found a reality congruous with it, but that on the contrary it stands in contradiction to the reality open to experience now and heretofore. It is only for that reason that the word of promise can give rise to the doubt that measures the word by the standard of given reality. And it is only for that reason that this word can give rise to the faith that measures present reality by the standard of the word. "Future" is here a designation of that reality in which the word of promise finds its counterpart, its answer, and its fulfillment, in which it discovers or creates a reality which accords with it and in which it comes to rest.

(e) The word of promise therefore always creates an interval of tension between the uttering and the redeeming of the promise. In so doing it provides man with a peculiar area of freedom to obey or disobey, to be hopeful or resigned. The promise institutes this period and obviously stands in correspondence with what happens in it. This, as [Walther] Zimmerli has illuminatingly pointed out, distinguishes the promise from the prophecies of a Cassandra and differentiates the resulting expectation of history from belief in fate.

(f) If the promise is not regarded abstractly apart from the God who promises, but its fulfillment is entrusted directly to God in his freedom and faithfulness, then there can be no burning interest in constructing a hard and fast juridical system of historical necessities according to a scheme of promise and fulfillment—neither by demonstrating the functioning of such a schema in the past nor by making calculations for the future. Rather, the fulfillments can very well contain an element of newness and surprise over against the promise as it was received. That is why the promise also does not fall to pieces along with the historical circumstance or the historical thought forms in which it was received, but can transform itself—by interpretation—without losing its character of certainty, of expectation, and of movement. If they are *God's* promises, then God must also be regarded as the subject of their fulfillment.

(g) The peculiar character of the Old Testament promises can be seen in the fact that the promises were not liquidated by the history of Israel—neither by disappointment nor by fulfillment—but that on the contrary Israel's experience of history gave them a constantly new and wider interpretation. This aspect comes to light when we ask how it came about that the tribes of Israel did not proceed to change their gods on the occupation of the promised land, but the wilderness God of promise remained their God in Canaan. Actually, the ancestral promises are fulfilled in the occupation of the land and the multiplication of the people, and the wilderness God of promise makes himself superfluous to the extent that his promises pass into fulfillment. The settled life to which they have attained in the land has little more to do with the God of promise on the journey through the wilderness. For the mastering of the agrarian culture the local gods are to hand. It could of course be said that the ancestral promises regarding the land have now been fulfilled and liquidated but that, for example, the promises of guidance and protection for the hosts of Israel in the holy wars continue and are still live issues. But it could also be said that the God who is recognized in his promises remains superior to any fulfillment that can be experienced, because in every fulfillment the promise, and what is still contained in it, does not yet become wholly congruent with reality and thus there always remains an overspill. The fulfillments in the occupation of the land do not fulfill the promise in the sense that they liquidate it like a check that is cashed and lock it away among the documents of a glorious past. The "fulfillments" are taken as expositions, confirmations, and expansions of the promise. The greater the fulfillments become, the greater the promise obviously also becomes in the memory of the expositor at the various levels of the tradition in which it is handed down. There is no trace here of what could be called the "melancholy of fulfillment." This peculiar fact of the promise that goes on beyond experiences of fulfillment could also be illustrated by the traces the promise leaves in the hopes and desires of men. It is ultimately not the delays in the fulfillment and in the parousia that bring men disappointment. "Disappointing experiences" of this kind are superficial and trite and come of regarding the promise in legalistic abstraction apart from the God who promises. On the contrary, it is every experience of fulfillment which, to the extent that we reflect on it as an experience behind us, ultimately contains disappointment. Man's hopes and longings and desires, once awakened by specific promises, stretch further than any fulfillment that can be conceived or experienced. However limited the promises may be, once we have caught in them a whiff of the future, we remain restless and urgent, seeking and searching beyond all experiences of fulfillment, and the latter leave us an aftertaste of sadness. The "not yet" of expectation surpasses every fulfillment that is already taking place now. Hence every reality in which a fulfillment is already taking place now, becomes the confirmation, exposition, and liberation of a greater hope. If we would use this as a help toward understanding the "expanding and broadening history of promise,"[8] if we ask the reason for the abiding overplus of promise as compared with history, then we must again abandon every abstract schema of promise and fulfillment. We must then have recourse to the theological interpretation of this process: the reason for the overplus of promise and for the fact that it constantly overspills history lies in the inexhaustibility of the God of promise, who never exhausts himself in any historic reality but comes "to rest" only in a reality that wholly corresponds to him.[9]

THE RESURRECTION AND THE FUTURE OF JESUS CHRIST
Source: Moltmann 1964; ET 1967/1993:139–43.

GOSPEL AND PROMISE

When we come to the question of the view of the revelation of God in the New Testament, then we discover the fact, already familiar from the Old Testament, that there is no unequivocal *concept* of revelation. What the New Testament understands by revelation is thus again not to be learned from the original content of the words employed, but only from the event to which they are here applied. The event to which the New Testament applies the expressions for revelation imparts to them a peculiar dynamic which is messianic in kind and implies a history of promise. The general impression could be described in the first instance by saying that with the cross and resurrection of Christ the one revelation of God, the glory of his lordship which embraces righteousness, life, and freedom, has begun to move towards man.[10] In the gospel of the event of Christ this future is already present in the promises of Christ. It proclaims the present breaking in of this future, and thus *vice versa* this future announces itself in the promises of the gospel. The proclamation of Christ thus places men in the midst of an event of revelation which embraces the nearness of the coming Lord. It thereby makes the reality of man "historic" and stakes it on history.

The eschatological tendency of the revelation in Christ is manifested by the fact that the revealing word is εὐαγγέλιον and ἐπαγγελία in one. . . . The gospel of the revelation of God in Christ is thus in danger of being incomplete and of collapsing altogether, if we fail to notice the dimension of promise in it. Christology likewise deteriorates if the dimension of the "future of Christ" is not regarded as a constitutive element in it.

But how is "promise" proclaimed in the New Testament as compared with the Old Testament history of promise? How is the future horizon of promise asserted in the New Testament as against the views of the Hellenistic mystery religions?

The approach to Christology has been sought in Christian dogmatics along different lines. We here select two basic types as illustrations of the problem.

Since the shaping of Christian dogmatics by Greek thought, it has been the general custom to approach the mystery of Jesus from the general idea of God in Greek metaphysics: the one God, for whom all men are seeking on the ground of their experience of reality, has appeared in Jesus of Nazareth—be it that the highest eternal idea of goodness and truth has found its most perfect teacher in him, or be it that in him eternal Being, the Source of all things, has become flesh and appeared in the multifarious world of transience and mortality. The mystery of Jesus is then the incarnation of the one, eternal, original, true, and immutable divine Being. This line of approach was adopted in the Christology of the ancient church in manifold forms. Its problems accordingly resulted from the fact that the Father of Jesus Christ was identified with the one God of Greek metaphysics and had the attributes of this God ascribed to him. If, however, the divinity of God is seen in his unchangeableness, immutability, impassibility, and unity, then the historic working of this God in the Christ event of the cross and resurrection becomes as impossible to assert as does his eschatological promise for the future.

In modern times the approach to the mystery of Jesus has often been from a general view of the being of man in history. History has always existed, ever since man has existed. But the actual experiencing and conceiving of the existence of man as historic, the radical disclosure of the historic character of human existence, came into the world with Jesus. The word and work of Jesus brought the decisive change in man's understanding of himself and the world, for by him man's self-understanding in history was given its true expression in an understanding of the historical character of human existence. Instead of a general question of God and a general idea of God, which finds its true expression in Jesus and is thus verified by him, what is here presupposed is a general concept of the being of man, a general questionableness of human existence, which finds its true expression in Jesus and is thus verified by him.

Both approaches to the mystery of Jesus set out from the universal, in order to find its true expression in the concrete instance of his person and his history. Neither of these approaches to Christology, to be sure, *need* bypass the Old Testament, but their way does not necessarily lie through it. The approach of Jesus to all men, however, has the Old Testament with its law and its promise as a necessary presupposition. It is therefore a real question whether we do not have to take seriously the importance for theology of the following two propositions:

1. It was *Yahweh*, the God of Abraham, of Jacob, the God of the promise, who raised Jesus from the dead. Who the God is who is revealed in and by Jesus, emerges only in his difference from, and identity with, the God of the Old Testament.

2. *Jesus was a Jew.* Who Jesus is, and what the human nature is which is revealed by him, emerges from his conflict with the law and the promise of the Old Testament.

If we take these starting points seriously, then the path of theological knowledge leads irreversibly from the particular to the general, from the historic to the eschatological and universal.

The first proposition would mean, that the God who reveals himself in Jesus must be thought of as the God of the Old Testament, as the God of the exodus and the promise, as the God with "future as his essential nature," and therefore must not be identified with the Greek view of God, with Parmenides's "eternal present" of Being, with Plato's highest Idea, and with the Unmoved Mover of Aristotle, not even in his attributes. Who he is, is not declared by the world as a whole, but is declared by Israel's history of promise. His attributes cannot be expressed by negation of the sphere of the earthly, human, mortal, and transient, but only in recalling and recounting the history of his promise. In Jesus Christ, however, the God of Israel has revealed himself as the God of all mankind. Thus the path leads from the *concretum* to the *concretum universale*, not the other way round. Christian theology has to think along *this* line. It is not that a general truth became concrete in Jesus, but the concrete, unique, historic event of the crucifying and raising of Jesus by Yahweh, the God of promise who creates being out of nothing, becomes general through the universal eschatological horizon it anticipates.[11] Through the raising of Jesus from the dead the God of the promises of Israel becomes the God of all men. The Christian proclamation of this God will accordingly always move within a horizon of general truth which it projects ahead of it and towards which it tends, and will claim in advance to be general in character and generally binding, even if its own universality is of an eschatological kind and does not come of abstract argument from the particular to the general.

If on the other hand theology takes seriously the fact that Jesus was a Jew, then this means that he is not to be understood as a particular case of human being in general, but only in connection with the Old Testament history of promise and in conflict with it. It is through the event of the cross and resurrection, which is understandable only in the context of the conflict between law and promise, that he becomes the salvation of all men, both Jews and Gentiles. It is the Christ event that first gives birth to what can be theologically described as "man," "true man, "humanity"—"neither Jew nor Greek, neither bond nor free, neither male nor female" (Gal. 3:28). Only when the real, historic, and religious differences between peoples, groups, and classes are broken down in the Christ event in which the sinner is justified, does there come a prospect of what true humanity can be and will be. The path leads here from the historic and unique to the universal, because it leads from the concrete event to the general in the sense of eschatological direction. Christian proclamation will consequently here again move within the horizon of general truth and make the claim to be universally binding. It will have to expound this claim in contra-distinction to other kinds of general anthropological concepts of *humanitas*, precisely because its own general concept of humanity has an eschatological content. It will not be able, for example, to set out from the fact that man is the being which possesses reason and language, and then go on to verify this aspect of his being by means of the event of justification, but it will set out on the contrary from the event of justification and calling, and then go on in face of other assertions as to the nature of man to uphold this event which makes man, theologically speaking, true man.

Exodus Church

Source: Moltmann 1964; ET 1967/1993:338 *(the book's concluding paragraph).*

As a result of this hope in God's future, this present world becomes free in believing eyes from all attempts at self-redemption or self-production through labor, and it becomes open for loving, ministering self-expenditure in the interests of a humanizing of conditions and in the interests of the realization of justice in the light of the coming justice of God. This means, however, that the hope of resurrection must bring about a new understanding of the world. This world is not the heaven of self-realization, as it as said to be in Idealism. This world is not the hell of self-estrangement, as it is said to be in romanticist and existentialist writing. The world is not yet finished, but is understood as engaged in a history. It is therefore the world of possibilities, the world in which we can serve the future, promised truth and righteousness and peace. This is an age of diaspora, of sowing in hope, of self-surrender and sacrifice, for it is an age which stands within the horizon of a new future. Thus self-expenditure in this world, day-to-day love in hope, becomes possible and becomes human within that horizon of expectation which transcends this world. The glory of self-realization and the misery of self-estrangement alike arise from hopelessness in a world of lost horizons. To disclose to it the horizon of the future of the crucified Christ is the task of the Christian church.

Notes

1. Ernst Bloch, *The Principle of Hope*, 3 vols., 1954–59, trans. Neville Plaice, Stephen Plaice, and Paul Knight (Cambridge, MA: MIT Press/Oxford: Basil Blackwell, 1986).

2. Jürgen Moltmann, *A Broad Place: An Autobiography* (Minneapolis: Fortress Press/London: SCM Press, 2008), 101.

3. John Calvin, *Institutes of the Christian Religion* III.2.42, trans. Ford Lewis Battles (London: SCM Press, 1961), 590.

4. Ludwig Feuerbach, *Das Wesen des Christentums* (Leipzig: Otto Wigand, 1848); trans. George Eliot as *The Essence of Christianity* (London: John Chapman, 1854).

5. Blaise Pascal, *Pensées*, No. 172, trans. W. F. Trotter, Everyman's Library #874 (London: J. M. Dent & Sons, 1943), 49f.

6. For the expression "guide-God," cf. Martin Buber, *Königtum Gottes*, 2d ed., 1936, xi; see *The Prophetic Faith*, trans. C. Witton Davies (New York: Macmillan, 1940).

7. For what follows, cf. the definitions of promise by Walther Zimmerli, "Verheissung und Erfüllung," *Evangelische Theologie* 12 (1952): 38ff.

8. Gerhard von Rad, "Typologische Auslegung des Alten Testaments," *Evangelische Theologie* 12 (1952): 25f.

9. Gerhard von Rad, "There Remains Still a Rest for the People of God," in *The Problem of the Hexateuch and Other Essays*, trans. E. W. T. Dickinson (London: SCM Press, 1966), 94ff.

10. Hannelis Schulte, "Der Begriff der Offenbarung im Neuen Testament," *Beiträge zur Evangelischen Theologie* 13 (1949): 23.

11. Cf. Ernst Käsemann, "The Problem of the Historical Jesus," in *Essays on New Testament Themes,* trans. W. J. Montague (London: SCM Press, 1964), 30f.

2

The Crucified God

The Crucified God *was published in 1972, eight years after* Theology of Hope. *But in his autobiography, Moltmann writes: "I had long been preoccupied with a theology of the cross before the theology of hope."*[1] *The book was essentially born, he says, "as part of my wrestling with God, my suffering under the dark side of God, his hidden face,* hester panim *as the Jews say, the side shown in the godlessness of the perpetrators and the God-forsakenness of the victims of injustice and violence in human history."*[2] *He sees his own experience during and after the war, and in the shadow of Auschwitz, in the light of "what we can say about God after Golgotha." The whole of* The Crucified God *can be seen as an attempt to wrestle with Christ's cry of abandonment, "My God, why have you forsaken me?," the cry that is at the heart of Moltmann's understanding of the cross. This understanding points away from the patristic church's tenet of God's "impassibility"—God's inability to suffer—for Christ's suffering is not separate from God. It is within God himself, so that it sets God beside us as we suffer. In taking upon himself the suffering of the cross, Christ has taken upon himself "all of life as it stands under death, law and guilt,"*[3] *"making peace by the blood of his cross" (Col. 1:20).*

IN EXPLANATION OF THE THEME

Source: Moltmann 1972; ET 1974/1993:1–6.

The cross is not and cannot be loved. Yet only the crucified Christ can bring the freedom which changes the world because it is no longer afraid of death. In his time the crucified Christ was regarded as a scandal and as foolishness. Today, too, it is considered old-fashioned to put him in the center of Christian faith and of theology. Yet only when men are reminded of him, however untimely this may be, can they be set free from the power of the facts of the present time, and from the laws and compulsions of history, and be offered a future which will never grow dark again. Today the church and theology must turn to the crucified Christ in order to show the world the freedom he offers. This is essential if they wish to become what they assert they are: the church of Christ, and Christian theology.

Since I first studied theology, I have been concerned with the theology of the cross. This may not have been so clear to those who liked *Theology of Hope*, which I published in 1964, as it was to its critics; yet I believe that it has been the guiding light of my theological thought. This no doubt goes back to the period of my first concern with questions of Christian faith and theology in actual life, as a prisoner of war behind barbed wire. I certainly owe it to the unforgettable lectures on Reformation theology which I heard from Hans Joachim Iwand, Ernst Wolf, and Otto Weber in 1948/49 in Göttingen. Shattered and broken, the survivors of my generation were then returning from camps and hospitals to the lecture room. A theology which did not speak of God in the sight of the one who was abandoned and crucified would have had nothing to say to us then. One cannot say, of course, whether as the result of our experiences we understood the crucified Christ better than anyone else. Experiences cannot be repeated. Moreover, one speaks of personal experiences only to explain why one is fascinated by what one is trying to communicate. It is not the experiences which are important, but the one who has been experienced in them. The theology of the cross which was meaningful to us then, and gave us firm ground beneath our feet, came to my mind again when the movements of hope in the 1960s met stiffer resistance and stronger opponents than they could stand, and many abandoned their hope, either to adapt themselves, half resigned, to the usual course of events, or to withdraw into themselves in total resignation. I can only speak for myself, but on my disappointment at the end of "socialism with a human face" in Czechoslovakia and the end of the civil rights movement in the USA, and at what I hope is only a temporary halt in the reforms in the ecumenical movement and the Catholic Church which began so confidently with the Second Vatican Council and the Uppsala Conference in 1968, the center of my hope and resistance once again became that which, after all, is the driving force of all attempts to open up new horizons in society and the church: the cross of Christ.

The criticism of the church and theology which we have been fortunate enough to experience, and which is justified on sociological, psychological, and ideological grounds, can only be accepted and made radical by a critical theology of the cross. There is an inner criterion of all theology, and of every church which claims to be Christian, and this criterion goes far beyond all political, ideological, and psychological criticism from outside. It is the crucified Christ himself. When churches, theologians, and forms of belief appeal to him—which they must, if they are to be Christian—then they are appealing to the one who judges them most severely and liberates them most radically from lies and vanity, from the struggle for power and from fear. The churches, believers, and theologians must be taken at their word. And this word is "the word of the cross." It is the criterion of their truth, and therefore the criticism of their untruth. The crisis of the church in present-day society is not merely the critical choice between assimilation or retreat into the ghetto, but the crisis of its own existence as the church of the crucified Christ. Any outside criticism which really hits the mark is merely an indication of its inner christological crisis. The question of ecclesiology, however unpleasant it may be for conservatives and progressives, is no more than a short prelude to its internal crisis, for only by Christ is it possible to tell what is a Christian church and what is not. Whether or not Christianity, in an alienated, divided, and oppressive society, itself becomes alienated, divided, and an accomplice of oppression, is ultimately decided only by whether the crucified Christ is a stranger to it or the Lord who determines the form of its existence. The objection has been made that it is still too early to raise this question in the churches and ecclesial communities, that the churches have not yet achieved the openness to the world which society has achieved, that in their ideology and practice they have not even admitted the justification of secular freedom movements and the criticisms which they make—and now their very basis is being questioned. I admit that this tactical question is justified, but do not believe that it leads any further than to the adaptation of antiquated forms of the church to newer forms. As far as I am concerned, the Christian church and Christian theology become relevant to the problems of the modern world only when they reveal the "hard core" of their identity in the crucified Christ and through it are called into question, together with the society in which they live. Ideological and political criticism from outside can only force theology and the church to reveal their true identity and no longer to hide behind an alien mask drawn from history and the present time. Faith, the church, and theology must demonstrate what they really believe and hope about the man from Nazareth who was crucified under Pontius Pilate, and what practical consequences they wish to draw from this. The crucified Christ himself is a challenge to Christian theology and the Christian church, which dare to call themselves by his name.

But what kind of theology of the cross does him justice, and is necessary today? There is a good deal of support in tradition for the theology of the cross, but it was never much loved. It begins with Paul, to whom its foundation is rightly attributed, and then leaps forward to Luther, in whom it is given explicit expression, and is present today in the persecuted churches of the poor and oppressed. It returned to life in a distinctive way in Zinzendorf. It left its mark on the better side of early dialectical theology and on the Luther renaissance of the 1920s. In a famous lecture in 1912, Martin Kähler described the cross of Christ as the "basis and standard of Christology," but unfortunately did not cling to the principle himself. In all the cases we have mentioned, the theology of the cross was relevant only within the framework of human misery and of salvation, even though attempts have been made to take it further.

To return today to the theology of the cross means avoiding one-sided presentations of it in tradition, and comprehending the crucified Christ in the light and context of his resurrection, and therefore of freedom and hope.

To take up the theology of the cross today is to go beyond the limits of the doctrine of salvation and to inquire into the revolution needed in the concept of God. Who is God in the cross of the Christ who is abandoned by God?

To take the theology of the cross further at the present day means to go beyond a concern for personal salvation, and to inquire about the liberation of man and his new relationship to the reality of the demonic crisis in his society. Who is the true man in the sight of the Son of man who was rejected and rose again in the freedom of God?

Finally, to realize the theology of the cross at the present day is to take seriously the claims of Reformation theology to criticize and reform, and to develop it beyond a criticism of the church into a criticism of society. What does it mean to recall the God who was crucified in a society whose official creed is optimism, and which is knee-deep in blood?

The final issue, however, is that of the radical orientation of theology and the church on Christ. Jesus died crying out to God, "My God, why hast thou forsaken me?" All Christian theology and all Christian life is basically an answer to the question which Jesus asked as he died. The atheism of protests and of metaphysical rebellions against God are also answers to this question.

Either Jesus who was abandoned by God is the end of all theology or he is the beginning of a specifically Christian, and therefore critical and liberating, theology and life. The more the "cross of reality" is taken seriously, the more the crucified Christ becomes the general criterion of theology. The issue is not that of an abstract theology of the cross and of suffering, but of a theology of the crucified Christ.

I may be asked why I have turned from "theology of hope" to the theology of the cross. I have given some reasons for this. But is it in itself a step backwards? "Why," asked Wolf-Dieter Marsch with approval, "has Moltmann come back from the all too strident music of Bloch, step by step to the more subdued *eschatologia crucis*?" For me, however, this is not a step back from the trumpets of Easter to the lamentations of Good Friday. As I intend to show, the theology of the cross is none other than the reverse side of the Christian theology of hope, if the starting point of the latter lies in the resurrection of the *crucified* Christ. As I said in *Theology of Hope*, that theology was itself worked out as an *eschatologia crucis*. This book, then, cannot be regarded as a step back. *Theology of Hope* began with the *resurrection* of the crucified Christ, and I am now turning to look at the *cross* of the risen Christ. I was concerned then with the remembrance of Christ in the form of the *hope* of his future, and I am now concerned with hope in the form of the *remembrance* of his death. The dominant theme then was that of *anticipations* of the future of God in the form of promises and hopes; here it is the understanding of the *incarnation* of that future, by way of the sufferings of Christ, in the world's sufferings. Moving away from Ernst Bloch's philosophy of hope, I now turn to the questions of "negative dialectic" and the "critical theory" of [Theodor] W. Adorno and [Max] Horkheimer, together with the experiences and insights of early dialectical theology and existentialist philosophy. Unless it apprehends the pain of the negative, Christian hope cannot be realistic and liberating. In no sense does this theology of the cross "go back step by step"; it is intended to make the theology of hope more concrete, and to add the necessary power of resistance to the power of its visions to inspire to action. I am aware that I am following the same course as Johann Baptist Metz, who for several years has been associating his politically critical eschatology more and more closely with the "dangerous remembrance" of the suffering and death of Christ. Ernst Bloch too is becoming more and more disturbed by the problem of evil, and the failure of both philosophy and theology to give it conceptual form. Nor need anyone feel comforted that the theme of the "theology of revolution" is no longer to be found in the chapter headings. The revolution of all religious, cultural, and

political values which proceeds from the crucified Christ will come in due time.
. . .

. . . In front of me hangs Marc Chagall's picture "Crucifixion in Yellow."
It shows the figure of the crucified Christ in an apocalyptic situation: people
sinking into the sea, people homeless and in flight, and yellow fire blazing in
the background. And with the crucified Christ there appears the angel with the
trumpet and the open roll of the book of life. This picture has accompanied me
for a long time. It symbolizes the cross on the horizon of the world, and can
be thought of as a symbolic expression of the studies which follow. A symbol
invites thought ([Paul] Ricoeur). The symbol of the cross invites rethinking.
And this book is not meant to bring the discussion to a dogmatic conclusion,
but to be, like a symbol, an invitation to thought and rethinking.

THE "CRUCIFIED GOD"

Source: Moltmann 1972; ET 1974/1993:235–49; 267–78.

TRINITARIAN THEOLOGY OF THE CROSS

In all the Christian churches, the cross has become the sign which distinguishes the churches from other religions and modes of belief. At the same time, it must be noted that in the ancient world of religion, the doctrine of the Trinity in the concept of God was the doctrine which marked off Christianity from polytheism, pantheism, and monotheism. When Islam conquered Asia Minor, Christian churches in many places were turned into mosques, and were given an inscription directed against Christians who still might be present: "God did not beget and is not begotten." The element in Christianity which was above all the object of passionate polemic from Islam monotheism was belief in the Trinity. Is this an indispensable part of Christian belief in God? Is there an inner logical connection between the two special features of Christianity, faith in the crucified Jesus and in the triune God? We are not concerned here to mediate in ecumenical fashion between two Christian traditions of which one has been fostered particularly in Protestantism and the other above all in Greek orthodoxy. Our question, rather, is: If we are to understand the "human," the "crucified" God, must we think of God in trinitarian terms? And conversely, can we think of God in trinitarian terms if we do not have the event of the cross in mind?

The doctrine of the Trinity enjoys no special significance in the history of Western theology. It seems to have been hard enough to speak of "God" at all in the life of the churches and in the understanding of believers with any degree of honesty. True, liturgies begin with the traditional formula "In the name of the Father, the Son, and the Holy Spirit," and the Apostles' Creed and its more modern versions have three articles and, in the view of many, claim to speak of God the Creator, the Reconciler, and the Redeemer.

In practice, however, the religious conceptions of many Christians prove to be no more than a weakly Christianized monotheism. However, it is precisely this general monotheism in theology and the belief of Christians which is involved in a crisis of identity. For this general religious monotheism is a permanent occasion for protest atheism, and rightly so. Karl Rahner is also right about Protestant theology when he observes that in theological and religious contexts people only say that "God" has been made man and not that "the Word has been made flesh" (John 3:16). "One could suspect that as regards the catechism of the head and the heart, in contrast to the catechism in books, the Christian idea of the incarnation would not have to change at all, if there were no Trinity."[4] Even the doctrine of grace is monotheistic, and not trinitarian, in practice. Man shares in the grace of God or the divine nature. It is still said that we acquire this grace through Christ, but no trinitarian differentiation in God seems to be necessary. The same thing is true of the doctrine of creation. Faith in the one creator God seems to be sufficient—as among Mohammedans. In eschatology, too, at best there is talk of the coming God and his kingdom or of God as the absolute future. Understandably, Christ then fades away to become the prophet of this future, who fills his function as the representative of the now absent God and can go when God himself comes to occupy his place. Finally, Christian ethics establishes the obedience of man under the rule of God and Christ, and rarely goes beyond a moral monarchy.

From the time of [Philipp] Melanchthon, and particularly since [Friedrich] Schleiermacher and the moral theology of the nineteenth century, the doctrine of the Trinity seems to have been regarded in Protestantism as no more than a theological speculation with no relevance for life, a kind of higher theological mystery for initiates. Although Melanchthon later thought completely in trinitarian terms, the only quotation to be made from his writings by liberal Protestantism in the nineteenth century was that passage from the *Loci communes* of 1521 which was so much in accord with the modern spirit:

> We do better to adore the mysteries of Deity than to investigate them. The Lord God Almighty clothed his Son with flesh that he might draw us from contemplating his own majesty to a consideration of the flesh, and especially of our weakness. . . . Therefore there is no reason why we should labour so much on those exalted topics such as "God," "The Unity and Trinity of God," "The Mystery of Creation," and "The Manner of the Incarnation." . . . To know Christ means to know his benefits, and not as they teach, to reflect upon his natures and the modes of his incarnation. . . . In his letter to the Romans when he was writing a compendium of Christian doctrine, did Paul philosophize about the mysteries of the Trinity, the mode of incarnation, or active and passive creation? . . . He takes up the law, sin, grace, fundamentals on which the knowledge of Christ exclusively rests.[5]

The transition among the Reformers from pure theological considerations to a critical theory of theological practice for faith in fact led to a surrender of the doctrine of the Trinity, because in the tradition of the early church the doctrine of the Trinity had its place in the praise and vision of God, and not in the economy of salvation. But does the doctrine of the Trinity in fact belong in the "consideration of the divine majesty," quite separately from the revelation of God through Christ for us, in our history and our flesh? Once this distinction is made, it is correct to turn from the doctrine of the Trinity as pure speculation and apply ourselves to the history of law, sin, and grace with which we are concerned. But such a distinction is itself fundamentally false. One does not "philosophize" speculatively about the mysteries of the Trinity, as Melanchthon put it, but stands before the question how God is to be understood in the event of the cross of Christ. This is a quite different set of problems.

The move from pure theory to the theory of practice is further demonstrated in the whole of modern thought. This is no longer contemplative thought but operational thought. Reason is no longer perceptive, but productive. It no longer seeks to recognize permanent being in reality, but seeks to recognize in order to change. Modern thought is thought concerned with work and production. It is pragmatic: reality is efficiency. Theories are not verified by eternal ideas but through practice and its results. As has been shown, this also dominated the hermeneutics of nineteenth-century theology. According to Kant, the canon of the interpretation of the biblical and theological traditions is "what is practical." He explains this in lapidary fashion:

> "Virtually no practical consequence can be drawn from the doctrine of the Trinity taken literally, if one seeks to understand it, and still less, once it is realized that it transcends all our concepts." For "by principles of belief is not to be understood that which should be believed (. . .) but that which is possible and purposeful to accept in a practical (moral) intent, though this cannot be demonstrated, but only believed." "Thus such a belief, because it neither makes a better man nor proves one to be such, is no part of religion."[6]

According to Schleiermacher, theological statements must be possible as statements of Christian self-awareness. He therefore put the doctrine of the Trinity at the end of *The Christian Faith* and indeed in an appendix, and remarked: "But this doctrine itself, as ecclesiastically framed, is not an immediate utterance concerning the Christian self-consciousness, but only a combination of several such utterances."[7] Nevertheless, Schleiermacher was open to a complete reshaping of the doctrine of the Trinity. "We have the less reason to regard this doctrine as finally settled since it did not receive any fresh treatment when the Evangelical (Protestant) Church was set up; and so there must still be in store for it a transformation which will go back to its very beginnings."[8]

Precisely this must be attempted today. We cannot achieve it in the form of the pure theory of antiquity; that appears to us to be pure speculation. *Quod supra nos nihil ad nos!* We cannot say of God who he is of himself and in himself; we can only say who he is for us in the history of Christ which reaches us in our history. Nor can we achieve it in the forms of modern thought which are so related to experience and practice. Or can we make something practical and relevant to Christian self-understanding out of the way in which God acts towards God? In that case we would have to give up the distinction made in the early church and in tradition between the "God in himself" and the "God for us," or between "God in his majesty" and "God veiled in the flesh of Christ," as Luther and Melanchthon put it. We would have to find the relationship of God to God in the reality of the event of the cross and therefore in our reality, and consider it there. In practice that would amount to a "complete reshaping of the doctrine of the Trinity," because in that case the nature of God would have to be the human history of Christ and not a divine "nature" separate from man.

Why did the doctrine of the Trinity become isolated speculation and a mere decoration for dogmatics after the Middle Ages? Karl Rahner has pointed out that after the supplanting of the *Sentences* of Peter Lombard by the *Summa* of Thomas Aquinas, a momentous distinction was introduced into the doctrine of God. This was the distinction between the tractates *De Deo uno* and *De Deo triuno* and the order in which they are put, which is still felt to be a matter of course even today. The purpose behind this separation and arrangement was apologetic. Following Thomas, one began with the question "Is there a God?," and demonstrated with the help of the natural light of human reason and the cosmological arguments for the existence of God that there was a God and that God was one. Then, with the same method, conclusions were drawn as to the metaphysical, non-human properties of the divine nature. This knowledge was assigned to natural theology. Only then was a move made to describe the inner being of God with the aid of the supernatural light of grace, a move towards *theologica christiana*, *theologia salvifica*, the saving knowledge of God.

In the first tractate there was a discussion of the metaphysical properties of God in himself, and in the second of his salvation-historical relationships to us. Even in Protestant orthodoxy, first a general doctrine of God "*De deo*" was outlined, after which there followed teaching on the "*mysterium de sancta trinitate.*" The great Greek theology of the Cappadocians certainly understood all theology as the doctrine of the Trinity. But it made a distinction between the "immanent Trinity" and the "Trinity in the economy of salvation," and thus distinguished in its own way between the inner being of God and salvation history, as between original and copy, idea and manifestation. Karl Barth, who differed from the Protestant tradition of the nineteenth century by making his *Church Dogmatics* begin not with apologetic prolegomena or with basic rules for hermeneutics but with the doctrine of the Trinity, which for him was the hermeneutic canon for understanding the Christian principle "Jesus Christ the Lord," followed the Cappadocians in distinguishing between the immanent Trinity and the economy of the Trinity. God is "beforehand in himself" everything that he reveals in Christ. God corresponds to himself.

Karl Rahner has advanced the thesis that both distinctions are inappropriate and that we must say: 1. The Trinity *is* the nature of God and the nature of God *is* the Trinity; 2. The economic Trinity *is* the immanent Trinity, and the immanent Trinity *is* the economic Trinity.

> God's relationship to us is three-fold. And this three-fold (free and unmerited) relationship to us is not merely an image or analogy of the immanent Trinity; it *is* this Trinity itself, even though communicated as free grace.[9]

Thus the unity and the Trinity of God belong together in one tractate. One cannot first describe the unity of the nature of God and then distinguish between the three divine persons or hypostases, as in that case one is essentially dealing with four beings. The being of God then becomes the hypostasis of God, so that the three persons can be renounced and one can think in monotheistic terms.

Before we consider this question further, we must also look at the particular context in which trinitarian thought is necessary at all. Otherwise these considerations could easily become a new version of traditional teaching under the changed conditions of modern times, just for the sake of a tradition which once existed. As Schleiermacher rightly said, any new version of the doctrine of the Trinity must be "a transformation which goes right back to its first beginnings." The place of the doctrine of the Trinity is not the "thinking of thought," but the cross of Jesus. "Concepts without perception are empty" (Kant). The perception of the trinitarian concept of God is the cross of Jesus. "Perceptions without concepts are blind" (Kant). The theological concept for the perception of the crucified Christ is the doctrine of the Trinity. The material principle of the doctrine of the Trinity is the cross of Christ. The formal principle of knowledge of the cross is the doctrine of the Trinity. Where do the first beginnings lie? As is well known, the New Testament does not contain any developed doctrine of the Trinity. That only arose in the controversies of the early church over the unity of Christ with God himself. I believe that [Bernhard] Steffen, in his long-forgotten book *Das Dogma vom Kreuz. Beitrag zu einer staurozentrischen Theologie* (1920: "The Dogma of the Cross. A Contribution to a Staurocentric Theology"), saw something quite astonishing:

> The scriptural basis for Christian belief in the triune God is not the scanty trinitarian formulas of the New Testament, but the thoroughgoing, unitary testimony of the cross; and the shortest expression of the Trinity is the divine act of the cross, in which the Father allows the Son to sacrifice himself through the Spirit.[10]

We must test this argument, according to which the theology of the cross must be the doctrine of the Trinity and the doctrine of the Trinity must be the theology of the cross, because otherwise the human, crucified God cannot be fully perceived.

What happened on the cross of Christ between Christ and the God whom he called his Father and proclaimed as "having come near" to abandoned men? According to Paul and Mark, Jesus himself was abandoned by this very God, his Father, and died with a cry of godforsakenness.

> That God delivers up his Son is one of the most unheard-of statements in the New Testament. We must understand "deliver up" in its full sense and not water it down to mean "send" or "give." What happened here is what Abraham did not need to do to Isaac (cf. Rom. 8:32): Christ was quite deliberately abandoned by the Father to the fate of death: God subjected him to the power of corruption, whether this be called man or death. To express the idea in its most acute form, one might say in the words of the dogma of the early church: the first person of the Trinity casts out and annihilates the second. . . A theology of the cross cannot be expressed more radically than it is here.[11]

Consequently we shall begin with a theological interpretation of those sayings which express the abandonment of Christ by God.

In the passion narratives, which present Jesus' death in the light of the life that he lived, the word for deliver up, παραδιδόναι, has a clearly negative connotation. It means: hand over, give up, deliver, betray, cast out, kill. The word "deliver up" (Rom. 1:18ff.) also appears in Pauline theology as an expression of the wrath and judgment of God and thus of the lostness of man. God's wrath over the godlessness of man is manifest in that he "delivers them up" to their godlessness and inhumanity. According to Israelite understanding, guilt and punishment lie in one and the same event. So too here: men who abandon God are abandoned by God. Godlessness and godforsakenness are two sides of the same event. The heathen turn the glory of the invisible God into a picture like corruptible being—"and God surrenders them to the lusts of their heart" (Rom. 1:24; par. 1:26 and 1:28). Judgment lies in the fact that God delivers men up to the corruption which they themselves have chosen and abandons them in their forsakenness. It is not the case that Paul threatens sinners, whether Jews or Gentiles, with a distant judgment; rather, he sees the wrath of God as now being manifest in the inhuman idolatry of the Gentiles and the inhuman righteousness by works of the Jews. Guilt and punishment are not separated temporally and juristically. In the godforsakenness of the godless idolaters Paul now already sees the revelation of the wrath of God, the judgment that is being accomplished. In this situation (Rom. 1:18) he proclaims the saving righteousness of God in the crucified Christ. But how can deliverance and liberation for godforsaken man lie in the figure of the godforsaken, crucified Christ?

Paul introduces a radical change in the sense of "deliver up" when he recognizes and proclaims the godforsakenness of Jesus in the eschatological context of his resurrection rather than in the historical context of his life. In Rom. 8:31f., we read: "If God is for us, who is against us? He who did not spare his own Son but gave him up for us all, will he not also give us all things with him?" According to this God gave up his own Son, abandoned him, cast him out, and delivered him up to an accursed death. Paul says in even stronger terms: "He made him sin for us" (2 Cor. 5:21) and "He became a curse for us" (Gal. 3:13). Thus in the total, inextricable abandonment of Jesus by his God and Father, Paul sees the delivering up of the Son by the Father for godless and godforsaken man. Because God "does not spare" his Son, all the godless are spared. Though they are godless, they are not godforsaken, precisely because God has abandoned his own Son and has delivered him up for them. Thus the delivering up of the Son to godforsakenness is the ground for the justification of the godless and the acceptance of enmity by God. It may therefore be said that the Father delivers up his Son on the cross in order to be the Father of those who are delivered up. The Son is delivered up to this death in order to become the Lord of both dead and living. And if Paul speaks emphatically of God's "own Son," the not-sparing and abandoning also involves the Father himself. In the forsakenness of the Son the Father also forsakes himself. In the surrender of the Son the Father also surrenders himself, though not in the same way. For Jesus suffers dying in forsakenness, but not death itself; for men can no longer "suffer" death, because suffering presupposes life. But the Father who abandons him and delivers him up suffers the death of the Son in the infinite grief of love. We cannot therefore say here in patripassian terms that the Father also suffered and died. The suffering and dying of the Son, forsaken by the Father, is a different kind of suffering from the suffering of the Father in the death of the Son. Nor can the death of Jesus be understood in theopaschite terms as the "death of God." To understand what happened between Jesus and his God and Father on the cross, it is necessary to talk in trinitarian terms. The Son suffers dying, the Father suffers the death of the Son. The grief of the Father here is just as important as the death of the Son. The Fatherlessness of the Son is matched by the Sonlessness of the Father, and if God has constituted himself as the Father of Jesus Christ, then he also suffers the death of his Fatherhood in the death of the Son. Unless this were so, the doctrine of the Trinity would still have a monotheistic background.

In Gal. 2:20 the "delivering up" formula also occurs with Christ as its subject: ". . . the Son of God, who loved me and gave himself for me." According to this it is not just the Father who delivers Jesus up to die godforsaken on the cross, but the Son who gives himself up. This corresponds to the Synoptic account of the passion story according to which Jesus consciously and willingly walked the way of the cross and was not overtaken by death as by an evil, unfortunate fate. It is theologically important to note that the formula in Paul occurs with both Father and Son as subject, since it expresses a deep conformity between the will of the Father and the will of the Son in the event of the cross, as the Gethsemane narrative also records. This deep community of will between Jesus and his God and Father is now expressed precisely at the point of their deepest separation, in the godforsaken and accursed death of Jesus on the cross. If both historical godforsakenness and eschatological surrender can be seen in Christ's death on the cross, then this event contains community between Jesus and his Father in separation, and separation in community.

As Rom. 8:32 and Gal. 2:20 show, Paul already described the godforsakenness of Jesus as a surrender and his surrender as love. Johannine theology sums this up in the sentence: "God so loved the world that he gave his only-begotten Son that all who believe in him should not perish but have everlasting life" (3:16). And 1 John sees the very existence of God himself in this event of love on the cross of Christ: "God is love" (4:16). In other words, God does not just love as he is angry, chooses, or rejects. He *is* love, that is, he exists in love. He constitutes his existence in the event of his love. He exists as love in the event of the cross. Thus in the concepts of earlier systematic theology it is possible to talk of a *homoousion*, in respect of an identity of substance, the community of will of the Father and the Son on the cross. However, the unity contains not only identity of substance but also the wholly and utterly different character and inequality of the event on the cross. In the cross, Father and Son are most deeply separated in forsakenness and at the same time are most inwardly one in their surrender. What proceeds from this event between Father and Son is the Spirit which justifies the godless, fills the forsaken with love, and even brings the dead alive, since even the fact that they are dead cannot exclude them from this event of the cross; the death in God also includes them.

In this way we have already used trinitarian phrases to understand what happened on the cross between Jesus and his God and Father. If one wanted to present the event within the framework of the doctrine of two natures, one could only use the simple concept of God (*esse simplex*). In that case one would have to say: what happened on the cross was an event between God and God. It was a deep division in God himself, insofar as God abandoned God and contradicted himself, and at the same time a unity in God, insofar as God was at one with God and corresponded to himself. In that case one would have to put the formula in a paradoxical way: God died the death of the godless on the cross and yet did not die. God is dead and yet is not dead. If one can only use the simple concept of God from the doctrine of two natures, as tradition shows, one will always be inclined to restrict it to the person of the Father who abandons and accepts Jesus, delivers him and raises him up, and in so doing will "evacuate" the cross of deity. But if one begins by leaving on one side any concept of God which is already presupposed and taken from metaphysics, one must speak of the one whom Jesus called "Father" and in respect of whom he understood himself as "the Son." In that case one will understand the deadly aspect of the event between the Father who forsakes and the Son who is forsaken, and conversely the living aspect of the event between the Father who loves and the Son who loves. The Son suffers in his love being forsaken by the Father as he dies. The Father suffers in his love the grief of the death of the Son. In that case, whatever proceeds from the event between the Father and the Son must be understood as the spirit of the surrender of the Father and the Son, as the spirit which creates love for forsaken men, as the spirit which brings the dead alive. It is the unconditioned and therefore boundless love which proceeds from the grief of the Father and the dying of the Son and reaches forsaken men in order to create in them the possibility and the force of new life. The doctrine of two natures must understand the event of the cross statically as a reciprocal relationship between two qualitatively different natures, the divine nature which is incapable of suffering and the human nature which is capable of suffering. Here we have interpreted the event of the cross in trinitarian terms as an event concerned with a relationship between persons in which these persons constitute themselves in their relationship with each other. In so doing we have not just seen one person of the Trinity suffer in the event of the cross, as though the Trinity were already present in itself, in the divine nature. And we have not interpreted the death of Jesus as a divine-human event, but as a trinitarian event between the Son and the Father. What is in question in the relationship of Christ to his Father is not his divinity and humanity and their relationship to each other but the total, personal aspect of the Sonship of Jesus. This starting point is not the same as that to be found in the tradition. It overcomes the dichotomy between immanent and economic Trinity, and that between the nature of God and his inner tri-unity. It makes trinitarian thought necessary for the complete perception of the cross of Christ.

Faith understands the historical event between the Father who forsakes and the Son who is forsaken on the cross in eschatological terms as an event between the Father who loves and the Son who is loved in the present spirit of the love that creates life.

If the cross of Jesus is understood as a divine event, i.e., as an event between Jesus and his God and Father, it is necessary to speak in trinitarian terms of the Son and the Father and the Spirit. In that case the doctrine of the Trinity is no longer an exorbitant and impractical speculation about God, but is nothing other than a shorter version of the passion narrative of Christ in its significance for the eschatological freedom of faith and the life of oppressed nature. It protects faith from both monotheism and atheism because it keeps believers at the cross. The content of the doctrine of the Trinity is the real cross of Christ himself. The form of the crucified Christ is the Trinity. In that case, what is salvation? Only if all disaster, forsakenness by God, absolute death, the infinite curse of damnation, and sinking into nothingness is in God himself, is community with this God eternal salvation, infinite joy, indestructible election, and divine life. The "bifurcation" in God must contain the whole uproar of history within itself. Men must be able to recognize rejection, the curse, and final nothingness in it. The cross stands between the Father and the Son in all the harshness of its forsakenness. If one describes the life of God within the Trinity as the "history of God" (Hegel), this history of God contains within itself the whole abyss of godforsakenness, absolute death, and the non-God. "*Nemo contra Deum nisi Deus ipse.*" Because this death took place in the history between Father and Son on the cross on Golgotha, there proceeds from it the spirit of life, love, and election to salvation. The concrete "history of God" in the death of Jesus on the cross on Golgotha therefore contains within itself all the depths and abysses of human history and therefore can be understood as the history of history. All human history, however much it may be determined by guilt and death, is taken up into this "history of God," i.e., into the Trinity, and integrated into the future of the "history of God." There is no suffering which in this history of God is not God's suffering; no death which has not been God's death in the history on Golgotha. Therefore there is no life, no fortune, and no joy which have not been integrated by his history into eternal life, the eternal joy of God. To think of "God in history" always leads to theism and to atheism. To think of "history in God" leads beyond that, into new creation and *theopoiesis*. To "think of history in God" however, first means to understand humanity in the suffering and dying of Christ, and that means all humanity, with its dilemmas and its despairs.

In that case, what sense does it make to talk of "God"? I think that the unity of the dialectical history of Father and Son and Spirit in the cross on Golgotha, full of tension as it is, can be described so to speak retrospectively as "God." In that case, a trinitarian theology of the cross no longer interprets the event of the cross in the framework or in the name of a metaphysical or moral concept of God which has already been presupposed—we have shown that this does not do justice to the cross, but evacuates it of meaning—but develops from this history what is to be understood by "God." Anyone who speaks of God in Christian terms must tell of the history of Jesus as a history between the Son and the Father. In that case, "God" is not another nature or a heavenly person or a moral authority, but in fact an "event." However, it is not the event of co-humanity, but the event of Golgotha, the event of the love of the Son and the grief of the Father from which the Spirit who opens up the future and creates life in fact derives.

In that case, is there no "personal God"? If "God" is an event, can one pray to him? One cannot pray to an "event." In that case there is in fact no "personal God" as a person projected in heaven. But there are persons in God: the Son, the Father, and the Spirit. In that case one does not simply pray to God as a heavenly Thou, but prays *in* God. One does not pray to an event but *in* this event. One prays through the Son to the Father in the Spirit. In the brotherhood of Jesus, the person who prays has access to the Fatherhood of the Father and to the Spirit of hope. Only in this way does the character of Christian prayer become clear. The New Testament made a very neat distinction in Christian prayer between the Son and the Father. We ought to take that up, and ought not to speak of "God" in such an undifferentiated way, thus opening up the way to atheism.

"God *is* love," says 1 John 4:16. Thus in view of all that has been said, the doctrine of the Trinity can be understood as an interpretation of the ground, the event, and the experience of that love in which the one who has been condemned to love finds new possibility for life because he has found in it the grace of the impossibility of the death of rejection. It is not the interpretation of love as an ideal, a heavenly power, or as a commandment, but of love as an event in a loveless, legalistic world: the event of an unconditioned and boundless love which comes to meet man, which takes hold of those who are unloved and forsaken, unrighteous or outside the law, and gives them a new identity, liberates them from the norms of social identifications and from the guardians of social norms and idolatrous images. What Jesus commanded in the Sermon on the Mount as love of one's enemy has taken place on the cross through Jesus' dying and the grief of the Father in the power of the spirit, for the godless and the loveless. Just as the unconditional love of Jesus for the rejected made the Pharisees his enemies and brought him to the cross, so unconditional love also means enmity and persecution in a world in which the life of man is made dependent on particular social norms, conditions, and achievements. A love which takes precedence and robs these conditions of their force is folly and scandal in this world. But if the believer experiences his freedom and the new possibility of his life in the fact that the love of God reaches him, the loveless and the unloved, in the cross of Christ, what must be the thoughts of a theology which corresponds to this love? In that case it is a love which creates its own conditions, since it cannot accept the conditions of lovelessness and the law. Further, it cannot command love and counterlove. As its purpose is freedom, it is directed towards freedom. So it cannot prohibit slavery and enmity, but must suffer this contradiction, and can only take upon itself grief at this contradiction and the grief of protest against it, and manifest this grief in protest. That is what happened on the cross of Christ. God is unconditional love, because he takes on himself grief at the contradiction in men and does not angrily suppress this contradiction. God allows himself to be forced out. God suffers, God allows himself to be crucified and is crucified, and in this consummates his unconditional love that is so full of hope. But that means that in the cross he becomes himself the condition of this love. The loving Father has a parallel in the loving Son and in the Spirit creates similar patterns of love in man in revolt. The fact of this love can be contradicted. It can be crucified, but in crucifixion it finds its fulfillment and becomes love of the enemy. Thus its suffering proves to be stronger than hate. Its might is powerful in weakness and gains power over its enemies in grief, because it gives life even to its enemies and opens up the future to change. If in the freedom given through experience of it the believer understands the crucifixion as an event of the love of the Son and the grief of the Father, that is, as an event between God and God, as an event within the Trinity, he perceives the liberating word of love which creates new life. By the death of the Son he is taken up into the grief of the Father and experiences a liberation which is a new element in this de-divinized and legalistic world, which is itself even a new element over against the original creation of the word. He is in fact taken up into the inner life of God, if in the cross of Christ he experiences the love of God for the godless, the enemies, insofar as the history of Christ is the inner life of God himself. In that case, if he lives in this love, he lives in God and God in him. If he lives in this freedom, he lives in God and God in him. If one conceives of the Trinity as an event of love in the suffering and the death of Jesus—and that is something which faith must do—then the Trinity is no self-contained group in heaven, but an eschatological process open for men on earth, which stems from the cross of Christ. By the secular cross on Golgotha, understood as open vulnerability and as the love of God for loveless and unloved, dehumanized men, God's being and God's life is open to true man. There is no "outside the gate" with God ([Wolfgang] Borchert), if God himself is the one who died outside the gate on Golgotha for those who are outside. . . .

THE EXPERIENCE OF HUMAN LIFE IN THE PATHOS OF GOD

Man develops his manhood always in relationship to the Godhead of his God. He experiences his existence in relationship to that which illuminates him as the supreme being. He orients his life on the ultimate value. His fundamental decisions are made in accordance with what unconditionally concerns him. Thus the divine is the situation in which man experiences, develops, and shapes himself. Theology and anthropology are involved in a reciprocal relationship. Therefore the theology of the "crucified God" also leads to a corresponding anthropology. Hitherto our dominant concern has been with the question of the history and the quality of the suffering of God; now we must inquire into the development of the humanity of man in this situation with God. A comparison of Christian theology with the *apathetic theology* of Greek antiquity and the *pathetic theology* of later Jewish philosophy of religion may help to define the context more clearly. We started by asserting that the adoption of the Greek philosophical concept of the "God incapable of suffering" by the early church led to difficulties in Christology which only more recent theology has set out to overcome. But before the "suffering of God" had become a theme of Christian theology in the present, Jewish theology had already been discussing the theme. Christian theology cannot but learn from this new Jewish exegesis of the history of God in the Old Testament and in the present suffering of the Jewish people.

(A) THE APATHEIA OF GOD AND THE FREEDOM OF MAN

In the ancient world, early Christianity encountered *apatheia* as a metaphysical axiom and an ethical ideal with irresistible force. On this concept were concentrated the worship of the divinity of God and the struggle for man's freedom. Like *pathos*, the word *apatheia* has many connotations. It means incapable of being affected by outside influences, incapable of feeling, as is the case with dead things, and the freedom of the spirit from inner needs and external damage. In the physical sense *apatheia* means unchangeableness; in the psychological sense, insensitivity; and in the ethical sense, freedom. In contrast to this, *pathos* denotes need, compulsion, drives, dependence, lower passions, and unwilled suffering. Since Plato and Aristotle the metaphysical and ethical perfection of God has been described as *apatheia*. According to Plato, God is good and therefore cannot be the cause of anything evil, of punishment and sorrow. The poetic conceptions of the gods as capricious, envious, vengeful, and punitive, which were meant to arouse emotions, *pathe*, among the audience of the tragedy, which would lead to *katharsis*, are rejected as "inappropriate to God." They do not fit the moral and political "guidelines for the doctrine of the gods." It is inappropriate to present God as the *auctor malorum*. As that which is perfect, the Godhead needs nothing. If it has no needs, it is therefore also unchangeable, for any change shows a deficiency in being. God does not need the services or the emotions of men for his own life. Because he is perfect, he needs no friends nor will he have any. "Friendship occurs where love is offered in return. But in friendship with God there is no room for love to be offered in return, indeed there is not even room for love. For it would be absurd if anyone were to assert that he loved Zeus."[12] As like is only known and loved by like, the Godhead is self-sufficient. From the time of Aristotle onwards, the metaphysical principle which has been derived from this has been θεὸς ἀπαθής.[13] As *actus purus* and pure causality, nothing can happen to God for him to suffer. As the perfect being, he is without emotions. Anger, hate, and envy are alien to him. Equally alien to him are love, compassion, and mercy. "The blessed and incorruptible being does not itself endure tribulation, nor does it burden others with it. Therefore it knows neither wrath nor favor. This sort of thing is to be found only in a weak being." God thinks himself eternally and in this is the thought of thought. God is ever-willing. Therefore both will and thought are part of his apathic being.

If it is the moral ideal of the wise man to become similar to the divinity and participate in its sphere, he must overcome needs and drives and lead a life free of trouble and fear, anger and love, in *apatheia*. He will find rest in God in the thinking of thought. He will find the eternal presence of God in the eternal will. The school of the Skeptics demanded the withholding of judgment (ἐποχή). The man of understanding must stand firm in *ataraxia*, and the wise man will possess *apatheia*. His knowledge is not disturbed by any emotions of the soul or any interests of the body. He lives in the higher sphere of the Logos. He does not even feel what other men regard as good or evil. He uses all things as though they had a value, although he ascribes no value to them. Imperturbability, dispassionateness, mildness follow the *epoche* of the Skeptics like a shadow. The middle situation (μετριοπάθεια) in the life of feeling and the senses which was originally praised, even by Aristotle, was then superseded by the Stoic ethic of the *apatheia* for which the wise man strives. In the struggle for virtue, the wise man acquires that which the Godhead possesses by nature.

Ancient Judaism, above all in the person of Philo, and ancient Christianity, took up this ideal of *apatheia* in theology and ethics and sought to fulfill it and go beyond it. Philo presents Abraham as the model of *apatheia*, but also praises his *metriopatheia*. He too regards *apatheia* as the goal of perfection. But man does not strive to be free for himself and content with himself. Rather, he strives to become free and without needs in the service of God who alone gives the power to achieve *apatheia*. Because Philo is in the area influenced by the Old Testament understanding of God, his doctrine of *apatheia* differs from that of the Stoics, although he has taken over their form of it. For him the *apatheia* strived for is indeed meant to lead to similarity with God, but in essence it leads to a different "situation of God."[14]

An examination of the discussion of *apatheia* in ancient Greece, Judaism, and Christianity shows that *apatheia* does not mean the petrification of men, nor does it denote those symptoms of illness which are today described as apathy, indifference, and alienation. Rather, it denotes the freedom of man and his superiority to the world in corresponding to the perfect, all-sufficient freedom of the Godhead. *Apatheia* is entering into the higher divine sphere of the Logos. On the other hand, only the lower drives and compulsions were understood as *pathos*. What today is described as the *pathos of life*, the meaning which fills a life, brings it alive and enhances it, was not included among the *pathe*. What Christianity proclaimed as the *agape* of God and the believer was rarely translated as *pathos*. Because true *agape* derives from liberation from the inward and outward fetters of the flesh (*sarx*), and loves without self-seeking and anxiety, without *ira et studio*, *apatheia* could be taken up as an enabling ground for this love and be filled with it. Love arises from the spirit and from freedom, not from desire or anxiety. The apathic God could therefore be understood as the free God who freed others for himself. The negation of need, desire, and compulsion expressed by *apatheia* was taken up and filled with a new positive content. The apathetic theology of antiquity was accepted as a preparation for the trinitarian theology of the love of God and of men. Only a long history of use in Judaism and Christianity changed the word and provided it with another context of meanings. It associated passion with love out of freedom for others and those who were different, and taught an understanding of the meaning of the suffering of love from the history of the passion of Israel and of Christ. These changes must be noted if justice is to be done to the apathetic theology of antiquity and its acceptance in Judaism and Christianity. Nevertheless, the question remains open whether the positive side of the new relationship with God did not inevitably have to break out of the framework of the presupposed negation of the negative, and still must do so.

(B) THE PATHOS OF GOD AND THE SYMPATHEIA OF MEN

It was Abraham Heschel who, in controversy with Hellenism and the Jewish philosophy of religion of Jehuda Halevi, Maimonides, and Spinoza which was influenced by it, first described the prophets' proclamation of God as *pathetic theology*.[15] The prophets had no "idea" of God, but understood themselves and the people in the *situation of God*. Heschel called this situation of God the *pathos of God*. It has nothing to do with the irrational human emotions like desire, anger, anxiety, envy, or sympathy, but describes the way in which God is affected by events and human actions and suffering in history. He is affected by them because he is interested in his creation, his people, and his right. The *pathos* of God is intentional and transitive, not related to itself but to the history of the covenant people. God already emerged from himself at the creation of the world "in the beginning." In the covenant he enters into the world and the people of his choice. The "history" of God cannot therefore be separated from the history of his people. The history of the divine *pathos* is embedded in this history of men. Because creation, covenant, and history of God spring from his freedom, his effective *pathos* is quite different from that of the capricious, envious, and heroic divinities of the mythical sagas, who are indeed subject to fate (*ananke*). It is the *pathos* of his free relationship to creation, to the people, and to history. The prophets never identified God's *pathos* with his being, since for them it was not something absolute, but the form of his relationship to others. The divine *pathos* is expressed in the relationship of God to his people. The concept of an apathic God was inevitably alien to them. Prophecy, therefore, is in essence not a looking forward into the future to see what is appointed in unalterable destiny or a predestined divine plan of salvation, but insight into the present *pathos* of God, his suffering caused by Israel's disobedience, and his passion for his right and his honor in the world. If the divine *pathos* is grounded in his freedom, it is not pure will, as in the Islamic concept of God. Rather, it is his interest in his creation and his people, by which God transfers his being into the history of his relationship and his covenant with man. God takes man so seriously that he suffers under the actions of man and can be injured by them. At the heart of the prophetic proclamation there stands the certainty that God is interested in the world to the point of suffering.

As Abraham Heschel shows in a comparison with Greek philosophy, with Confucianism, Buddhism, and Islam, the Israelite understanding of the *pathos* of God is unique.[16] But in a way parallel to that taken by Christian theology, Jewish scholasticism in the Middle Ages also sought to adapt itself to the idea of the *theos apathes*. "Any passion is evil." Therefore Jehuda Halevi thought that compassion and sympathy could only be signs of weakness in the soul and were not appropriate to God. "He is a just judge; he ordains the poverty of one individual and the wealth of another without any change in his nature, without feelings of sympathy with one or anger against another." According to Maimonides, no predicate which involves corporeality and the capacity for suffering may be applied to God. "God is free from passions; he is moved neither by feelings of joy nor feelings of grief." So too Spinoza asserted that strictly speaking "God neither loves nor hates." So for a long time the apathic God became a fundamental principle for Jewish theology too.

Now if one starts from the *pathos* of God, one does not think of God in his absoluteness and freedom, but understands his passion and his interest in terms of the history of the covenant. The more the covenant is taken seriously as the revelation of God, the more profoundly one can understand the historicity of God and history in God.[17] If God has opened his heart in the covenant with his people, he is injured by disobedience and suffers in the people. What the Old Testament terms *the wrath of God* does not belong in the category of the anthropomorphic transference of lower human emotions to God, but in the category of the divine *pathos*. His wrath is injured love and therefore a mode of his reaction to men. Love is the source and the basis of the possibility of the wrath of God. The opposite of love is not wrath, but indifference. Indifference towards justice and injustice would be a retreat on the part of God from the covenant. But his wrath is an expression of his abiding interest in man. Anger and love do not therefore keep a balance. "His wrath lasts for the twinkling of an eye," and, as the Jonah story shows, God takes back his anger for the sake of his love in reaction to human repentance. As injured love, the wrath of God is not something that is inflicted, but a divine suffering of evil. It is a sorrow which goes through his opened heart. He suffers in his passion for his people.[18]

In the sphere of the apathic God man becomes a *homo apatheticus*. In the situation of the pathos of God he becomes a *homo sympatheticus*.[19] The divine *pathos* is reflected in man's participation, his hopes, and his prayers. Sympathy is the openness of a person to the present of another. It has the structure of dialogue. In the *pathos* of God, man is filled with the spirit of God. He becomes the friend of God, feels sympathy with God and for God. He does not enter into a mystical union but into a sympathetic union with God. He is angry with God's wrath. He suffers with God's suffering. He loves with God's love. He hopes with God's hope. Abraham Heschel has developed his theology of the divine *pathos* as a *dipolar theology*. God is free in himself and at the same time interested in his covenant relationship and affected by human history. In this covenant relationship he has spoken of the *pathos* of God and the *sympatheia* of man, and in so doing has introduced a second bipolarity. For the *sympatheia* of man answers the *pathos* of God in the spirit. The prophet is an *ish haruach*, a man driven and emboldened by the spirit of God. There is probably a hint here of the idea of a dual personality in God. Both notions can be followed further in the theology of the rabbis and are further deepened by them.

As [Peter] Kuhn has demonstrated,[20] the rabbis at the turn of the ages spoke of a number of stages in the self-humiliation of God: in the creation, in the call of Abraham, Isaac, and Jacob and the history of Israel, in the exodus and in the exile. Psalm 18:36—"When you humble me you make me great"—was understood to mean: "You show me that you are great by your humiliation of yourself." God dwells in heaven and among those who are of a humble and contrite spirit. He is the God of gods and brings justice to widows and orphans. He is lofty and yet looks upon the lowly. So he is present in two opposite ways. God already renounces his honor in the beginning at creation. Like a servant, he carries the torch before Israel into the wilderness. Like a servant he bears Israel and its sins on his back. He descends into the thornbush, the ark of the covenant, and the temple. He meets men in those who are in straits, in the lowly and the small. These *accommodations* of God to the limitations of human history at the same time contain *anticipations* of his future indwelling in his whole creation, when in the end all lands will be full of his glory. He enters not only into the situation of the limited creature, but even into the situation of the guilty and suffering creature. His lamentation and sorrow over Israel in the exile show that God's whole existence with Israel is in suffering. Israel is "the apple of his eye." He cannot forget Israel's suffering, for were he to do that he would have to forget "his own rights." So God goes with Israel into the

Babylonian exile. In his "indwelling" in the people he suffers with the people, goes with them into prison, feels sorrow with the martyrs. So conversely the liberation of Israel also means the liberation of that "indwelling of God" from its suffering. In his Shekinah the Holy One of Israel shares Israel's suffering and Israel's redemption, so that in this respect it is true that "God has redeemed himself from Egypt together with his people: 'The redemption is for me and for you.' God himself 'was led out (with Israel from Egypt).'"[21] Because his name has been bound up with Israel, Israel is redeemed when God has redeemed himself, that is, has glorified his name; and the suffering of God is the means by which Israel is redeemed. God himself is "the ransom" for Israel.[22]

A shattering expression of the *theologia crucis* which is suggested in the rabbinic theology of God's humiliation of himself is to be found in *Night*, a book written by [Elie] Wiesel, a survivor of Auschwitz:

> The SS hanged two Jewish men and a youth in front of the whole camp. The men died quickly, but the death throes of the youth lasted for half an hour. "Where is God? Where is he?" someone asked behind me. As the youth still hung in torment in the noose after a long time, I heard the man call again, "Where is God now?" And I heard a voice in myself answer: "Where is he? He is here. He is hanging there on the gallows . . ."[23]

Any other answer would be blasphemy. There cannot be any other Christian answer to the question of this torment. To speak here of a God who could not suffer would make God a demon. To speak here of an absolute God would make God an annihilating nothingness. To speak here of an indifferent God would condemn men to indifference.

But theological reflection must draw the consequence from such experiences of the suffering of God in suffering which cannot be accounted for in human terms. Rabbinic talk of God's humiliation of himself presses towards a distinction in God between God himself and his "indwelling" (Shekinah), between God and the indwelling spirit of God. Judaism of the rabbinic period developed the notion of such a dual personality in God in order to be able to express the experience of the suffering of God with Israel and in suffering to protect that "religion of sympathy," the openness for God against the curse of God (Job 2:9), hardening of the heart, and the surrender of hope. But the intrinsic theological problem arises when one asks what is the cause of the suffering of the God who suffers with imprisoned, persecuted, and murdered Israel. Does he merely suffer for human injustice and human wickedness? Does the Shekinah, which wanders with Israel through the dust of the streets and hangs on the gallows in Auschwitz, suffer in the God who holds the ends of the earth in his hand? In that case not only would suffering affect God's *pathos* externally, so that it might be said that God himself suffers at the human history of injustice and force, but suffering would be the history in the midst of God himself. We are not concerned here to set up paradoxes, but to ask whether the experiences of the passion and the suffering of God lead into the inner mystery of God himself in which God himself confronts us.

(C) THE FULLNESS OF LIFE IN THE TRINITARIAN HISTORY OF GOD

Christian faith does not believe in a new "idea" of God. In the fellowship of the crucified Christ it finds itself in a new "situation of God" and participates in that with all its existence.

Christian theology can only adopt the insight and the longing of Hellenistic *apathetic theology* as a presupposition for the knowledge of the freedom of God and the liberation of fettered man. For its own concerns it completely reverses the direction of that theology: it is not the ascent of man to God but the revelation of God in his self-emptying in the crucified Christ which opens up God's sphere of life to the development of man in him. This situation is related to the situation of the Jews, for the *pathos* of God perceived and proclaimed by the prophets is the presupposition for the Christian understanding of the living God from the passion of Christ. But the *pathetic theology* of Judaism must begin from the covenant of God with the people and from membership of this people of God. Therefore there is for it a direct correspondence between the *pathos* of God and the *sympatheia* of men. On the basis of the presupposition of election to the covenant and the people it is necessary only to develop a dipolar theology which speaks of God's passion and the drive of the spirit in the suffering and hopes of man. This presupposition does not exist for the Christian, especially for the Gentile Christian. Where for Israel immediacy with God is grounded on the presupposition of the covenant, for Christians it is Christ himself who communicates the Fatherhood of God and the power of the Spirit. Therefore Christian theology cannot develop any dipolar theology of the reciprocal relationship between the God who calls and the man who answers; it must develop a trinitarian theology, for only in and through Christ is that dialogical relationship with God opened up. Through Christ, God himself creates the conditions of entering into that relationship of *pathos* and *sympatheia*. Through him he creates it for those who cannot satisfy these conditions: the sinners, the godless, and those forsaken by God. In Christian terms, therefore, no relationship of immediacy between God and man is conceivable which is separated from this person and his history. But in that God himself creates the conditions for communion with God through his self-humiliation in the death of the crucified Christ and through his exaltation of man in the resurrection of Christ, this community becomes a gracious, presuppositionless, and universal community of God with all men in their common misery. For the sake of the unconditionality and universality of God's community of grace, Christian theology must therefore think simultaneously in both christocentric and trinitarian terms. Only the covenant founded one-sidedly by God and opened to all in the cross of Christ makes possible the covenant relationships of dialogue in the spirit, in *sympatheia*, and in prayer. "God was in Christ"—that is the presupposition for the fellowship of sinners and godless with God, since it opens up God's sphere for the whole of man and for all men. "We live in Christ"—that is the consequence for the faith which experiences the full communion with God in communion with Christ.

But how can this sphere of God opened up in Christ be described? Is it comparable to the field of action of God's apathic freedom or to the field of force of God's *pathos*?

Following Philippians 2, Christian theology speaks of the final and complete self-humiliation of God in man and in the person of Jesus. Here God in the person of the Son enters into the limited, finite situation of man. Not only does he enter into it, descend into it, but he also accepts it and embraces the whole of human existence with his being. He does not become spirit so that man must first soar to the realm of the spirit in order to participate in God. He does not merely become the covenant partner of an elect people so that men must belong to this people through circumcision and obedience to the covenant in order to enter into his fellowship. He lowers himself and accepts the whole of mankind without limits and conditions, so that each man may participate in him with the whole of his life.

When God becomes man in Jesus of Nazareth, he not only enters into the finitude of man, but in his death on the cross also enters into the situation of man's godforsakenness. In Jesus he does not die the natural death of a finite being, but the violent death of the criminal on the cross, the death of complete abandonment by God. The suffering in the passion of Jesus is abandonment, rejection by God, his Father. God does not become a religion, so that man participates in him by corresponding religious thoughts and feelings. God does not become a law, so that man participates in him through obedience to a law. God does not become an ideal, so that man achieves community with him through constant striving. He humbles himself and takes upon himself the eternal death of the godless and the godforsaken, so that all the godless and the godforsaken can experience communion with him.

The incarnate God is present, and can be experienced, in the humanity of every man, and in full human corporeality. No one need dissemble and appear other than he is to perceive the fellowship of the human God with him. Rather, he can lay aside all dissembling and sham and become what he truly is in this human God. Furthermore, the crucified God is near to him in the forsakenness of every man. There is no loneliness and no rejection which he has not taken to himself and assumed" in the cross of Jesus. There is no need for any attempts at justification or for any self-destructive self-accusations to draw near to him. The godforsaken and rejected man can accept himself where he comes to know the crucified God who is with him and has already accepted him. If God has taken upon himself death on the cross, he has also taken upon himself all of life and real life, as it stands under death, law, and guilt. In so doing he makes it possible to accept life whole and entire and death whole and entire. Man is taken up, without limitations and conditions, into the life and suffering, the death and resurrection of God, and in faith participates corporeally in the fullness of God. There is nothing that can exclude him from the situation of God between the grief of the Father, the love of the Son, and the drive of the Spirit.

Life in communion with Christ is full life in the trinitarian situation of God. Dead in Christ and raised to new life, as Paul says in Rom. 6:8, the believer really participates in the suffering of God in the world, because he partakes in the suffering of the love of God. Conversely, he takes part in the particular suffering of the word, because God has made it his suffering in the cross of his Son.[24] The human God who encounters man in the crucified Christ thus involves man in a realistic divinization (*theosis*). Therefore in communion with Christ it can truly be said that men live *in God* and *from God*, "that they live, move, and have their being in him" (Acts 17:28). Understood in pantheistic terms, that would be a dream which would have to ignore the negative element in the world. But a trinitarian theology of the cross perceives God in the negative element and therefore the negative element in God, and in this dialectical way is panentheistic. For in the hidden mode of humiliation to the point of the cross, all being and all that annihilates has already been taken up in God and God begins to become "all in all." To recognize God in the cross of Christ, conversely, means to recognize the cross, inextricable suffering, death, and hopeless rejection in God.

A "theology after Auschwitz" may seem an impossibility or blasphemy to those who allowed themselves to be satisfied with theism or their childhood beliefs and then lost them. And there would be no "theology after Auschwitz" in retrospective sorrow and the recognition of guilt, had there been no "theology in Auschwitz." Anyone who later comes up against insoluble problems and despair must remember that the *Shema* of Israel and the Lord's Prayer were prayed in Auschwitz.

It is necessary to remember the martyrs, so as not to become abstract. Of them and of the dumb sacrifices it is true in a real, transferred sense, that God himself hung on the gallows, as [Elie] Wiesel was able to say. If that is taken seriously, it must also be said that, like the cross of Christ, even Auschwitz is in God himself. Even Auschwitz is taken up into the grief of the Father, the surrender of the Son, and the power of the Spirit. That never means that Auschwitz and other grisly places can be justified, for it is the cross that is the beginning of the trinitarian history of God. As Paul says in 1 Corinthians 15, only with the resurrection of the dead, the murdered and the gassed, only with the healing of those in despair who bear lifelong wounds, only with the abolition of all rule and authority, only with the annihilation of death will the Son hand over the kingdom to the Father. Then God will turn his sorrow into eternal joy. This will be the sign of the completion of the trinitarian history of God and the end of world history, the overcoming of the history of man's sorrow and the fulfillment of his history of hope. God in Auschwitz and Auschwitz in the crucified God—that is the basis for a real hope which both embraces and overcomes the world, and the ground for a love which is stronger than death and can sustain death. It is the ground for living with the terror of history and the end of history, and nevertheless remaining in love and meeting what comes in openness for God's future. It is the ground for living and bearing guilt and sorrow for the future of man in God.

Notes

1. Jürgen Moltmann, *A Broad Place*, trans. Margaret Kohl (Minneapolis: Fortress Press/London: SCM Press), 189.

2. Ibid.

3. Moltmann 1972; ET 1974/1993:277.

4. Karl Rahner, *Theological Investigations*, vol. 4, trans. Kevin Smyth (Baltimore: Helicon, 1966), 79.

5. Philipp Melanchthon, *Loci communes theologici* (1521), trans. Lowell J. Satre, in Wilhelm Pauck, ed., *Melanchthon and Bucer*, Library of Christian Classics (London: SCM Press, 1969), 21f.

6. Immanuel Kant, *Der Streit der Fakultäten,* A 50, 57.

7. Friedrich Schleiermacher, *The Christian Faith,* §170.

8. Ibid., §172.

9. Rahner, *Theological Investigations*, 4:96.

10. Ibid., 4:152.

11. Wiard Popkes, *Christus Traditus. Eine Untersuchung zum Begriff der Dahingabe im Neuen Testament*, ATANT 49 (Zurich: Zwingli, 1967), 286f.

12. Aristotle, *Magna Moralia* II, 1208b.

13. Aristotle, *Metaphysics* XII, 1073 a 11.

14. Theodor Rüther, *Die sittliche Forderung der Apatheia in den beiden ersten christlichen Jahrhunderten und bei Klemens von Alexandrinus* (Freiburg: N.P., 1949), 11f.

15. Abraham Heschel, *The Prophets* (New York: Harper & Row, 1962).

16. However, there are also beginnings in this direction in Islam, as has been shown by Henry Corbin, "Sympathie et Theopathie chez les Fidèles d'amour en Islam," *Eranos* 24 (1956): 199–301.

17. Heschel, *The Prophets*, 252.

18. Ibid., 209ff.

19. Ibid., 307ff.

20. Peter Kuhn, *Gottes Selbsterniedrigung in der Theologie der Rabbinen,* SANT 17 (Munich: Kösel, 1968).

21. Ibid, 89.

22. Ibid, 90.

23. Elie Wiesel, *Night* (New York: Hill and Wang, 1960), 75f.

24. Dietrich Bonhoeffer, "The Bible directs man to God's powerlessness and suffering: only the suffering God can help. . . . Man is summoned to share in God's sufferings at the hands of a godless world. . . . It is not the religious act that makes the Christian, but participation in the sufferings of God in the secular life. It is allowing oneself to be caught up into the messianic suffering of God in Jesus Christ." In *Letters and Papers from Prison*, enl. ed., trans. Reginald Fuller, et al. (London: SCM Press, 1971), 282, 337. Similarly, too, Dorothee Sölle, *Christ the Representative: An Essay in Theology after the 'Death of God'* (London: SCM Press, 1967), 150ff.

3

The Trinity and the Kingdom

In 1980, Moltmann published the first of what he described as "systematic contributions to theology" in The Trinity and the Kingdom: The Doctrine of God *(ET: 1981). Whereas in* Theology of Hope *and* The Crucified God *he had considered the whole of theology from a single focus, his intention now was to "treat important doctrines in systematic sequence." The doctrine of the Trinity was already intrinsic to his consideration of the cross, which he interprets as an experience within the Trinity itself, but he now developed this viewpoint more generally into a "social" doctrine of the Trinity. "My concern here," he wrote later, "was to perceive the relationships of sociality in God and to practice a new 'trinitarian thinking.' By that I meant thinking in relationships, in communities, and in transitions. . . . I called this generally trinitarian thinking, and in particular perichoretic thinking. Perichoresis means reciprocal indwelling and mutual interpenetration."[1] The trinitarian unity of God embraces the community of believers with God and with each other. A key text for Moltmann's exposition is Jesus' High Priestly prayer (John 17:21):*

> *That they may all be one,*
> *even as Thou, Father, art in me, and I in thee,*
> *that they also may be in us.*

Trinitarian Theology Today

Source: Moltmann 1980; ET 1981/1993:1–20.

What do we think of when we hear the name of the triune God? What ideas do we associate with the Trinity? What do we experience in the fellowship of the Father, the Son, and the Holy Spirit?

The answers will vary greatly, if indeed an answer is attempted at all. Some people will think of the traditional rituals and symbols of Christian worship, baptism, the Lord's Supper, and the blessing. Other people are reminded of passionate disputes in the early church. Some will see in their mind's eye the pictures of Christian art depicting three divine persons, or two persons and the Holy Spirit in the form of a dove. Many people view the theological doctrine of the Trinity as a speculation for theological specialists, which has nothing to do with real life. That is why modern Protestants like to content themselves with the young [Philipp] Melanchthon's maxim: "We adore the mysteries of the Godhead. That is better than to investigate them."[2] It is difficult enough to believe that there is a God at all and to live accordingly. Does belief in the Trinity not make the religious life even more difficult, and quite unnecessarily? Why are most Christians in the West, whether they be Catholics or Protestants, really only "monotheists" where the experience and practice of their faith is concerned? Whether God is one or triune evidently makes as little difference to the doctrine of faith as it does to ethics. . . . In the attempts that are being made to justify theology today—whether it is hermeneutical theology or political theology, process theology or the theological theory of science—the doctrine of the Trinity has very little essential importance.

In this chapter we shall try to demolish some explicit objections and some tacit inhibitions, and shall try to uncover ways of access to an understanding of the triune God. . . . And in the course of this discussion we shall have to consider critically different views about what reason is, theologically speaking.

§1 Return to Trinitarian Thinking

1. Experience as a Means of Access?

The first group of express objections and tacit reservations towards the doctrine of the Trinity come from experience; they are related to the limitations of the experience open to us. By experience the modern person means perceptions which *he himself* can repeat and verify. They are perceptions, moreover, which affect *him himself*, because they crystallize out in some alteration *of* his self; that is to say, they are related to his subjectivity. Must not truth be something we can experience? Can we experience God? Is it possible to talk about the triune God out of personal experience?

It was Friedrich Schleiermacher who first understood the way in which this modern concept of experience and truth was related to actual existence, and it was he who consistently remolded "dogmatic theology" into "the doctrine of faith." The piety which is faith's expression is "neither knowledge nor action, but a determination of feeling or immediate self-consciousness." By this Schleiermacher does not mean psychologically ascertainable emotions; he means that the whole human existence is affected. That is why he talked about "*immediate* self-consciousness."[3] In this immediate self-consciousness we experience ourselves as "quite simply dependent," that is to say, we become aware of ourselves in relation to God, the reason and the ground of our own selves. For Schleiermacher, therefore, the experience of the self in faith points towards God. God is indirectly experienced in the experience of the absolute dependency of our own existence. This means that all statements about God are bound to be at the same time statements about the personal existence determined by faith. Statements about God which do not include statements about the immediate self-consciousness of the believer belong to the realm of speculation, because they are not verifiable by personal experience. It was therefore quite consistent for Schleiermacher to put the doctrine of the Trinity at the end of his doctrine of faith: the doctrine of the triune God is "not a direct statement about Christian self-consciousness, but only a web of several such statements"—i.e., a construction which gathers together a number of different statements of faith." As the transcendent ground of our sense of absolute dependence, God is one. Schleiermacher therefore understood Christianity as a "monotheistic mode of belief." The church's doctrine of the three divine Persons is secondary, because it is a mere web of different statements about the Christian self-consciousness; it does not alter Christianity's monotheism at all. Consequently it is enough to talk about the one God, by talking about one's own Christian self-consciousness. The doctrine of the Trinity is superfluous. Assuming the presuppositions of our modern, subjective concept of experience, the transformation of dogmatics into the doctrine of faith, and the conversion of the church's doctrine of the Trinity into abstract monotheism, is inescapable.

But can faith's experience of God be adequately expressed in this concept? Must not faith for its part fundamentally alter the concept? If faith is a living relationship, then faith conceived of as "a determination of feeling or immediate self-consciousness" can only grasp one side of the matter. The other side of the relationship, the side we term "God," remains unknown if we ascribe to it no more than the reason behind the definition of one's own self. Even if we relate "experience" to the experiencing subject, concentrating it solely on the experience of the self in experience, it will still be permissible to ask, not only: *How do I experience God?* What does God mean for me? How am I determined by him? We must also ask the reverse questions: *How does God experience me?* What do I mean for God? How is he determined by me?

Of course the relationship between God and man is not a reciprocal relationship between equals. But if it is not a one-sided relationship of causality and dependency either—if it is a relationship of covenant and love—then for man's experience of himself this question is not merely valid; it is actually necessary. Can a person experience "himself" in his relationship to God as person if God is certainly supposed to mean everything to him, but if he is not supposed to mean anything to God? In faith the person experiences God in God's relationship to him, and himself in his relationship to God. If he experiences God in this, then he also thereby experiences the way God has "experienced"—and still "experiences"—him. If one were only to relate the experience of God to the experience of the self, then the self would become the constant and "God" the variable. It is only when the self is perceived in the experience which God has with that self that an undistorted perception of the history of one's own self with God and in God emerges.

The expression "experience of God" therefore does not only mean our experience of God; it also means God's experience with us. Consequently we are not using the concept of experience in quite the same way in both cases. God experiences people in a different way from the way people experience God. He experiences them in his divine manner of experience. The Bible is the testimony of God's *history* with men and women, and also the testimony of God's *experiences* with men and women. If a person experiences in faith how God has experienced—and still experiences —him, for that person God is not the abstract origin of the world or the unknown source of his absolute feeling of dependency; he is *the living God*. He learns to know himself in the mirror of God's love, suffering, and joy. In his experience of God he experiences—fragmentarily,   indeed,   and   certainly   "in   a   glass, darkly"—something of God's own experience with him. The more he understands God's experience, the more deeply the mystery of God's passion is revealed to him. He then perceives that the history of the world is the history of God's suffering. At the moments of God's profoundest revelation there is always suffering: the cry of the captives in Egypt; Jesus' death cry on the cross; the sighing of the whole enslaved creation for liberty. If a person once feels the infinite passion of God's love which finds expression here, then he understands the mystery of the triune God. God suffers with us—God suffers from us—God suffers for us: it is this experience of God that reveals the triune God. It has to be understood, and can only be understood, in trinitarian terms. Consequently fundamental theology's discussion about access to the doctrine of the Trinity is carried on today in the context of the question about God's capacity or incapacity for suffering. That is why here we have put [a] chapter on the passion of God before our account of the doctrine of the Trinity in the narrower sense.

From time immemorial, experience has been bound up with wonder or with pain. In wonder the subject opens himself for a counterpart and gives himself up to the overwhelming impression. In pain the subject perceives the difference of the other, the contradiction in conflict and the alteration of his own self. In both modes of experience the subject enters entirely into his counterpart. The modern concept of experience, which has discovered and stressed its subjective components, threatens to transform experience into experience of the self. But the justifiable perception of the determinations of the individual self in any objective experience must not lead to obsessedly preoccupied interest in mere experience of the self; that would be narcissism. The only experiences perceived would then be those which confirmed the self and justified its condition; and interest in experience of the self is then in fact fear of experiencing the other. This means that the capacity for wonder and the readiness for pain are lost. The modern culture of subjectivity has long since been in danger of turning into a "culture of narcissism,"[4] which makes the self its own prisoner and supplies it merely with self-repetitions and self-confirmations. It is therefore time for Christian theology to break out of this prison of narcissism, and for it to present its "doctrine of faith" as a doctrine of the all-embracing "history of God." This does not mean falling back into objectivistic orthodoxy. What it does mean is that experience of the self has to be integrated into the experience of God, and experience of God has to be integrated into the trinitarian history of God with the world. God is no longer related to the narrow limits of a fore-given, individual self. On the contrary, the individual self will be discovered in the over-riding history of God, and only finds its meaning in that context.

2. PRACTICE AS A MEANS OF ACCESS?

A second group of objections and reservations towards the doctrine the Trinity come from the sphere of practical application and are connected with the practicability of the truth. The modern has become pragmatic. What does not turn into act has no value. It is only practice that verifies a theory, for reality has become identical with the historical world. People understand themselves as historical beings. For them the only possible correspondence between being and consciousness is to be found in actual historical practice. For them truth only comes about in what is truly act. Hence for men and women today the truth, as [Bertolt] Brecht says, must "always be concrete." And that means it must "be performed." That is the modern turn from the pure theory of truth to the practical theory of it. But is truth, which under certain given circumstances is incapable of realization, therefore to be despised and thrown away simply because of that? Is the truth which God himself is, so "practicable" that people have to "realize God," "put God into practice"? Is the doctrine of the Trinity a practical truth?

It was [Immanuel] Kant who elevated moral practice into the canon by which the interpretation of all biblical and ecclesiastical traditions is to be judged. The interpretation is to be ruled by practical reason, for interpretation also means application:

> Passages of Scripture which contain certain *theoretical* doctrines, proclaimed as sacred but going beyond all concepts of reason (even the moral ones) *may* be interpreted to the advantage of the latter; and those which contain statements contradictory to reason *must* so be interpreted.[5]

The first example he takes is the doctrine of the Trinity:

> From the doctrine of the Trinity, taken literally, nothing whatsoever can be gained for practical purposes, even if one believed that one comprehended it—and less still if one is conscious that it surpasses all our concepts.[6]

Whether we have to worship three or ten persons in the deity is unimportant, Kant claimed, because "it is impossible to extract from this difference any different rules for practical living." For theoretical reason God is unknowable, because he exceeds the limits of any possible experience; so it is only in the postulates of practical reason that Kant brings God to the fore, together with "liberty" and "immortality." Here the transcendental definition "God" is sufficient; for moral monotheism is enough to provide the foundation for free and responsible conduct.

Given the presupposition of the modern comprehensive, moral, political, or revolutionary concept of practice, the transformation of theological dogmatics into ethics or politics is quite understandable. But do the experience and practice of the Christian faith find adequate expression in this modern concept of practice? Does not this faith have to burst apart that concept, changing it fundamentally, if it wants to bring out its own truth?

The modern understanding of the Christian faith as a practice of living which tries to conform to the life of Jesus, in order to carry on his cause, is only half the truth, because it only perceives one side of what the believer has to give.

The person who acts has God behind him and the world in front of him, so to speak. For him, the world is the domain to which he is sent, the domain where the gospel is to be proclaimed, where we are to love our neighbor and liberate the oppressed. The future is the domain of open potentialities. It depends on him, ultimately, which of these potentialities he realizes and which he rejects. He thinks in the movement of God to the world and is himself part of this movement. He works in the movement from potentiality to reality and is himself the realizer. Whether it is a question of ethical theology or political theology or revolutionary theology, it is always *the theology of action*. In this theology practice takes precedence over reflection and theory. "The first thing is the obligation to love and serve. Theology only comes *after* this, and is a second act."[7] The practical act which is necessary in today's misery is the liberation of the oppressed. Theology is hence the critical reflection about this essential practice in the light of the gospel. It does not merely aim to understand the world differently; it wants to change the world as well. It sees itself as one component in the process through which the world is liberated. That is the fundamental idea underlying the new theology of liberation. Today it is the best ethical and political theology, because it tries to do, and teaches us to do, what is needful today for the needs of the oppressed.

But Christian love is not merely a motivation, and Christian faith is more than the point from which action takes its bearings. Being a Christian is also characterized by gratitude, joy, praise, and adoration. Faith lives in meditation and prayer as well as in practice. Without the *vita contemplativa* the *vita activa* quickly becomes debased into activism, falling a victim to the pragmatism of the modern meritocratic society which judges by performance. Of course there is a speculative trivialization of the concept of God. But it can be pragmatically trivialized too.

In meditation and contemplation man turns to the God in whom he believes, opening himself to his reality. Without any alibi in what he does, he stands before what [Karl] Barth called "the all transforming fact" and surrenders himself wholly to it. "To know God means to suffer God" says a wise old theological saying. To suffer God means experiencing in oneself the death pangs of the old man and the birth pangs of the new. The Old Testament already tells us that "He who looks upon God must die." The closer people come to the divine reality, the more deeply they are drawn into this dying and this rebirth. This becomes vividly present and experienceable in the figure of the crucified Jesus. Christian meditation and contemplation are therefore at their very heart *meditatio crucis*, the stations of the cross, meditation on the passion. The person who turns to the God who encounters us visibly in the person of the crucified Jesus, accepts this transformation. In the pain of repentance and a new beginning he experiences the joy of God's fellowship. The practice of his own life is thereby changed, and changed much more radically than is possible within the potentialities open to the "active" person. The man or woman who suffers God in the fellowship of the crucified Jesus can also praise God in the fellowship of the Jesus who is risen. The theology of the cross becomes the theology of doxology.

Action and meditation are related to one another in many different ways. The point of intersection emerges from the situation in which the individual finds himself. But the one always conditions the other. Meditation can never lead to flight from the Christian practice required of us because, being Christian meditation, it is *meditatio passionis et mortis Christi*. Practice can never become the flight from meditation because, as Christian practice, it is bound to discipleship of the crucified Jesus. Consequently theology in action and theology in doxology belong together. There must be no theology of liberation without the glorification of God and no glorification of God without the liberation of the oppressed.

The modern world's devotion to what is ethical and pragmatic has led to the disintegration of the doctrine of the Trinity in moral monotheism. The reduction of faith to practice has not enriched faith; it has impoverished it. It has let practice itself become a matter of law and compulsion.

If we are to be freed for practice—not from it!—it is important for meditation, contemplation, and doxology to be rediscovered. It is only together, not each for itself, that practice and adoration lead men and women into the history of God. The rediscovery of the meaning of the doctrine of the Trinity begins when the one-sidedness of a merely pragmatic thinking is overcome, and when practice is liberated from activism, so that it can become a liberated practice of the gospel. This has consequences for the nature of knowing itself—for the way in which we arrive at knowledge.

In the pragmatic thinking of the modern world, knowing something always means dominating something: "Knowledge is power." Through our scientific knowledge we acquire power over objects and can appropriate them. Modern thinking has made reason operational. Reason recognizes only "what reason herself brings forth according to her own concept."[8] It has become a productive organ—hardly a perceptive one any more. It builds its own world and in what it has produced it only recognizes itself again. In several European languages, understanding a thing means "grasping" it. We grasp a thing when "we've got it." If we have grasped something, we take it into our possession. If we possess something we can do with it what we want. The motive that impels modern reason *to know* must be described as the desire to conquer and to dominate.

For the Greek philosophers and the Fathers of the church, knowledge meant something different: it meant knowing in *wonder*. By knowing or perceiving one participates in the life of the other. Here knowing does not transform the counterpart into the property of the knower; the knower does not appropriate what he knows. On the contrary, he is transformed through sympathy, becoming a participator in what he perceives. Knowledge confers fellowship. That is why knowing, perception, only goes as far as love, sympathy, and participation reach. Where the theological perception of God and his history is concerned, there will be a modern discovery of trinitarian thinking when there is at the same time a fundamental change in modern reason—a change from lordship to fellowship, from conquest to participation, from production to receptivity. A new theological penetration of the trinitarian history of God ought also to free the reason that has been made operational—free it for receptive perception of its Other, free it for participation in that Other. Trinitarian thinking should prepare the way for a liberating and healing concern for the reality that has been destroyed.

§2 ON THE WAY TO THE TRIUNE GOD

The question about the reality of God has been answered in various different ways in the history of Western theology. One answer was given by Greek antiquity, continued to be given in the Middle Ages, and still counts as valid in the present-day definitions of the Roman Catholic Church: God is the supreme substance. The cosmological proofs of God claim to offer sufficient grounds for this assumption at every period. The other answer springs from the special tradition of the Old Testament and, by way of medieval nominalism, passed down to the Idealist philosophy of the nineteenth century. According to this answer, God is the absolute subject. The biblical testimonies of salvation history and the present experience of the world as history force us to think of God, not merely as the supreme substance but as the absolute subject as well. The specific answer given by Christian theology goes beyond these two answers: God, it claims, is the triune God. But what does this characteristically Christian answer mean in relation to those other concepts of God, which theology took over for itself in the course of its history? How are we to understand the reality of the world if we are to understand God, not as supreme substance and not as absolute subject, but as triunity, the three-in-one?

1. GOD AS SUPREME SUBSTANCE

The cosmological proofs of God proceed from the finitude of the world and contrast this with infinite being. Because finitude has several definitions, there are several cosmological proofs. Their common starting point is the finitude of the world, and this can be so classified that they follow one another as steps on a single path. According to Aquinas there are "five ways" of cosmological proof. Some neo-Thomist theologians believe that they are the only convincing proofs of God at all; all the others are either fallacies or proofs which can be traced back to the "five ways." In 1871 the First Vatican Council defined the fundamental demonstrability of God for Roman Catholic theology by stating "that God, the origin and goal of all things, can be known with certainty from created things, with the help of the natural light of human reason."[9] In 1907 the anti-modernist oath restricted this to "the five ways," with the declaration "that God can be known with certainty and can hence also be proved, as cause can be proved from effects."[10]

The cosmological proofs of God start from the world and presuppose that the world is cosmos, not chaos, well ordered by means of eternal laws, and beautiful in its protean forms. The proofs derive from Greek philosophy, and Greek philosophy of course presupposes the spirit of the Greek religion, for it grew up out of the Enlightenment of this religion. In Greek "God" is a predicate, not a name. The Divine Ones are present in all worldly happenings. They need no special revelations. Consequently life in the eternal orders of the cosmos is a plenitude of all that is divine. Human life is led in the presence and in the fellowship of the gods if it is in correspondence with the orders and movements of the cosmos, Πάντα πλήρη θεῶν, said Thales, in a phrase frequently quoted by Plato and Aristotle. It was on the basis of this cosmic religion that Greek religious philosophy grew up, a philosophy which inquires about the origin of the gods and about their divine nature. The divine nature, the Deity, τὸ θεῖον is one, necessary, immovable, infinite, unconditional, immortal, and impassible. What is divine is defined by certain characteristics of the finite cosmos, and these are marked by negation. That is the *via negativa*. Because the Divine is one, it is the origin and measure of the Many in the cosmos.

This philosophical inference about the nature of the divine presupposes a divinely ordered cosmos. The existence of the divine essence is not in question. It is already presupposed by the existence of the cosmos. The divine essence is indirectly manifested in the mirror of that cosmos. The deity can be known from the world, by a process of deduction. Conversely, the world as cosmos, which reflects the divine essence and the divine wisdom, is comprehended from the presence of the divine. Here deity and cosmos provide mutual evidence for one another, thereby opening up a space for living in the chaos of the world, and order in the terrors of time. The cosmological proof of God based on the world is always at the same time the theological proof of the world based on God. That is why the concept of the world as cosmos is fundamental.

Aquinas's "five ways" go back to Aristotle and Cicero. They presuppose the Greek concept of a cosmos which is a hierarchical order, graduated into different strata of being. The proofs are so ordered that each demonstration explains what the preceding one had implicitly presupposed; so the "five ways" belong together in a single demonstrative process. They start from general phenomena in the world and inquire about their ultimate foundation, beyond which nothing can be asked at all. The first starts from movement in the world and arrives at the concept of the *primum movens*; the second proceeds from effects in the world and arrives at the concept of the *causa prima*; the third starts from the potential being of all things and arrives at the concept of the *ens per se necessarium*; the fourth begins with the gradations of being in the world and arrives at the concept of the *maxime ens*; the fifth, finally, starts from the order of the world and arrives at the concept of the highest *intellectus*. To these five definitions Aquinas adds in each case: "*et hoc dicimus Deum.*"

The cosmological proof of God was supposed by Thomas to answer the question *Utrum Deus sit?* But he did not really prove the *existence* of God; what he proved was the *nature* of the divine. The divine nature is the moving, causing, necessary, pure, and intelligent Being for being that is moved, caused, possible, intermingled, and ordered: that was how he understood the *via eminentiae*. In this way Aquinas answered the question: "What is the nature of the divine?," but not the question: "Who is God?" With the help of his proof, God as the supreme essence or being has become conceivable, although we are not compelled to call this highest substance "God." The fact that "all" human beings call this substance "God" is due to the *consensus gentium* which Aquinas himself says is not conclusive, but merely provides the general linguistic rule, which may in certain circumstances be relative.

The five ways of the cosmological proof of God are certainly cogent on the basis of the cosmology and metaphysics they presuppose. But is this cosmology itself convincing? If the human understanding of reality changes fundamentally, these proofs of God lose their power, like all other proofs as well. They are irrefutable from the standpoint of their own premises; but these premises can quite well be cut from under their feet. What separates modern thinking from Greek and medieval metaphysics is a changed view of reality as a whole.

2. GOD AS ABSOLUTE SUBJECT

The method of the cosmological proofs of God rests on the premise that there is an ordered cosmos. The perceiving person finds himself existing *in* this order as a living being endowed with soul and spirit. The "house of being" is his worldly home. This thinking in terms of being was superseded by the rise of modern, European *subjectivity*. Once man makes himself the subject of his own world by the process of knowing it, conquering it, and shaping it, the conception of the world as cosmos is destroyed. Descartes split the world into *res cogitans* and *res extensa*; and this modern dichotomization has made the ontological order of being obsolete, and the monarchy of the highest substance obsolete at the same time.[11] Reality is no longer understood as the divine cosmos, which surrounds and shelters man as his home. It is now seen as providing *the material* for the knowledge and appropriation of the world of man. The center of this world and its point of reference is the human subject, not a supreme substance. There is no higher reality encompassing man, the sphere of his experience, and the realm of his awareness. It is *he himself* who opens up reality and makes it accessible. So the unity of what is real is determined anthropologically, no longer cosmologically and theocentrically. The cosmos shows no "traces" of the deity; on the contrary, it is full of traces of man. This transition to modern time has been called "the anthropological turning point" (Martin Buber), "the uprising to subjectivity" (Martin Heidegger), and the path "from ontocracy to technocracy" (A. T. van Leeuwen). It was out of this transition that Western atheism grew up. A world which has in principle become man's object proves only the existence of man and no longer the existence of a God. Is this the beginning of European nihilism?

> What did we do when we unchained this earth from its sun? Where is it moving to now? Away from all the suns? Do we not continually stumble and fall? Backwards, sideways, forwards, in all directions? Is there still an above and a below? Are we not wandering through an infinite nothingness? Do we not feel the breath of empty space? Do

we not continually encounter night and still more night? Do we not
have to light our lanterns before noon? . . . God is dead! God remains
dead! And we have killed him.[12]

If man can no longer understand himself in the light of the world and its
cohesions, but has to comprehend the world and its cohesions in the light of
his own plans for its domination, then it would seem the obvious course for
him to look for the mirror in which knowledge of God is to be found in his
own subjectivity. But of course in the same degree to which he discovers his
subjectivity in its superiority to the world, he also discovers that subjectivity's
finitude. So he will inquire about an infinite, absolute, and perfect subjectivity
which lends his own subjectivity bearings, thus sustaining it and giving it
permanence. The proof of God drawn from the world gives way to the proof
of God drawn from existence, from the soul, from the immediate self-
consciousness. That is not an objective proof; it is a subjective one. It is not
theoretical; it is practical. People no longer need God in order to explain the
world, but they do need him in order to exist with self-confidence, with self-
certainty, and with self-respect.

   This notion of God has a long history. We find the first theological traces
of it in Augustine: knowledge of the self is no longer part of knowledge of the
world, but is related exclusively to knowledge of God. "O eternal God, could
I but know who I am and who thou art." "My desire is to know God and the
soul. Nothing else? No, nothing else."[13] The subject becomes directly certain
of itself. Certainty of God becomes the correlative of direct certainty of the self.
This means of access to God has a biblical foundation. The world is God's work,
but man is God's image. That means that every human being finds in himself
the mirror in which he can perceive God. The knowledge of God in his image
is surer than the knowledge of God from his works. So the foundation of true
self-knowledge is to be found in God.

   It was Descartes who finally stripped the world of God, making it an affair
of mathematics; and it was he who made this idea the basis of his philosophy
of subjectivity: a person can doubt all the experiences mediated by the senses,
but not the fact that it is he himself who doubts. In the process of thinking
he becomes directly conscious of himself. This certainty of the self is the
fundamentum inconcussum. But he is conscious of himself as a finite being.
Consequently the notion of a finite being is already presupposed and inherent in
the notion of his self-consciousness: "The mere fact that I exist and that a certain
idea of a completely perfect being . . . is within me is the most convincing
demonstration that God exists."[14] The more, therefore, man experiences himself

as subject—even if finite subject—over against the world of objects he has subjected, the more he recognizes in God, not the supreme substance of the world, but the infinite, perfect, and absolute subject, namely the archetype of himself. God is for him no longer the ground of the world, but the ground of the soul. He is sought, not as the secret of the world, but as the secret of his own soul.

It was only after Kant had confuted the proofs of God from the world through his critique of pure reason that Protestant theology began to concern itself seriously with reflections about subjectivity. Influenced by Kant and Schleiermacher, the ethical theology grew up—in Protestantism particularly—for which faith means moral certainty of God; and the theology of experience, for which God is experienced in the believing person's experience of his own self. God is not to be found in the explicable world of things; he has to be sought for in the experienceable world of the individual self. It is only possible to talk about God when one talks about man or, to be more precise, about oneself, and out of one's own experience of the self: this, Rudolf Bultmann declared, is the fundamental principle of existential theology. "For if the realization of our own existence is involved in faith and if our existence is grounded in God and is non-existent outside God, then to apprehend our existence means to apprehend God."[15]

But it was [Johann Gottlieb] Fichte and [G. W. F.] Hegel who went over to a consideration of God's absolute subjectivity for the first time. If, for the anthropological reasons we have mentioned, God has to be understood as the absolute, perfect subject, then we must also think of God as the subject of his own revelation and as the subject of man's knowledge of him. Consequently his revelation can only be "self-revelation" and man's knowledge of him can only be man's own "self-knowledge." Really, there can be no indirect communication of God by way of his works in the world or through his image in man; there can only be his direct "self-communication." God understood as absolute subject presupposes free will in God, which is not necessary in the concept of the supreme substance. God reveals himself where and when he likes. He reveals himself in a certain person and a certain history, determined by him.

God, thought of as subject, with perfect reason and free will, is in actual fact the archetype of the free, reasonable, sovereign person, who has complete disposal over himself. That is why, in the bourgeois world of the nineteenth and twentieth centuries, this concept of God was developed further into the concept of "*absolute personality*" and, in simpler phraseology, to the idea of "*the personal God.*" The starting point and goal of this modern concept of God was and is the interpretation of the person as subject, and stress on the subjectivity of all his knowledge and all his relationships.

3. THE TRIUNE GOD

The churches' traditional doctrine of the Trinity derives from the specifically Christian tradition and proclamation. In order to comprehend the New Testament's testimony to the history of Jesus Christ, the Son of God, theology had to develop the trinitarian concept of God. The history of Jesus the Son cannot be grasped except as part of the history of the Father, the Son, and the Spirit. . . . Here we shall simply ask how the specifically Christian doctrine of the Trinity fits in with the general concepts of God as supreme substance and absolute subject, and what problems emerge at this point; and we shall ask too whether the doctrine of the Trinity itself cannot provide us with the matrix for a new kind of thinking about God, the world, and man.

Ever since Tertullian, the Christian Trinity has always been depicted as belonging within the general concept of the divine substance: *una substantia—tres personae*. The one, indivisible, homogeneous, divine substance is constituted as three individual, divine persons. Consequently the converse also applies: the three persons are certainly different from one another, but they are one in their common divine substance. It is understandable that for Augustine and Thomas Aquinas this one, common, divine substance counted as being the foundation of the trinitarian persons and was hence logically primary in comparison. Augustine proceeded from the one God, whose unity he apprehended in the concept of the one divine essence, only after that arriving at the concept of the trinitarian persons. According to Aquinas, when we generalize, or abstract, from the trinitarian persons, what remains for thought is the one divine nature. It is this, he claimed, which is in general to be called "God," not the three persons, or only one of them.

This presentation of the trinitarian persons in the one divine substance had considerable consequences for Western theology, and even for Western thinking in general. In theological textbooks ever since Aquinas, the article on God has been divided into the treatise *De Deo uno* and the treatise *De Deo trino*. Even Protestant orthodoxy took over this twofold division. First of all comes the proof and the assurance that there is a God and that God is one. Only after that is the doctrine of the triune God developed. First of all we have general, *natural* theology; the special *theology of revelation* comes afterwards. Natural theology, accordingly, provides the general framework within which the theology of revelation draws the special Christian picture of God. The framework makes the picture possible, but it also restricts it. The metaphysical characteristics of the supreme substance are determined on the basis of the cosmological proofs of God. The divine being is one, immovable, impassible, and so forth. The specifically Christian doctrine of God can change nothing about all this, even though it has to talk about the triune God and the sufferings of the Son of God on the cross. Natural theology's definitions of the nature of the deity quite obviously become a prison for the statements made by the theology of revelation. That is clearly evident in the definition of God's unity. If natural theology's article *De Deo uno* is put before the article *De Deo trino*, then what is really being taught is a double divine unity—a unity of the divine essence, and the union of the triune God. The result is that the first unity forces out the second. Consequently, not only is there undue stress on the unity of the triune God, but there is also a reduction of the triunity to the One God. The representation of the trinitarian persons in a homogeneous divine substance, presupposed and recognizable from the cosmos, leads unintentionally but inescapably to the disintegration of the doctrine of the Trinity in abstract monotheism.

Ever since Hegel in particular, the Christian Trinity has tended to be represented in terms belonging to the general concept of the absolute subject: *one subject—three modes of being.* The one, identical divine subject can only be thought of as perfect subject if it can relate to itself. If it relates to itself this must be viewed as an eternal process of self-differentiation and self-identification of the absolute subject. It is only on the basis of the presupposed self-differentiation of the absolute subject that we can talk about God's "self"-revelation and "self"-communication. The reflection process of the absolute subject has—like the reflection process of every finite subject as well—this triadically conceivable structure of self-distinction and self-identification.

A Christian doctrine of the Trinity which is to be presented in the medium of the modern concept of God as absolute subject must renounce the trinitarian concept of person, because the concept of person also contains the concept of the subject of acts and relationships. It must surrender the concept of person to the one, identical God-subject, and choose for the trinitarian persons another, non-subjective expression. For this, Western tradition would seem to offer the neuter concept of "mode of being." Out of the necessity of its being, the one identical divine subject reflects on itself in three modes of being, communicating itself in this triadic way: God reveals himself through himself. The Father is assigned to the "I," the Son to the "self," and the Spirit to the identity of the divine "I-self"; and this becomes the basic structure of modern doctrines of the Trinity. What the traditional doctrine of the Trinity meant, is supposed to be reproduced by talking about "the self-relationships and self-mediations of the one, united God."

The later notion of "absolute personality" does at least take us a step further. The human personality is the result of a historical maturing process of the person; and in a similar way the absolute personality of God must be seen as the result of his eternal life process, eternally present in himself. The absolute personality of God fulfills its eternal being in three different modes of being. The effect of its triadic life on earth is therefore a process of self-emptying and re-appropriation of absolute personality.

Here the problems for the doctrine of the Trinity resemble those we discovered in the earlier Trinity of substance: the unity of the absolute subject is stressed to such a degree that the trinitarian persons disintegrate into mere aspects of the one subject. But the special Christian tradition and proclamation cannot be conceived of within the concept of the absolute subject. To represent the trinitarian persons in the one, identical, divine subject leads unintentionally but inescapably to the reduction of the doctrine of the Trinity to monotheism.

A new treatment of the doctrine of the Trinity today has to come to terms critically with these philosophical and theological traditions. A return to the earlier Trinity of substance is practically impossible, if only because the return to the cosmology of the old way of thinking about being has become impossible too, ever since the beginning of modern times. To carry on with the more modern "subject" Trinity is not in fact very fruitful either, because modern thinking in terms of "subject" is increasingly losing force and significance. Anthropological thinking is giving way to the new, relativistic theories about the world, and anthropocentric behavior is being absorbed into social patterns. "The belief that the most important thing about experience is the experiencing of it, and about deeds the doing of them, is beginning to strike most people as naïve."[16] The world of growing interdependencies can no longer be understood in terms of "my private world." Today the appeal to pure subjectivity is viewed as an inclination towards escapism.

The present book is an attempt to start with the special Christian tradition of the history of Jesus the Son, and from that to develop a historical doctrine of the Trinity. Here we shall presuppose the unity of God neither as homogenous substance nor as identical subject. Here we shall inquire about that unity in the light of this trinitarian history and shall therefore develop it too in trinitarian terms. The Western tradition began with God's unity and then went on to ask about the trinity. We are beginning with the trinity of the persons and shall then go on to ask about the unity. What then emerges is a concept of the divine unity as the union of the tri-unity, a concept which is differentiated and is therefore capable of being thought first of all.

In distinction to the trinity of substance and to the trinity of subject we shall be attempting to develop a social doctrine of the Trinity. We understand the scriptures as the testimony to the history of the Trinity's relations of fellowship, which are open to men and women, and open to the world. This trinitarian hermeneutics leads us to think in terms of relationships and communities; it supersedes the subjective thinking which cannot work without the separation and isolation of its objects.

Here, thinking in relationships and communities is developed out of the doctrine of the Trinity, and is brought to bear on the relation of men and women to God, to other people and to mankind as a whole, as well as on their fellowship with the whole of creation. By taking up panentheistic ideas from the Jewish and the Christian traditions, we shall try to think *ecologically* about God, man, and the world in their relationships and indwellings. In this way it is not merely the Christian *doctrine* of the Trinity that we are trying to work out anew; our aim is to develop and practice trinitarian *thinking* as well.

THE MYSTERY OF THE TRINITY

Source: Moltmann 1980; ET 1981/1993:129–39; 148–54; 156–61.

§1 A CRITICISM OF CHRISTIAN MONOTHEISM

1. MONOTHEISM AND MONARCHY

The patristic doctrine of the Trinity does not originate in an absorption of the philosophical doctrine of the Logos, and of neo-Platonic triadologies, as has often been maintained. Its source is to be found in the New Testament witness to the trinitarian history of the Son, and in the church's practice of baptism in the name of the triune God.

The early church's doctrine of the Trinity took on form during its resistance against dangerous heresies, in which the unity of Christ with God was called in question, either on God's behalf or on Christ's. It was only in these controversies that trinitarian dogma grew up; and with the dogma grew its formulation, as philosophical terminology was given a new theological mold.

The necessary resistance against Arianism on the one hand, and the laborious surmounting of Sabellianism on the other, led to the development of an explicit doctrine of the Trinity. Both heresies are christological in nature. Consequently the dogma of the Trinity was evolved out of Christology. It is designed to preserve faith in Christ, the Son of God, and to direct the Christian hope towards full salvation in the divine fellowship. The doctrine of the Trinity cannot therefore be termed "a speculation." On the contrary, it is the theological premise for Christology and soteriology.

The heresies which forced the church to formulate the doctrine of the Trinity in its early centuries, are by no means historically fortuitous and a thing of the past. They are permanent dangers to Christian theology. The deviations which are called by the names of Arius and Sabellius are continually among us theologically. Consequently it is useful to repeat the fundamental decisions of the early creeds, in spite of all the hermeneutical differences which we today, rightly, feel and perceive. These heresies have to be treated typologically and systematically, not merely historically.

The Second Epistle of Clement (1.1) already puts its finger on the fundamental problem when it demands that Christians think about Jesus "as they do about God" (ὡς περὶ θεοῦ). The reason it gives is a soteriological one: "For if we think any less of him than this, then we expect but little of him." Even externally, the adoration of Christ as God must be clearly recognizable. Pliny the Younger reported to Rome in the first century that the Christians in Bithynia praised Christ in their worship as if he were God (quasi Deo). Ignatius of Antioch called Christ God without any differentiation at all, even though he generally added "my" God or "our" God, which permits the distinction compared with "God *per se*." It is here that the theological problem arises.

What is the relationship between Christ and God, and how is the divine revelation in Christ related to God himself? How is the differentiable relationship of Christ to God the Father related to the unity of God himself? And how is the adoration of Christ as God reconcilable with God's unity?

These questions became all the more important because, from the time of the Christian apologists onwards, Christians won over the educated in the Roman Empire by proclaiming the One God: "ΕΙΣ ΘΕΟΣ." It was the acceptance of philosophical monotheism and the idea of the universal monarchy of the one God that made Christianity a "world religion," and that got over Christianity's appearance of being a Jewish messianic sect, or a private religion. But monotheism and monarchianism are only the names for two sides of the same thing: the One is the principle and point of integration for the Many. The One is the measure of the Many. The One God has always been appealed to and comprehended in the context of the unity of the world. . . .

. . . Let me point out at once here that this monotheistic monarchianism was, and is, an uncommonly seductive religious-political ideology. It is the fundamental notion behind the universal and uniform religion: One God—one Logos—one humanity; and in the Roman empire it was bound to seem a persuasive solution for many problems of a multi-national and multi-religious society. The universal ruler in Rome had only to be the image and correspondence of the universal ruler in heaven.

Both the acceptance of the fundamental monotheistic monarchical idea and its conquest through the doctrine of the Trinity must be counted among the great theological achievements of the early church; and this is true, not merely in the sphere of the doctrine of faith, but in the realm of political theology as well. For monotheism was, and is, always a "political problem" too.

Strict monotheism has to be theocratically conceived and implemented, as Islam proves. But once it is introduced into the doctrine and worship of the Christian church, faith in Christ is threatened: Christ must either recede into the series of the prophets, giving way to the One God, or he must disappear into the One God as one of his manifestations. The strict notion of the One God really makes theological Christology impossible, for the One can neither be parted nor imparted. It is ineffable. The Christian church was therefore right to see monotheism as the severest inner danger, even though it tried on the other hand to take over the monarchical notion of the divine lordship.

Strict monotheism obliges us to think of God without Christ, and consequently to think of Christ without God as well. The questions whether God exists and how one can be a Christian then become two unrelated questions. But if on the other hand trinitarian dogma maintains the unity of essence between Christ and God, then not only is Christ understood in divine terms; God is also understood in Christian ones. The intention and consequence of the doctrine of the Trinity is not only the deification of Christ; it is even more the Christianization of the concept of God. God cannot be comprehended without Christ, and Christ cannot be understood without God. If we are to perceive this, we not only have to reject the Arian heresy; the Sabellian heresy must be dismissed with equal emphasis.

2. MONOTHEISTIC CHRISTIANITY: ARIUS

The first possible way of abandoning Christ's divinity in favor of the One God can be found in what is known as *subordinationism*. The doctrine of Jesus' divinity grew up out of the biblical testimony to Jesus' sonship, and out of the Johannine doctrine of the Logos. The alternative, on the other hand, has its roots in early Christian *Spirit Christology*. According to this pneumatological Christology, it was not the eternal Son of the Father who in Jesus became man; it was the divine Spirit, who took up his dwelling in him. That is to say, Jesus taught and ministered as a man imbued with the Spirit. His power was the power of the divine Spirit. Through the power of the Spirit he led a perfect life which provides an authoritative model for all believers. This can be termed dynamistic subordinationism. It sets Jesus among the prophets, even if as the last and most perfect of them. Spirit Christology dominates *adoptionist subordinationism* as well. According to this, Jesus was adopted as Son of God through the Spirit, so that he might become the first-born among many brethren. The strength of these Christologies lies in the fact that they bring out the force of the Spirit as subject in Jesus' life and ministry. Their weakness is that, for the sake of the One God, they are unable to bring Jesus into any essential unity with the Father. This means that although they can find in him the foundation for a new morality, they cannot arouse any hope for full fellowship with God through him. The confession of faith in Christ does not burst apart the concept of the One God. Consequently Christ has to be subordinated to this One God. . . .

. . . Arius, a pupil of Lucian of Antioch, then became the advocate of subordinationism in its fullest form. He too starts from the idea of the One God. He thinks of God as the simple, supreme substance which, by virtue of its indivisible unity, also represents the ground of all being. The One is the cause of the many and their measure, but it is not caused itself. The One God is therefore the causeless Cause of all things. But because the One is indivisible, it is also ineffable. The One God is by definition "incommunicable." Consequently, for the fellowship of God and all things, there has to be a mediation through intermediaries. Arius called the mediating intermediary between the One God and the manifold world "Son" (in terms of Christian tradition) and (in philosophical terminology) "Logos." He is the creation of the One God, but the first, and hence the created being who is prototypical for all others. If he occupies this first mediating position, then he must himself, like all created beings, be alterable, mutable, and temporal. If he were not, he could neither form the world nor rule over it. Arius can only see "the Son" as "the first-born of creation," not as the only begotten Son of the Father, because he feels compelled to adhere to the unity of the One God.

This first-born of all creation, God's Wisdom and Reason, has appeared in Jesus. Consequently, Jesus can be called the first-born Son, but not the only begotten Son. Arianism's greatness lay in the way it brought Jesus and the divinity manifested in him as close as possible to the One God, yet without destroying God's undivided unity. Its monarchianism took the form: One God—one Logos—one world—one world monarchy. Its Christology of the first-born Son permitted only this graduated succession of being and authority.

Arianism is monotheistic Christianity in its purest form. Its mediator Christology admittedly moves Christ into the sphere of mythical intermediaries. . . . A Christology of this kind cannot provide any foundation for the redemption that makes full fellowship with God possible; it can only offer the basis for a new morality, for which Jesus' life provides the pattern and standard.

It was with difficulty, and only with the help of Constantine's imperial authority, that the Council of Nicaea was able to condemn Arianism in 325, and that it was able to win acceptance for (and establish as dogma) the complete unity of nature between Jesus Christ "the only begotten Son," and the Father. "The only begotten Son of God" (μονογενής) is "God of God, light of light, very God of very God, begotten not made, being of one substance with the Father." But this thesis of the *homousios* cast up a whole series of new problems.

What is the relation between the only begotten Son of the Father and the first-born of creation?

If Jesus, the only begotten Son, is "of one substance" with God the Father, how are we to understand God's unity?

If the Father is "of one substance" with the only begotten Son, how are we to interpret the sovereignty of God?

If the *homousios* does not merely identify Christ with God, but identifies God with Christ as well, then the divine unity can no longer be interpreted monadically. It has to be understood in trinitarian terms. But that leads to fundamental changes in the doctrine of God, in Christology, and in politics. Christian faith can then no longer be called "monotheistic" in the sense of the One God. God's sovereignty can then no longer be understood as the "universal monarchy" to which everything is subjected. It has to be interpreted and presented as the redeeming history of freedom.

3. CHRISTIAN MONOTHEISM: SABELLIUS

The other form of Christian monotheism is to be found in *modalism*. It is often viewed as the other extreme from subordinationism and its precise opposite; but in fact it is only the reverse side of the same thing. For modalism too is dominated by the basic idea of the One God and of the universal monarchy, which can be exercised only by this one subject. Of course the method of safeguarding this undivided unity of God's is a different one: Christ is no longer subordinated to the one God; he is dissolved, dissipated in that one God.

"We must think about Jesus Christ as we do about God," the Second Epistle of Clement demands. This is modalism's starting point: Jesus Christ is God, he is our God. This was undoubtedly the belief of the early Christian community. But theologically it gives rise to a problem: if Christ is our God, then the Father and the Son must be, not merely *one* but in fact *one and the same*. The One God is then called Father, inasmuch as he makes himself the subject of his revelation. He is then called "Son" and "Holy Spirit," inasmuch as he becomes the object and power of his own revelation.

An early form of maintaining God's simple unity in this way can be found in Syrian patripassianism: "The Father himself appeared in the flesh by making himself the Son; he himself suffered; he himself died; he himself raised himself." According to this thesis, the history of Christ can have only *one* subject. It is the One God who appears to us *as* Father, *as* Son, and *as* Spirit. The *trias* only comes into being in the revelation of the *monas*.

In the Christian community modalistic piety was, and is, often supported by bishops who think that they are standing on the sure ground of the church when they declare that Christ is God. In Rome this was apparently the church's official teaching in the second century. It was only the theological polemic of Hippolytus against Noetus, and Tertullian's struggle against Praxeas, which showed the dangers inherent in this view and which made it obvious that it was in fact a heresy.

It was Sabellius who gave modalism its theological formulation, and it was he who later gave his name to this whole trend. The basic ideas are not at all complicated. In the history of his revelation and his communication of salvation, the One God takes on three forms: in the form of the Father he appears to us as the *creator* and law-giver; in the form of the Son he appears as the *redeemer*; in the form of the Holy Spirit he appears as the *giver of life*. Father, Son, and Spirit are the three manifestations or modes of appearance of the One God. But this One God himself is as unknowable, unnameable, and ineffable as the "One" itself.

Sabellius called the three modes of appearance of the One God not merely manifestations, but also ἰδία/περιγραφή, that is to say, "something in God, something indwelling in him." The One God therefore does not merely appear to us in a threefold manner: in salvation history he is actually threefold to a certain degree, insofar as he is "the indweller" of his own manifestations and, through them, dwells in the world. Sabellius distinguishes between the One God and his indwellings. The One God himself is without distinction, incommunicable, and hence unknowable. But he allows himself to be known in history in the indwellings which are known by the three names. Sabellius even succeeds in thinking of God's monadic unity, not rigidly but (with the help of Stoic terms) as containing movement. It can expand itself and contract, develop, and gather together. Of course, as Marcellus of Ancyra critically added, this does not mean expanding the divine being; it means expansion of the divine will and activity. This already indicates that the One God is not merely to be thought of as monadic substance but at the same time as identical subject as well.

Sabellius and Marcellus reduced the one God and the Christian Trinity to a common denominator in what seems at first sight to be a quite convincing way. The One God is the eternal, uncompounded, undivided light whose rays are refracted in different ways, according to receptivity, in the world of men and women. But if the One God only appears *as* Father, *as* Son, and *as* Spirit, then this phraseology already indicates the "unreal" nature of the manifestations. Who or what the One God himself is cannot be perceived, because it cannot be communicated. Consequently the recognition of the manifestations of God *as . . .* cannot communicate any fellowship with *God himself* either.

This modalism is only seemingly a theology of Christ's divinity. In actual fact it leads to the dissolution of Christ's divinity in the ineffable and incommunicable Oneness of the Godhead *per se*. The statement that "Christ is God" ultimately makes Christ disappear in the One God. Conversely, the manifestation of the One God as Christ is condemned to unreality. In this way too the intellectual compulsions of monotheistic thinking prevail. Monotheism is common to both Sabellianism and Arianism. But whereas throughout the history of the church Arianism was always tainted with "liberalism" and heresy, Sabellian modalism was at times established church doctrine; and whether it has really been overcome even now is the question which the Eastern church still puts to the whole trinitarian doctrine of the churches of the West. . . .

4. THE FOUNDATION OF THE DOCTRINE OF THE TRINITY: TERTULLIAN

With his treatise against Praxeas (c. 215) Tertullian counts as being the initiator of a trinitarian solution of the problems in the Christian doctrine of God which were thrown up by subordinationism and modalism. The Fathers learnt from Tertullian, even if they did not mention his name. He perceived the problems more clearly than anyone before him, and the brilliance of his language and his skill in definition made new answers possible. Through him the theological discussion moved on to a new level. . . .

For Tertullian, God is from all eternity One, but not alone. His Reason (*logis, ratio*) or Wisdom (*sophia, sermo*) must be called equally eternal. The One God is in reality not a numerical or monadic One, but a unity which is differentiated in itself. The Logos proceeds from God through the act of eternal *generatio*, thereby becoming "the Son." Tertullian interprets this process as *prolatio*, in order to be able to say that the Son and the Father are *distincti* but not *divisi*, *discreti* but not *separati*. They are distinguished in their divine unity and are hence in their distinction one. The third to issue forth is the Holy Spirit. The Father sends him through the Son, and he is bound to the Father and the Son through the unity of the divine substance. In order to make this differentiated unity clear, Tertullian draws on Gnostic and neo-Platonic images such as sun—ray—reflection; or source—brook—river. The images are used to describe distinguishable individualities of the same matter. The monarchy of God is not abolished through this trinitarian differentiation, for the Son and the Spirit are subordinated to the Father. The Father is at the same time the whole divine substance. As *portiones totius* the Son and the Spirit have their being from him, and they carry out his will. When the work of the world's redemption and perfecting has been fulfilled, they will give back their authority to the Father.

The remarkable features of this initial outline are:

1. The trinitarian differentiation of the divine *monas*: *una substantia—tres personae*;

2. The distinctions in the unity: *distincti, non divisi; discreti, non separati*;

3. The new verbal coinage *trinitas*, which now takes the place of the divine *monas*.

But Tertullian was only able to develop these trinitarian differentiations in God because he replaced the θεὸς ἐστὶν εἷς by θεὸς ἐστὶν ἕν. Yet if God is *one*, and not one-and-the-same, who exercises the monarchy? The Father: for the Father is at the same time the total substance; the Son is a derivation and the Spirit is a part of him. But are the trinitarian differentiations then not after all merely modes of manifestation of the One God in the work of redemption? Tertullian tried to fend off this conclusion by distinguishing between monarchy and economy. The monarchy of the Father belongs within the divine Trinity itself, and it must be distinguished from the dispensation of salvation (economy) in creation. The Son is begotten, the world is created. The Holy Spirit goes forth, the world is redeemed.

Yet the line which Tertullian draws between the immanent and the economic Trinity is a fluid one, for if the Son and the Spirit proceed from the Father for the purpose of creating the world and for the work of redemption, then they must also return into the Oneness of the Father when these purposes are fulfilled, so that "God may be all in all."

The original One would then only differentiate itself in a trinitarian sense, in order to complete and perfect itself into the All-One. But that would mean that God is only to be thought of in trinitarian terms where his creative and redemptive self-communication is concerned, and not for his own sake. In these ideas the category of unity after all prevails over the triunity once more. This proves that it is not merely the concept of the *monas* which is the basic problem of the Christian concept of God. It is the concept of *monarchia* too. If these terms are not differentiated and altered, a Christian doctrine of God is not really possible. . . .

7. WHAT DIVINE UNITY?

Trinitarian theology grew up through the theological remolding of philosophical terms. This can be seen very well from the history of the concept "person." The remolding of the concept of God's unity necessary for an understanding of the triune God and his history, on the other hand, was evidently much more difficult. The philosophical starting point, which was the monadic interpretation of the One God, continually asserted itself in the history of the early church, even though Arianism was rejected and Sabellianism was overcome. Even where people were able to differentiate the concept of God's unity in trinitarian terms, the monadic interpretation held its ground in the concept of monarchy, whether it was understood as the monarchy of the Father within the Trinity or as the extra-trinitarian divine monarchy over the world.

The early creeds, which set the trend for tradition, remain ambivalent where the question of God's unity is concerned. The Nicene Creed, with its use of *homousios* as keyword, suggests a unity of substance between Father, Son, and Spirit. But the Athanasian Creed, with the thesis "*unus Deus*," maintains the identity of the one divine subject.

So are Father, Son, and Spirit one in their possession of the same divine substance, or *one and the same*, in being the same divine subject? Can the unity of the three distinct Persons lie in the homogeneity of the divine substance, which is common to them all, or does it have to consist in the sameness and identity of the one divine subject?

In the first case we should have to think of the unity of God as neuter, as the terms οὐσία or *substantia* suggest. In the second case we ought really only to talk about the One God, as the concept of the absolute subject demands.

In the first case the threeness of the persons is in the foreground, while the unity of their substance is the background. In the second case the unity of the absolute subject is in the foreground, and the three persons recede into the background. The first case is obviously open to the charge of tritheism; the second case to the reproach of modalism. In the first case the word tri-unity is used, while in the second case the threefold God (the *Dreifaltigkeit*) is the preferred term. In the first case we proceed from the three persons and inquire about their unity; in the second case we start from the One God and ask about his trinitarian self-differentiation. If the biblical testimony is chosen as point of departure, then we shall have to start from the three persons of the history of Christ. If philosophical logic is made the starting point, then the inquirer proceeds from the One God.

After considering all this, it seems to make more sense theologically to start from the biblical history, and therefore to make the unity of the three divine persons the problem, rather than to take the reverse method—to start from the philosophical postulate of absolute unity, in order then to find the problem in the biblical testimony. The unity of the Father, the Son, and the Spirit is then the eschatological question about the consummation of the trinitarian history of God. The unity of the three persons of this history must consequently be understood as a *communicable* unity and as an *open, inviting unity, capable of integration*. The *homogeneity* of the divine substance is hardly conceivable as communicable and open for anything else, because then it would no longer be homogeneous. The *sameness* and the identity of the absolute subject is not communicable either, let alone open for anything else, because it would then be charged with non-identity and difference. Both these concepts of unity—like the monadic concept—are exclusive, not inclusive. If we search for a concept of unity corresponding to the biblical testimony of the triune God, the God who unites others with himself, then we must dispense with both the concept of the one substance and the concept of the identical subject. All that remains is: the unitedness, the at-oneness of the three persons with one another, or: the unitedness, the at-oneness of the triune God. For only the concept of unitedness is the concept of a unity that can be communicated and is open. The one God is a God *at one* with himself. That presupposes the personal self-differentiation of God, and not merely a modal differentiation, for only persons can be at one with one another, not modes of being or modes of subjectivity. The at-oneness of the three divine persons is neither presupposed by these persons as their single substance nor is it brought about as the sameness or identity of the divine lordship or self-communication. The unitedness, the at-oneness, of the triunity is already given with the fellowship of the Father, the Son, and the Spirit. It therefore does not need to be additionally secured by a particular doctrine about the unity of the divine substance, or by the special doctrine of the one divine lordship.

The Father, the Son, and the Spirit are by no means merely *distinguished* from one another by their character as persons; they are just as much united with one another and in one another, since personal character and social character are only two aspects of the same thing. The concept of person must therefore in itself contain the concept of unitedness or at-oneness, just as, conversely, the concept of God's at-oneness must in itself contain the concept of the three persons. This means that the concept of God's unity cannot in the trinitarian sense be fitted into the homogeneity of the one divine substance, or into the identity of the absolute subject either; and least of all into one of the three persons of the Trinity. It must be perceived in the *perichoresis* of the divine persons. If the unity of God is not perceived in the at-oneness of the triune God, and therefore as a perichoretic unity, then Arianism and Sabellianism remain inescapable threats to Christian theology.

§2 THE DOXOLOGICAL TRINITY

1. THE ECONOMY AND DOXOLOGY OF SALVATION

Ever since the repulse of modalism through Tertullian, it has been usual to distinguish between the economic and the immanent Trinity. The economic Trinity designates the triune God in his dispensation of salvation, in which he is revealed. The economic Trinity is therefore also called the revelatory Trinity.

The immanent Trinity is the name given to the triune God as he is in himself. The immanent Trinity is also called the substantial Trinity. This distinction cannot mean that there are two different Trinities. It is rather a matter of the same triune God as he is in his saving revelation and as he is in himself.

Is the distinction between *God for us* and *God in himself* a speculative one? And if it is speculative, is it necessary? This distinction is usually substantiated by the freedom of the divine decision and by human salvation's character of grace. God is perfect; he is self-sufficient; he is not bound to reveal himself. We experience our salvation by his grace, undeservedly and beyond our deserts. The distinction between an immanent Trinity and an economic Trinity secures God's liberty and his grace. It is the logically necessary presupposition for the correct understanding of God's saving revelation.

This distinction between immanent and economic Trinity would be necessary if, in the concept of God, there were really only the alternative between liberty and necessity. But if God *is* love, then his liberty cannot consist of loving or of not loving. On the contrary, his love is his liberty and his liberty is his love. He is not compelled to love by any outward or inward necessity. Love is self-evident for God. So we have to say that the triune God loves the world with the very same love that he himself *is*. The notion of an immanent Trinity in which God is simply by himself, without the love which communicates salvation, brings an arbitrary element into the concept of God which means a break-up of the Christian concept. Consequently this idea safeguards neither God's liberty nor the grace of salvation. It introduces a contradiction into the relationship between the immanent and the economic Trinity: the God who loves the world does not correspond to the God who suffices for himself. Before the unchangeable God, everything is equal and equally indifferent. For the loving God, nothing is a matter of indifference. Before an equivocal, an undecided God, nothing is significant. For the God who in his love is free, everything is infinitely important. But the immanent and the economic Trinity cannot be distinguished in such a way that the first nullifies what the second says. The two rather form a continuity and merge into one another.

The other and specific starting point for distinguishing between the economic and the immanent Trinity is to be found in *doxology*. The assertions of the immanent Trinity about eternal life and the eternal relationships of the triune God in himself have their *Sitz im Leben,* their situation in life, in the praise and worship of the church:

Glory be to the Father and to the Son and to the Holy Ghost!

Real theology, which means the knowledge of God, finds expression in thanks, praise, and adoration. And it is what finds expression in doxology that is the real theology. There is no experience of salvation without the expression of that experience in thanks, praise, and joy. An experience which does not find expression in this way is not a liberating experience. Only doxology releases the experience of salvation for a full experience of that salvation. In grateful, wondering, and adoring perception, the triune God is not made man's object; he is not appropriated and taken possession of. It is rather that the perceiving person participates in what he perceives, being transformed into the thing perceived through his wondering perception. Here we know only insofar as we love. Here we know in order to participate. Then to know God means to participate in the fullness of the divine life. That is why in the early church the doxological knowledge of God is called *theologia* in the real sense, being distinguished from the doctrine of salvation, the *oeconomia Dei*. The "economic Trinity" is the object of kerygmatic and practical theology; the "immanent Trinity" the content of doxological theology.

If we start from this distinction, then it becomes clear that doxological theology is *responsive* theology. Its praise and its knowledge of God are a response to the salvation that has been experienced. If the immanent Trinity is the counterpart of praise, then knowledge of the economic Trinity (as the embodiment of the history and experience of salvation) precedes knowledge of the immanent Trinity. In the order of being it succeeds it.

But how and why do we arrive at the one perception from the other? In doxology the thanks of the receiver return from the goodly gift to the giver. But the giver is not thanked merely for the sake of his good gift; he is also extolled because he himself is good. So God is not loved, worshiped, and perceived merely because of the salvation that has been experienced, but for his own sake. That is to say, praise goes beyond thanksgiving. God is recognized, not only in his goodly works but in his goodness itself. And adoration, finally, goes beyond both thanksgiving and praise. It is totally absorbed into its counterpart, in the way that we are totally absorbed by astonishment and boundless wonder. God is ultimately worshiped and loved for himself, not merely for salvation's sake. Of course all the terms of doxology crystallize out of the experience of salvation. But they grow up out of the conclusion drawn from this experience about the transcendent conditions which make the experience possible. And in this way they necessarily go beyond any individual experience and arrive at that experience's transcendent ground. In this way doxological terms remain inescapably bound to the experience of salvation and do not go speculatively beyond it. They remain related to the experience of salvation precisely because they are directed towards the God himself whose salvation and love has been experienced.

It follows from this interlacing of the doctrine of salvation with doxology that we may not assume anything as existing in God himself which contradicts the history of salvation; and, conversely, may not assume anything in the experience of salvation which does not have its foundation in God. The principle that the doctrine of salvation and doxology do not contradict one another is founded on the fact that there are not two different Trinities. There is only one, single, divine Trinity and one, single, divine history of salvation. The triune God can only appear in history as he is in himself, and in no other way. He is in himself as he appears in salvation history, for it is he himself who is manifested, and he is just what he is manifested as being. Is this a law which infringes God's liberty? No, it is the quintessence of God's truth. God can do anything, but "he cannot deny himself" (2 Tim. 2:13): "God is faithful." . . . God's truth is his faithfulness. Consequently we can rely on his promises and on himself. . . . The true God is the God of truth, whose nature is eternal faithfulness and reliability. That is why the principle behind the Christian doctrine of the Trinity is:

Statements about the immanent Trinity must not contradict statements about the economic Trinity. Statements about the economic Trinity must correspond to doxological statements about the immanent Trinity.

2. THE HISTORICAL EXPERIENCE OF SALVATION

. . . [Earlier] we interpreted salvation history as "the history of the Son" of God, Jesus Christ. We understood this history as the trinitarian history of God in the concurrent and joint workings of the three subjects, Father, Son, and Spirit; and we interpreted it as the history of God's trinitarian relationships of fellowship. The history of the Son is not implemented by a single subject. Consequently even the divine life itself cannot be implemented by a single subject either. So we have to comprehend the triune God as the "transcendent primal ground" of this trinitarian history of God if we are to praise him, to magnify him, and to know him as the one who he himself is. In contrast to the psychological doctrine of the Trinity, we are therefore developing a social doctrine of the Trinity, and one based on salvation history.

The reduction of the Trinity to a single identical subject (even if the subject is a threefold one) does not do justice to the trinitarian history of God. The reduction of the three persons to three modes of subsistence of the one God cannot illuminate salvation history in the fullness of God's open trinitarian relationships of fellowship. We have understood the unity of the divine trinitarian history as the open, unifying at-oneness of the three divine persons in their relationships to one another. If this uniting at-oneness of the triune God is the quintessence of salvation, then its "transcendent primal ground" cannot be seen to lie in the one, single, homogeneous divine essence (*substantia*), or in the one identical, absolute subject. It then lies in the eternal *perichoresis* of the Father, the Son, and the Spirit. The history of God's trinitarian relationships of fellowship corresponds to the eternal *perichoresis* of the Trinity. For this trinitarian history is nothing other than the eternal *perichoresis* of Father, Son, and Holy Spirit in their dispensation of salvation, which is to say in their opening of themselves for the reception and unification of the whole creation.

The history of salvation is the history of the eternally living, triune God who draws us into and includes us in his eternal triune life with all the fullness of its relationships. It is the love story of the God whose very life is the eternal process of engendering, responding, and blissful love. God loves the world with the very same love which he is in himself. If, on the basis of salvation history and the experience of salvation, we have to recognize the unity of the triune God in the perichoretic at-oneness of the Father, the Son, and the Holy Spirit, then this does not correspond to the solitary human subject in his relationship to himself; nor does it correspond, either, to a human subject in his claim to lordship over the world. It only corresponds to a human fellowship of people without privileges and without subordinances. The perichoretic at-oneness of the triune God corresponds to the experience of the community of Christ, the community which the Spirit unites through respect, affection, and love. The more open-mindedly people live with one another, for one another, and in one another in the fellowship of the Spirit, the more they will become one with the Son and the Father, and one in the Son and the Father (John 17:21).

God as almighty power and lordship—this notion of God is mediated and enforced from "above to below." But God as love is experienced in the community of brothers and sisters through mutual acceptance and participation. That applies too to any human order of society which deserves the name of "human" in the Christian sense: the further the acceptance of the other goes, the deeper the participation in the life of the other is, the more united people who have been divided by the perversions of rule will become. In the community of Christ it is *love* that corresponds to the perichoretic unity of the triune God as it is manifested and experienced in the history of salvation; in human society it is solidarity that provides this correspondence. . . .

3. THE RELATIONSHIP BETWEEN THE IMMANENT AND THE ECONOMIC TRINITY

. . . The meaning of the cross of the Son on Golgotha reaches right into the heart of the immanent Trinity. From the very beginning, no immanent Trinity and no divine glory is conceivable without "the Lamb who was slain." So in Christian art too there are hardly any representations of the Trinity in heaven without the cross and the One crucified. If we start from the assumption that the perceptions and conceptions about the immanent Trinity in doxology are built up on the basis of the experience of salvation, then this immediately becomes comprehensible: anyone who owes his salvation to the delivering up of the Son to death on the cross can never think of God in the abstract, apart from the cross of Christ. For him, God is from eternity to eternity "the crucified God." Only "the Lamb that was slain is worthy to receive power, and riches, and wisdom, and strength, and honor, and glory and blessing" (Rev. 5:12). . . .

. . . The relationship of the triune God to himself and the relationship of the triune God to his world is not to be understood as a one-way relationship—the relation of image to reflection, idea to appearance, essence to manifestation—but as a mutual one. The concept "mutual relationship" does not equate God's relationship to the world with his relationship to himself. But it says that God's relationship to the world has a retroactive effect on his relationship to himself—even though the divine relationship to the world is primarily determined by that inner relationship. The growth of knowledge of the immanent Trinity from the saving experience of the cross of Christ makes this necessary. The pain of the cross determines the inner life of the triune God from eternity to eternity. If that is true, then the joy of responsive love in glorification through the Spirit determines the inner life of the triune God from eternity to eternity too. Just as the cross of the Son puts its impress on the inner life of the triune God, so the history of the Spirit molds the inner life of the triune God through the joy of liberated creation when it is united with God. That is why Christian doxology always ends with the eschatological prospect, looking for "the perfecting of thy kingdom in glory, when we shall praise and adore thee, Father, Son, and Holy Spirit, for ever and ever."[17]

If it is the quintessence of doxology, then the doctrine of the immanent Trinity is part of eschatology as well. The economic Trinity completes and perfects itself to immanent Trinity when the history and experience of salvation are completed and perfected. When everything is "in God" and "God is all in all," then the economic Trinity is raised into and transcended in the immanent Trinity. What remains is the eternal praise of the triune God in his glory.

The Kingdom of Freedom

Source: Moltmann 1980; ET 1981/1993:191–202.

§1 Criticism of Political and Clerical Monotheism

The functional problem of the doctrine of the Trinity lies in its relationship to the doctrine of the kingdom. How are God's Trinity and his kingdom related to one another? Is the doctrine of the Trinity the appropriate interpretation of the one divine lordship (Barth's view), or does the history of the kingdom of God reveal the divine life of the Father, the Son, and the Spirit? Does the divine Trinity act only inwardly in its threefold nature, acting outwardly "without division" (as Augustine taught)? Or are the "works of the Trinity" defined in a trinitarian sense as well? The more we stress the economy of salvation and the lordship of God, the more we are compelled to stress God's unity, for this divine rule would seem only capable of being exercised by a single, identical subject. But the further doxology is developed, the more it is possible already to perceive the triunity in the history of salvation and in the lordship that makes us free; and the more this will be praised to all eternity.

We have developed the doctrine of the Trinity in the context of the surmounting of religious monotheism, monotheistic Christianity, and Christian monotheism. We must therefore now go on to see its bearings on the criticism of political and clerical monotheism as well. We have said that monotheism is monarchism. The question: Does God exist? is an abstract one. Theology is never concerned with the actual existence of a God. It is interested solely in the rule of this God in heaven and on earth. The notion of a divine monarchy in heaven and on earth, for its part, generally provides the justification for earthly domination—religious, moral, patriarchal, or political dominion—and makes it a hierarchy, a "holy rule." . . .

. . . The doctrine of the Trinity which, on the contrary is developed as a theological doctrine of freedom must for its part point towards a community of men and women without supremacy and without subjection.

1. Political Monotheism

What is the relationship between the religious ideas of any given era and the political constitution of its societies? That is the question asked by political theology. . . .

. . . The idea of theocracy was very much alive among the martyrs, during the Christian persecutions, and among the theological apologists of Christianity in the first three centuries. Consequently, from a very early period there was a Christian preference for the Roman empire. Remembrance of the Emperor Augustus's peaceful empire outshone even the remembrance of the Christ crucified by Pontius Pilate. . . .

. . . The doctrine of sovereignty suggested by Christian monotheism . . is more absolutist than the theories based on Aristotle or the Stoics: the one almighty emperor is to a preeminent degree *the visible image* of the invisible God. His "glory" reflects God's glory. His rule represents God's rule. . . . The idea of unity in God therefore provokes both the idea of the universal, unified church, and the idea of the universal, unified state: one God—one emperor—one church—one empire. . . .

. . . It is only when the doctrine of the Trinity vanquishes the monotheistic notion of the great universal monarch in heaven, and his divine patriarchs in the world, that earthly rulers, dictators, and tyrants cease to find any justifying religious archetypes any more.

How must a doctrine of the Trinity be formulated if it is to have this intention?

(a) The Christian doctrine of the Trinity unites God, the almighty Father, with Jesus the Son, whom he delivered up and whom the Romans crucified, and with the life-giving Spirit, who creates the new heaven and the new earth. It is impossible to form the figure of the omnipotent, universal monarch, who is reflected in earthly rulers, out of the unity of this Father, this Son, and this Spirit.

(b) If we see the Almighty in trinitarian terms, he is not the archetype of the mighty ones of this world. He is the Father of the Christ who was crucified and raised for us. As the Father of Jesus Christ, he is almighty because he exposes himself to the experience of suffering, pain, helplessness, and death. But what he *is* is not almighty power; what he *is* is love. It is his passionate, passible love that is almighty, nothing else.

(c) The glory of the triune God is reflected, not in the crowns of kings and the triumph of victors, but in the face of the crucified Jesus, and in the faces of the oppressed whose brother he became. He is the one visible image of the invisible God.

(d) Seen in trinitarian terms, the life-giving Sprit, who confers on us the future and hope, does not proceed from any accumulation of power, or from the absolutist practice of lordship; he proceeds from the Father of Jesus Christ and from the resurrection of the Son. The resurrection through the life-quickening energy of the Holy Spirit is experienced, not at the spearheads of progress, but in the shadow of death. . . .

. . . The monotheistic God is "the Lord of the world." He is defined simply through his power of disposal over his property, not through personality and personal relationships. He really has no name—merely legal titles. But the triune God represents an inexhaustible life, a life which the three persons have in common, in which they are present with one another, for one another and in one another. What the doctrine of the Trinity calls *perichoresis* was also understood by patristic theologians as the sociality of the three divine persons. Two different categories of analogy have always been used for the eternal life of the Trinity: the category of the individual person, and the category of community. . . . [T]he image of God must not merely be sought for in human individuality; we must look for it with equal earnestness in human sociality.

The Christian doctrine of the Trinity provides the intellectual means whereby to harmonize personality and sociality in the community of men and women, without sacrificing the one to the other. . . . If today we understand person as the unmistakeable and untransferable individual existence, we owe this to the Christian doctrine of the Trinity. But why was the concept of the *perichoresis*—the unity and fellowship of the persons—not developed with equal emphasis? The disappearance of the social doctrine of the Trinity has made room for the development of individualism, and especially "possessive individualism," in the Western world: everyone is supposed to fulfill "himself," but who fulfills the community? It is a typically Western bias to suppose that social relationships and society are less "primal" than the person. . . .

2. CLERICAL MONOTHEISM

. . . In the period of the apostolic Fathers, Christianity spread rapidly in Asia Minor. . . . It was at that time that Ignatius of Antioch formulated the principle of the episcopate which has remained valid in many churches until the present day: one bishop—one church. He founded this episcopal unity of the church by means of the following theological hierarchy: one God—one Christ—one bishop—one church. The bishop represents Christ to his church just as Christ represents God. This representative derivation of divine authority is obviously monarchical monotheism. . . .

. . . In the Middle Ages and in the nineteenth century the doctrine of the monarchical episcopate was developed further in the theology of the papacy. . . . Papal authority guarantees the unity of the church. That authority is itself guaranteed by the Petrine apostolic succession. Peter's authority is itself guaranteed by the words of the historical Jesus (Matt. 16:18). . . .

. . . To base a justification of the church's unity and the pope's "ministry of unity" on Matthew 16 is not only dubious and fraught with assumptions historically; it is also theologically weak. . . .

. . . But there is another, different justification for the church's unity—a trinitarian one. We find it in Jesus' High Priestly prayer in John 17:20f.: "That they may all be one; even as thou, Father, art in me, and I in thee, that they also may be in us, so that the world may believe that thou hast sent me." Here the unity of the Christian community is a trinitarian unity. It *corresponds* to the indwelling of the Father in the Son, and of the Son in the Father. It *participates* in the divine triunity, since the community of believers is not only fellowship *with* God but *in* God too. The unity of the church is already given through the prayer of Jesus, which the church can be sure was heard by the Father.

. . . Monarchical monotheism justifies the church as hierarchy, as sacred dominion. The doctrine of the Trinity constitutes the church as "a community free of dominion." . . . What stands at the center is not faith in God's revelation on the basis of ecclesiastical authority, but faith on the basis of individual insight into the truth of revelation. The hierarchy which preserves and enforces unity is replaced by the brotherhood and sisterhood of the community of Christ.

Notes

1. Jürgen Moltmann, *A Broad Place: An Autobiography*, trans. Margaret Kohl (Minneapolis: Fortress Press/London: SCM Press, 2008), 287f.

2. Philipp Melanchthon, *Loci Communes* (1521), *Werke* II, ed. Robert Stupperich (Gütersloh: Bertelsmann, 1952), 7.

3. Friedrich Schleiermacher, *Glaubenslehre*, 2d ed., §§ 3 and 4.

4. Cf. here now Christopher Lasch, *The Culture of Narcissism: American Life in an Age of Diminishing Expectations* (New York: Norton, 1978).

5. Immanuel Kant, *Der Streit der Fakultäten* (1798), Philosophische Bibliothek [hereafter PhB] 252 (1959): 33.

6. Ibid., 34.

7. Cf. Gustavo Gutiérrez, *A Theology of Liberation: History, Politics, and Salvation*, trans. Caridad Inda and John Eagleson (Maryknoll, NY: Orbis, 1973), 11.

8. Immanuel Kant, *Critique of Pure Reason*, preface to the 2d ed.

9. Heinrich Denzinger, *Enchiridion Symbolorum et Definitionum* (1854) (Freiburg: Herder, 195726), 1785.

10. Ibid., 2071.

11. René Descartes, *Discours de la méthode* (1637), PhB 26 a (1870): esp. 25ff.

12. Friedrich Nietzsche, "Der tolle Mensch," in *Die fröhliche Wissenschaft*, no. 125.

13. Augustine, *Soliloquia*, I, 2 and II, 1.

14. René Descartes, 3. *Meditation* (1641), PhB 27 (2003): 42.

15. Rudolf Bultmann, "What Does It Mean to Speak of God?" in *Faith and Understanding*, trans. Louise Pettibone Smith (London: SCM Press, 1969), 63.

16. Robert Musil, *The Man without Qualities*, trans. Eithne Wilkins and Ernst Kaiser, 3 vols. (1953–60) (London: Secker & Warburg), 1:175.

17. This Doxology is used by the Reformierte Kirche in Deutschland.

4

God in Creation

Moltmann's longstanding concern with ecology found fullest expression in the Gifford Lectures for 1984–85, published under the title God in Creation: An Ecological Doctrine of Creation. *The doctrine of creation he put forward was based on the guiding concept of "creation's indwelling divine Spirit." Creation should be seen not as a single act on God's part, finished and done with, but as an "open system," open for redemptive history and for disaster, open for relationships and interactions in which all created being is involved, since the whole creation is waiting to obtain the glorious liberty of the children of God (Rom. 8:21) in the eschatological goal, when "God will be all in all."*

Although God in Creation *is the fullest and richest exposition of Moltmann's ecological ideas, these are already a theme in a previous work,* The Future of Creation *(1977), published in English in 1979. A first excerpt is therefore taken from this earlier book, and is followed by passages from his more comprehensive exposition in* God in Creation.

THE FUTURE OF CREATION: CREATION AS AN OPEN SYSTEM
Source: Moltmann 1977; ET 1979/2007:115–30.

1. TWO PROBLEMS

(*i*) We all know that since the beginning of modern times there has been a crisis in the relationship between science and belief in creation. Science emancipated itself from the religious culture of the Middle Ages and founded the secular culture of modern times. Theology became apologetic, fighting a mere rearguard battle against the triumphal progress of science—either by limiting belief in creation *deistically* to the original contingency of the universe; or by limiting it *existentially* to the personal contingency of human existence; or by cutting off *church dogmatics* so completely from the sciences that the two neither interfere with one another nor have anything to say to one another. If today we are striving for a convergence between science and belief in creation, this presupposes a revision both of theology's traditional concept of creation, and of classical science's concept of nature. The ecological crisis caused by the progressive destruction of nature was brought about by Christianity and science together; and if man and nature want to win a chance to survive, then Christianity and science must together revise both the picture of man found in the traditional belief in creation ("subdue the earth," Gen. 1:28) and the picture of man reflected in Cartesian science ("*Maître et possesseur de la nature*").

(*ii*) Since the development of Christian dogmatics within the sphere of Greek thinking, theological method has always begun with the description of the creation of the world, and has finally arrived at the idea of the world's redemption. By thinking in this way, it always related redemption to creation and understood redemption in its light. The creation of the world was really the foundation of everything. In the beginning was God, the Creator, and his creation was very good and perfect. At the end it will be again as it was at the beginning: τὰ ἔσχατα ὡς τὰ πρῶτα. Redemption is then nothing other than the restoration of original creation with all its goodness: *restitutio in integrum*. If we understand redemption in this way, in the light of creation and for the sake of creation, then we have a *protological understanding of eschatology*. History between creation and redemption is then primarily the history of the Fall. It cannot bring anything new, except the increasing deterioration and aging of the earth. Only redemption will restore creation. The revision of the doctrine of creation which is, in my view, necessary today (both for exegetical reasons, and for reasons of experience and our dealings with nature) is a changeover to an *eschatological understanding of creation*. If we make this changeover, not only will eschatology continue to be understood in the light of creation, but creation will also be understood in the light of eschatology.

2. IS CREATION A CLOSED SYSTEM OR AN OPEN ONE?

The final syllable of *Schöpfung*—the German word for creation—indicates the completed process of creative activity and its result. Consequently when we talk about creation, we instinctively think, theologically, about the original state of the world and the beginning of all things, imagining them as a condition that was once finished, complete in itself and perfect. Belief in creation repeats the judgment of the Creator over his creation: "Behold, it was very good."

Unfortunately man cannot, like his Creator, rest at this point. For experience tells him, "Behold, it is unfortunately not very good." This difference between the judgment of faith and the judgment of experience has led people to put the "very good" creation before history and to describe it in terms of an image of religious memory, by means of religious symbols of origin. Dogma called Adam's status in paradise the *status integritatus*. As the man whose creation was "very good," Adam possessed *justitia et sanctitas originalis*. The first man and woman were driven out of this perfect state because of their sin. To this perfect state redemption will lead them back.

What, then, is history? It is first of all paradise lost, then the road to exile. What is redemption? It is the way back and, as the final outcome, paradise regained. Sin perverts the good creation. Grace restores it. What emerges from the history of sin and grace is the good creation as it was originally. In the history of religion this corresponds to "the myth of eternal return," described by Mircea Eliade.[1] Did Thomas Aquinas mean anything different when he said: "*Finis rerum respondet principio, Deus enim principium et finis rerum. Ergo et exitus rerum a principio respondet reductioni rerum in finem*"? At all events for Thomas time has a symmetrical, circular structure. . . . Does not Rudolf Bultmann have the same thing in mind when he writes:

> No light shone in Jesus other than the light that always shone in creation. In the light of the revelation of redemption, man does not have to understand himself any differently from the way he was always supposed to understand himself in the face of revelation in creation and law: as God's creation.[2]

At all events, time has a symmetrical, circular structure for Bultmann too:

> So what meaning has the divine righteousness or the forgiveness of
> sins? . . . Its meaning is that the original relationship of creation will
> be restored.[3]

According to what its wording would seem to suggest, as well as traditional
interpretations of it, original creation is non-historical. History only begins
with the Fall of man and ends with the restoration of creation in redemption.
Creation itself has neither time nor history. The picture of creation which is
painted in this way is the picture of a closed system, perfect in itself and totally
self-sufficient.

Modern exegesis of the Old and New Testaments will not allow us to
maintain this notion of creation. Biblically, faith in salvation as a historical
process determines belief in creation; and insofar as redemption determines faith
in salvation as a historical process, eschatology also determines the experience
of history and belief in creation. We may mention the following as being
systematically important findings of Old Testament exegesis:

(*i*) The Israelite belief in creation developed out of Israel's historical
experience of God—the exodus, the covenant, the occupation of the promised
land—and is molded by this experience. Israel had a "soteriological
understanding of creation."[4]

(*ii*) In both the Yahwist and the Priestly Documents, creation in the
beginning does not mean an unscathed primal condition; it means the history
that precedes salvation history. That is why creation, with its various orders, is
itself understood as the work of Yahweh's grace and is narrated in the form of
the *toledoth*. Creation in the beginning "opens up the historical prospect." God's
historical relation with the world does not merely begin after the Fall; it begins
with creation. Creation is aligned towards the future, so that we can say: "In
Old Testament theology creation is an eschatological concept."[5]

(*iii*) The information "in the beginning God created" establishes time
together with creation. But if time begins simultaneously with "creation in the
beginning," then creation must be subject to change from the beginning, for
time is only perceived from alteration. But if creation is subject to change and
is open to time from the beginning, then it cannot be a closed system; it must
be an open one. Consequently the time that begins with creation does not
have a symmetrical structure either, in which future and past, goal and origin
correspond to one another, like the two halves of a circle. Time's structure is a-
symmetrical. It is open for a future which does not have to be the return of what
was at the beginning, in the form of a *restitutio in integrum*. Some scholars have
thought that "creation in the beginning" already envisages the consummation

of creation "at the end" because the idea of *acharith* and the idea of *reshith* belong together. Even if this does not follow directly from the concept "in the beginning," according to the Priestly Document creation at the beginning does point forward towards "God's resting," and, according to the Yahwist, towards the universal fulfillment of the blessing to Abraham. This determination of a goal may be termed eschatological. "To the beginning there corresponds an end, to creation there corresponds a consummation, to the 'very good' here a 'perfectly glorious' there."[6]

It follows from this that theology must talk about creation not only at the beginning, but also in history and at the end. That is to say, we must have in view the total process of divine creative activity. "Creation" as the quintessence of God's creative activity comprehends creation at the beginning, the creation of history, and the creation of the endtime. It embraces the initial creative activity, creative activity in history, and the eschatological consummation. The reduction of the concept of creation to creation in the beginning has led traditionally either to the cleavage between "creation and redemption" and between "nature and super-nature," or to a division between "the first and the second creation." But this calls in question the continuity and unity of the divine creative activity itself. The concept of the unity of God in the unity of meaning of his creative activity can, in my view, only be preserved through the concept of the coherent, eschatologically orientated process of creation. If this is correct, then the position of man with regard to creation changes as well. He no longer merely confronts God's non-human creation as its lord, the creature who was made in the image of God; together with all other things, he also stands in the Becoming of the still-open, uncompleted process of creation. Creation is then not a *factum* but a *fieri*. This leads to a new interpretation of man's destiny in creation; and "subdue the earth" cannot be this destiny's final word.

If theology wants to sum up God's creative activity, then it must view creation as the still-open, creative process of reality. In traditional terms, we mean by this the unity of the *regnum naturae*, the *regnum gratiae*, and the *regnum gloriae*, each viewed eschatologically, in respect of its particular time. The initial creation points towards salvation history, and both point beyond themselves to the kingdom of glory. It is not the covenant of grace which already provides the "inner ground" for creation in the beginning; the inner ground is only given with the kingdom of glory. For the kingdom of glory is the inner motivation of the divine history of the covenant. At the same time, in the process of creation which is totally aligned towards glory, we can distinguish between the following, according to their different conditions:

(*a*) creation in the beginning;
(*b*) creative acts in history;
(*c*) the creation of the endtime.

3. CREATION IN THE BEGINNING

According to the texts, creation in the beginning is evidently creation without any presuppositions. The expression *creatio ex nihilo* is intended to convey the liberty of the Creator and the contingency of all being—both its initial contingency and its permanent, fundamental contingency. The question: Why is there something rather than nothing? cannot be answered by pointing to any necessity. But it cannot be answered by pointing to pure chance either. *Creatio ex nihilo* defines in a negative way the positive ground of creation in God's good pleasure. Out of "the inner necessity of his love," to use Barth's phrase, the Creator makes something that corresponds to him and gives him pleasure. That is why creation has a meaning in its contingency. . . .

Creation in the beginning is also the creation of time. It must therefore be understood as *creatio mutabilis*. It is perfectible, not perfect, for it is open for the history of both disaster and salvation, for both destruction and consummation. If we understand creation individually and as a whole as *an open system*, then its beginning is at the same time the condition for its history and its completion. Creation at the beginning is the creation of conditions for the potentialities of creation's history. It pegs out the experimental field of constructive and destructive possibilities. It is open for time and for its own alteration in time. We cannot see in initial creation the invariant nature of history, but we can see the beginning of nature's history.

The creation accounts tell us that the initial creation out of chaos is also a creation of order in chaos. In the symbolic language of the Bible, the forces of chaos—night and the sea—thrust themselves into creation, even though they are excluded and confined by God. *Creatio ex nihilo* is therefore *creatio in nihilo* as well and is consequently creation that is threatened, and only protected to a limited degree against that threat. In the apocalyptic visions of the creation of the endtime, on the other hand, the encroaching forces of chaos are absent (Rev. 21:1; 22:5). The creation of glory is to be a creation that is no longer threatened and no longer vulnerable. In it God will be "all in all" (1 Cor. 15:28, KJV), for then his glory is apparently to interpenetrate everything and overcome not only death but even the possibility of death. The Augustinian doctrine of freedom says the same thing: the initial *posse non peccare* is to be overcome by the *non posse peccare* of the endtime, and the initial *posse non mori* by the endtime's *non posse mori*. The inference is that man was created as "potentiality *for*." He is certainly destined for righteousness and not for sin, and for glory, not death. But he can still fall short of what his potentiality is destined for. This cannot be said to be what Barth calls an "impossible possibility" in the ontological sense; but it can in the ethical sense be called a potentiality which ought not to be realized.

4. CREATIVE ACTS IN HISTORY

In ascribing to Israel a soteriological understanding of creation in the beginning, we must also, on the other hand, recognize that Israel had an understanding of salvation in history which was based on creation. The prophets use the word *bara* more frequently for the divine creation of new, unexpected, and unmerited salvation in history than for creation in the beginning. Like the Psalms, the prophets saw the exodus and the creation of the world, the creation of the world and the universal exodus of the endtime as belonging to a single perspective. Consequently belief in creation also serves faith in salvation, because for that faith, salvation proceeds from God's new creations. That is why creation in the beginning can be praised as an act of salvation, and the redemption can be expected in terms of a new creation.

The *bara* events of history are God's free acts and hence contingent. But they are not without premises, as was creation in the beginning. They are depicted as the creation of something new out of something old—of salvation out of wretchedness and life from dead bones. The divine creative activity at the beginning is conceived of as being an effortless creating through the Word; but the divine creative activity of redemption is understood as God's weariness and labor (Isa. 43:24; Isaiah 55). The creating of salvation for those who are without it proceeds from the suffering of God's love for his people. Because Israel understood itself as being exemplary for the nations and for the whole of creation, we can view its experience of history as exemplary for the understanding of history in general. Here the hidden actions of God in history are manifest in an exemplary way.

What are God's creative acts in history related to? Theological language related salvation to sin, and redemption to slavery. But what are sin and slavery? Having called creation in the beginning a system open for time and potentiality, we can understand sin and slavery as the self-closing of open systems against their own time and their own potentialities. If a person closes himself against his potentialities, then he is fixing himself on his present reality and trying to uphold what is present, and to maintain the present against possible changes. By doing this he turns into *homo incurvatus in se*. If a human society settles down as a closed system, seeking to be self-sufficient, then something similar happens: a society of this kind will project its own present into the future and will merely repeat the form it has already acquired. For this society the future ceases to offer scope for possible change; and in this way the society also surrenders its freedom. Natural history demonstrates from other living things as well that closing up against the future, self-immunization against change, and the breaking off of communication with other living things leads to self-destruction and death. Although isolation in man and human society can hardly be compared with other phenomena (insofar as man and human societies have particular destinies), analogous phenomena can be shown in other living things too. Whereas the word "sin" only means human misdemeanor, the concept of deadly self-isolation can lead to a fuller understanding of the "subjection of creation to futility" which Paul talks about in Rom. 8:19ff.

If in history God creates salvation for the people that lacks it, then he liberates that people from slavery, whether it is self-imposed or imposed from outside. If he creates grace for the sinner, then he frees him from his self-isolation. But because closed or isolated systems can only be opened again by means of renewed communications with others (if they are not to be destroyed), the opening to God takes place through God's suffering over their isolation. Because God himself suffers over man's closedness towards him, he keeps his communication with man alive in spite of opposition, creating the domain where isolated man can open up and transform himself. Thus man's openness to God is brought about by grace, and grace springs from the suffering of God in his faithfulness to isolated man. The opening of man's closed society for openness towards man's neighbor and towards the world can be conceived analogously. Closed systems bar themselves against suffering and self-transformation. They grow rigid and condemn themselves to death. The opening of closed systems and the breaking down of their isolation and immunization will have to come about through the acceptance of suffering. But the only living beings that are capable of doing this are the ones which display a high degree of vulnerability and capacity for change. They are not merely alive; they can make other things live as well.

Anyone who looks for statements about creation in the New Testament often finds the results disappointing. Apart from the beautiful "lilies of the field," creation does not seem to be a new theme. But we only get this impression if we are looking for statements about creation at the beginning. The New Testament testimony to creation is embedded in the kerygma about the resurrection, and in pneumatology. In these God's creative activity is understood eschatologically as καλεῖν ("to call to life"), as ἐγείρειν ("to raise"), and as ξωοποιοῦν ("to make alive"), for they are related to the creation of the endtime or "the new creation."

For Paul the creation of the endtime begins with the raising from the dead of the Christ who had been surrendered to death. He describes creation as a process which has begun with the raising of Christ, which continues to be efficacious in the revelation of the Spirit, and which will end with the quickening of mortal bodies—that is to say, the resurrection of the dead. For Paul the perfect tense of the resurrection of Christ always points to the future tense of our own resurrection.

When quickening and resurrection are described in the categories of divine creative activity, it is because this event is supposed to correspond to creation in the beginning (Rom. 4:17; 2 Cor. 4:6). Insofar as they have as their premise the surrender, the suffering, and the death of Christ in our stead and for our sakes, the historical weariness and labor of the Creator is completed in them. Because God in Christ has suffered our isolation—that is to say our death—he opens the fullness of his eternal life to us through Christ's resurrection. Eternal life is no longer a life which is merely preserved from death; it is life that has overcome death. Consequently this opening up of eternal life through Christ's death and resurrection must be understood as the completion of the process of creation. According to Paul, the crucified Christ has been raised to be the *Kyrios* and transformed into the "life-giving Spirit." Consequently the quickening powers of the Spirit proceed from him to the church. In the Pauline doctrine of the charismata, the Spirit is the power of the new creation, as well as the power of the resurrection. The powers of the new creation are to descend on "flesh" in the community of Christ and through it, in order to quicken that flesh for eternal life.

If we want to interpret salvation in this perspective, then we shall have to see it as the ultimate and, in trend, universal opening of closed and isolated men and women and this closed world for the fullness of divine life. God's openness for the world becomes manifest in Christ's suffering and death. That is why Christ's resurrection brings about, in faith, limited openness to God on the part of men and women. The "revelation of the Spirit" in the charismata of the community of Christ makes this mutual opening of God and man specific in the opening of the frontiers which men and women set up in order to cut themselves off from others: Jews and Gentiles, Greeks and barbarians, bond and free, male and female (Gal. 3:28). The liberation created through Christ's passion and glorification works in a liberating way through the charismatic quickening of the world. Openness to God, openness to our world are established wherever possible; and community in freedom is conferred.

5. THE CONSUMMATION OF CREATION

Statements about the future of creation and of history in the kingdom of glory can only be made along the guiding lines of historical experience and hope. Ideas which we form in the midst of history about its end take the form of anticipation. In the prophetic and apocalyptic visions we find two formal principles: first the negation of the negative and, secondly, the fulfillment of anticipations. In this double form the visions remain both realistic and futuristic. The negation of what is negative—"death shall be no more, nether shall there be mourning nor crying nor pain any more" (Rev. 21:4)—defines the space that is open for the positive reality that is to come. The vision of "the classless society" also follows this method of describing the future by means of a negation of the negative. But the mere negation of the negative does not necessarily lead to a definition of the positive. Consequently eschatology too cannot be developed merely as negative theology. The negation of the negative must itself be founded on an anticipation of the positive, latent though this anticipation may be. If this were not the case, the negative could not be experienced as negative and judged accordingly. For biblical eschatology, the negation of what is negative is rooted in experiences of the divine promissory history, which lets us seek for fulfillment. The pattern of promise and fulfillment and the negation-of-the-negative scheme together mold the pattern of the eschatological visions.

The completion of the creative process in the kingdom of glory is presented as God's indwelling in the new creation. "Behold, the dwelling of God is with men. He will dwell with them, and they shall be his people" (Rev. 21:3). It is no longer merely heaven that is named as the place where God dwells; heaven and earth are now newly created, so that God himself may dwell in them: *finitum capax infiniti*. In the consummation, the hidden, anticipatory indwelling of God in temple and people are to be universally fulfilled. At the creation in the beginning there was as yet no talk of such an indwelling. But creation was to be open for that, and for that it was designed. First Corinthians 15 links this fulfillment of creation and promissory history with the negation of the negative: "[He will destroy] every rule and every authority and power . . . The last enemy to be destroyed is death" (vv. 24-26). The Son is to fulfill his liberating rule by giving over the kingdom to the Father "so that God may be all in all" (v. 28 KJV). Moreover, according to Paul the Creator does not remain confronting his creation but enters into it with his glory, so permeating everything. This includes the destruction of all destructive forces and therefore the new creation of all things out of the divine glory. Man is not merely restored as the image of God; he is "glorified" (Rom. 3:23; 8:30). That is to say, he acquires a part in the life and glory of God. Together with man, the whole creation will be free from the enslavement of futility and so participate in the all-permeating glory of God. Glorified man and glorified creation are consequently finite but no longer mortal; temporal but no longer transitory. The patristic doctrine of *theosis* tried to think this through against the background of the life of the risen and transfigured Christ. If we understand finitude as a qualitative and not a quantitative term (as we must do, if infinity is to be anything different from endlessness)—if we perceive time from change and not merely from transience, so that a change from "glory into glory" becomes conceivable, then these ideas do not seem so unusual.

We have now termed creation at the beginning an open system, and have understood the history of God as being the opening up in time of closed systems. This gives rise to the further question, whether the completion of the process of creation is to be conceived of as the final end of the open and opened systems. Is the kingdom of glory the universal system which has finally come to a close? The new creation would then be the end of time and in itself timeless. The open system "man" would then only be an unfinished system, and the open systems of nature would be only systems that are not yet closed. History would be the condition of a cosmos that was not yet thoroughly determined. And in this case the consummation would be the end of human liberty and the end of God's potentialities. Time would be abolished in eternity, and possibility in reality. But completion cannot be thought of in this way theologically. If the process of creation is to be completed through God's indwelling, then the unlimited fullness of divine potentiality dwells in the new creation; and through his participation in the unbounded liberty of God, glorified man is free. The indwelling of the limitless fullness of God's potentialities therefore means the openness of all systems of life *par excellence*, and hence that they will be eternally living systems. It will therefore be permissible for us to assume that there will be time and history, future and possibility in the kingdom of glory as well, and that they will be present in unimpeded measure and in a way that is no longer ambivalent. Instead of timeless eternity we would therefore do better to talk about eternal time, and instead of the end of history to speak of the end of pre-history and the beginning of the eternal history of God, man, and nature. We must then, however, think of change without transience, time without the past, and life without death. But it is difficult to do this in the history of life and death, growth and decay, because all our concepts are stamped by these experiences.

Yet both the structure of the natural system and human experience of history point in this direction. The material structures already show a margin of undetermined behavior. When we pass from atomic structures to more complex systems, we discover greater openness to time and a growing wealth of

potentiality. With the evolution of more complex systems, the indefinabilty of
behavior grows, because the possibilities increase. The human person and man's
social systems are the most complex systems that we know. They show the
highest degree of indeterminate behavior and the widest measure of openness
to time and the future. Every realization of potentiality through open systems
creates new openness for potentiality; it is by no means the case that potentiality
is merely realized and that the future is transformed into the past. Consequently
it is impossible to imagine the kingdom of glory (which perfects the process
of creation through the indwelling of God) as a system that has finally been
brought to a close, i.e., a closed system. We must conceive of it as the openness
of all finite life systems for infinity. This of course means among other things
that the being of God must no longer be thought of as the highest reality for
all realized potentialities, but as the transcendent making-possible of all possible
realities.

6. ASSOCIATIONS OF MAN AND NATURE THAT ARE CAPABLE OF SURVIVAL

The misunderstanding of creation as a primal, finished, and in–itself–perfect
condition has meant traditionally that the designation of Gen. 1:28, "Be fruitful
and multiply, and fill the earth and subdue it," has been seen as man's true and
essential destiny. People did not read this designation in the Priestly Document
in the light of the history of tradition, seeing it in the context of earlier texts
such as the Yahwist (who interpreted this "having dominion" as "tilling and
keeping"), or in the light of later Old and New Testament passages. Instead
they related all the later texts to this single "creation text." What followed was a
one–sided stress on man's special position in the cosmos. Man is the subject who
rules; all other creatures are subject to him and are his objects. His rule over the
world was understood as the proof that he was made in the image of God.

In modern times there followed from this the division of reality into subject
and object, the *res cogitans* and the *res extensa*. Through science man was to
become, according to Descartes, "*maître et possesseur de la nature*"—i.e., was
to fulfill the destiny for which he had been created. Because he understood
redemption from the Fall as being the restoration of original creation, Francis
Bacon declared that the goal of the scientific knowledge of nature was "the
restitution and reinvesting (in great part) of man to the sovereignty and power
. . . which he had in his first state of creation." The restoration of man's universal
rule through science and technology was to make man again God's image on
earth. In Bacon and Descartes we can see the fatal reversal of biblical thinking
which, with the rise of technology, has led today to the world-wide ecological
crisis. According to the Bible, man's lordship over the world is justified because

he is made in the image of God. According to Bacon and Descartes, it is man's rule over the world that substantiates his divinity.

The triumphal progress of classical science and modern technology dates from the time when Bacon and Descartes described the relationship between man and the world as the relation between a subject and an object, and this pattern came to be generally accepted. It is a pattern of domination and exploitation. Quantum physics has not made this pattern totally outdated, but it has relativized it:

> The old division of the world into objective processes in space and time and the mind in which these processes are mirrored—in other words the Cartesian difference between *res cogitans* and *res extensa*—is no longer a suitable starting point for our understanding of modern science. Science, we find, is now focussed on the network of relationships between man and nature, on the framework which makes us as living beings dependent parts of nature, and which we as human beings have simultaneously made the object of our thoughts and actions. Science no longer confronts nature as an objective observer, but sees itself as an actor in this interplay between man and nature.[7]

It is precisely this reciprocal play which is not comprehended in the pattern of rule and subjection. So it is necessary for us to develop a new scheme. According to the model of communication and co-operation, nature is no longer the subjugated object of man, but a cohesion of open life systems with its own subjectivity. The Cartesian phase, in which nature was objectified, has been fundamentally exhausted, scientifically speaking, and offers no new insights. The recognition of complex open systems in the environment demands a model based on a theory of communication. Two subjects with, of course, different subjectivity enter into a mutual relationship with one another. Wherever we come across undetermined behavior in natural systems, we can talk about a certain subjectivity or "freedom of choice." The more science advances towards a recognition of more complex systems, the more it will cease to provide merely technically applicable results, but will also offer findings showing that, out of consideration for our partner "environment," we must not do what we would be able to do. Investigations into the ecology of survival on the sub-human level have shown that in "the struggle for existence" symbioses between competing organisms have a far greater chance of survival than conflicts of competing organisms. The subject-object relationship of man to nature, and the pattern of domination and exploitation, do not lead to any symbiosis between human and non-human systems that would be capable of survival; they lead to the silencing of nature and to the ecological death of both nature and man.

Because, now, all processes which change our natural environment have their roots in economic and social processes in human societies, and because these in their turn are based on man's interpretation of himself, it would seem a task for Christian theology to work for the revaluation of previously accepted values. Man will not again become God's image here on earth by subjecting nature to himself, demolishing the natural systems and exploiting them for his own purposes.

For Christian faith, Christ is "true man" and "the image of God" on earth. That is why "all authority in heaven and one earth" has been given to him (Matt. 28:18). But he came "not to be served"—not to rule—"but to serve." And he served in order to make us free for fellowship with God and for openness for one another. In the light of Christ's mission, Gen. 1:28 will have to be interpreted in an entirely new way: not "subdue the earth" but "free the earth through fellowship with it." For according to Romans 8, the whole enslaved creation waits for the revelation of "the glorious liberty of the children of God," so that it itself may thereby be free. Karl Marx called this "the true resurrection of nature" and hoped that it would come from "a naturalization of man" and from the "humanization of nature."[8]

The conclusion to be drawn from this for the ethics of human society is that we need a new orientation, away from the will to power towards solidarity, away from the struggle for existence towards peace in existence, and away from the pursuit of happiness towards fellowship. The most important element in the further development of civilization is social justice, not the growth of economic power. We shall not be able to achieve social justice without justice for the natural environment, and we shall not be able to achieve justice for nature without social justice. For the pattern of exploitation has dominated both human labor and the resources or "wealth" of nature. If today the "limits of growth" are becoming visible, and if we are entering a situation where there is going to be a general shortage of foodstuffs, "doing without" will be unavoidable. Solidarity and fellowship are the values which make unavoidable suffering and necessary sacrifices endurable.

Justice is the form of authentic interdependence between people, and between society and the environment. It comes into being in the symbioses between different systems of life, and is the basis for common survival. Its presupposition is the recognition of the independence and subjectivity of the other life-system.

> Independence, in the sense of liberation from oppression of others, is a requirement of justice. But independence in the sense of isolation from the human community is neither possible nor just. We—human persons—need each other within communities. We—human communities—need each other within the community of mankind. We—the creation—need God, our Creator and Recreator. Mankind faces the urgent task of devising social mechanisms and political structures that encourage genuine interdependence, in order to replace mechanisms and structures that sustain domination and subservience.[9]

This outline of an eschatological doctrine of creation with the help of a theory of open systems and their mutual communication, is designed to serve this task. For if the task is not fulfilled, man and nature have no chance of survival.

PREFACE TO *GOD IN CREATION*

Source: Moltmann 1985; ET 1985/1993: xiii–xv.

PREFACE TO THE PAPERBACK EDITION

. . . Faced as we are with the progressive industrial exploitation of nature and its irreparable destruction, what does it mean to say that we believe in God the Creator, and in this world as his creation? What we call the environmental crisis is not merely a crisis in the natural environment of human beings. It is nothing less than a crisis in human beings themselves. It is a crisis of life on this planet, a crisis so comprehensive and so irreversible that it cannot unjustly be described as apocalyptic. It is not a temporary crisis. As far as we can judge, it is the beginning of a life and death struggle for creation on this earth. . . .

. . . By the title *God in Creation* I mean God the Holy Spirit. God is "the lover of life" and his Spirit is *in* all created beings. In order to understand this, I have dropped the earlier divisions of theology, which followed the pattern of the three articles of the Apostles' Creed. Instead I have interwoven these three articles together in a trinitarian sense so that I was able to develop a pneumatological doctrine of creation. This doctrine of creation, that is to say, takes as its starting point the indwelling divine Spirit of creation. . . .

The [subtitle of chapter 1] describes this doctrine of creation as an "ecological doctrine." This is of course intended first of all to point to the ecological crisis of our time, and the ecological thinking which we have to learn. But in a deeper sense it is also a reference to the symbolism of "home" and "dwelling" which I have employed in this book. According to the Greek derivation, the word *ecology* means "the doctrine of the house" (οἶκος). What does the Christian doctrine of creation have to do with "a doctrine of the house"? If we see only a Creator and his work, there is no connection. But if we understand the Creator, his creation, and the goal of that creation in a trinitarian sense, then the Creator, through his Spirit, *dwells* in his creation as a whole, and in every individual created being, by virtue of his Spirit holding them together and keeping them in life. The inner secret of creation is this *indwelling of God*, just as the inner secret of the Sabbath of creation is *God's rest*. If we ask about creation's goal and future, we ultimately arrive at the transfiguring indwelling of the triune God in his creation, which through that indwelling becomes a new heaven and a new earth (Revelation 21), and at God's eternal Sabbath, in which the whole creation will find bliss. The divine secret of creation is the Shekinah, God's indwelling; and the purpose of the Shekinah is to make the whole creation the house of God.

If this is the theological side of the ecological doctrine of creation, the anthropological side must correspond to it. Existence can only become a home if the relationship between nature and human beings is without stresses and strains—if it can be described in terms of reconciliation, peace, and a viable symbiosis. The indwelling of human beings in the natural system of the earth corresponds, for its part, to the indwelling of the Spirit in the soul and body of the human being, which puts an end to the alienation of human beings from themselves.

GOD IN CREATION

Source: Moltmann 1985; ET 1985/1993:1–19.

SOME GUIDING IDEAS FOR AN ECOLOGICAL DOCTRINE OF CREATION

With this doctrine of creation I am taking a further step along the road on which I started out with *The Trinity and the Kingdom of God* (1980; ET 1981). In that book I developed a social doctrine of the Trinity. Here my subject is the corresponding ecological doctrine of creation.

It is easy to see the connection between the two.

As long as God was thought of as the absolute subject, the world had to be viewed as the object of his creation, preservation, and redemption. The more transcendent the conception of God became, the more immanent were the terms in which the world was interpreted. Through the monotheism of the absolute subject, God was increasingly stripped of his connection with the world, and the world was increasingly secularized. As a result, the human being—since he was God's image on earth—had to see himself as the subject of cognition and will, and was bound to confront his world as its ruler. For it was only through his rule over the earth that he could correspond to his God, the Lord of the world. God is the Creator, Lord, and owner of the world; and in the same way the human being had to endeavor to become the lord and owner of the earth. This was the idea behind the centralistic theologies, and the foundation of the hierarchical doctrines of sovereignty.

Our standpoint is a different one. We have begun to understand God, in the awareness of his Spirit, for Christ's sake, as the triune God, the God who in himself constitutes the unique and perfect fellowship of the Father and the Son and the Holy Spirit. If we cease to understand God monotheistically as the one, absolute subject, but instead see him in a Trinitarian sense as the unity of the Father, the Son, and the Spirit, we can then no longer, either, conceive his relationship to the world he has created as a one-sided relationship of domination. We are bound to understand it as an intricate relationship of community—many-layered, many-faceted, and at many levels. This is the fundamental idea behind non-hierarchical, decentralized, confederate theology. In this introduction we shall formulate a few guiding ideas which will provide the points of reference for this doctrine of creation.

1. KNOWLEDGE OF NATURE AS GOD'S CREATION IS PARTICIPATING KNOWLEDGE

If a doctrine of creation is to be ecological, it must try to get away from analytical thinking, with its distinctions between subject and object, and must strive to learn a new, communicative, and integrating way of thought. This means that it will have to revert to the pre-modern concept of reason as the organ of perception and participation (*methexis*).

Modern thinking has developed by way of an objectifying, analytical, particularizing, and reductionalistic approach. The aim is to reduce an object or fact to its smallest possible, no-longer-divisible components, and from that point to reconstruct it. This is a trend in all modern disciplines which are designed to be what are called "exact" sciences, on the model of physics. It is therefore quite true to say that we know more and more about less and less; and it is not without reason that people deplore the domination of the specialists. The concern and the methods of this kind of thinking are directed towards the domination of objects and facts. The old Roman principle for successful rule, *divide et impera*, also provides the guideline for modern methods of dominating nature.

Yet modern sciences, especially nuclear physics and biology, have now proved that these forms and methods of thinking do not do full justice to reality, and hardly bring any further advances in knowledge. On the contrary, objects can be known and understood very much better if they are seen in their relationships and co-ordinations with their particular environments and surroundings (which include the human observer)—if, that is to say, they are integrated, not isolated; perceived in their totality, not split up. This perception of things-as-a-whole is inevitably less sharply defined than the segmenting knowledge which aims to dominate; but it is richer in connections and relationships.

To be alive means existing in relationship with other people and things. Life is communication in communion. And, conversely, isolation and lack of relationship means death for all living things, and dissolution even for elementary particles. So if we want to understand what is real *as* real, and what is living *as* living, we have to know it in its own primal and individual community, in its relationships, interconnections, and surroundings.

But we shall then have to conceive of the inversion of this as well. We shall have to understand that everything real and everything living is simply a concentration and manifestation of its relationships, interconnections, and surroundings. Integrating, and integral, thinking moves purposefully in this social direction towards the goal of an inclusiveness that is many-sided, and ultimately fully comprehensive.

When this happens, of course, the concern that motivates cognition changes. We no longer desire to know in order to dominate, or analyze and reduce in order to reconstruct. Our purpose is now to perceive in order to participate, and to enter into the mutual relationships of the living thing.

Integrating and integral thinking serves to generate the community between human beings and nature which is necessary and promotes life. And here "nature" means both the natural world in which we share, and our own bodily nature. As a network and interplay of relationships is built up, a symbiotic life comes into being. This life has to be differently defined on its different levels.

On the legal and political level, we have to see it as a "covenant with nature," in which the rights of human beings and the rights of the earth are respected and balanced out. Nature must no longer be viewed as "unclaimed property."

On the medical level, this symbiotic life must be defined as "the psychosomatic totality" of the human being who stands over against himself. The body must no longer be seen as something which we "possess."

On the religious level, it has to be interpreted as "a community of creation." Creation is certainly not the world which human beings are supposed to "subdue."

Integrating and integral thinking is impelled by the will to find a way into this covenant, this totality, this community; to arrive at an awareness of these things, to deepen them after they have been ignored for so long, and to restore them when they have been destroyed.

In this sense, a theological doctrine of creation . . . cannot be one-dimensional. It must use multifarious ways of access to the community of creation, and make people aware of them. We find these approaches in both tradition and experience, in science as well as in wisdom, in intuition but also in deduction. We shall try to look critically at theological traditions in the doctrine of creation. But I should also like to take up new, post-critical scientific methods and ways of thinking. And the approaches of poetic perception must be integrated as well. . . . Theology always includes the imagination, fantasy for God and his kingdom. If we were to ban the images of the imagination from theology, we should be robbing it of its best possession. Eschatologically oriented theology is dependent on a messianic imagination of the future, and sets this imagination free.

2. CREATION FOR GLORY

It is my intention to present a deliberately and emphatically Christian doctrine of creation. In this context I understand the word "Christian" in its original sense, as "messianic"; but messianic as the word has been molded by Jesus' proclamation and his history. So a Christian doctrine of creation is a view of the world in the light of Jesus the Messiah; and it will be determined by the points of view of the messianic time which has begun with him and which he defines. It is directed towards the liberation of men and women, peace with nature, and the redemption of the community of human beings and nature from negative powers, and from the forces of death.

The messianic doctrine of creation therefore sees creation together with its future—the future for which it was made and in which it will be perfected. Ever since ancient times "the future of creation" has been termed "the kingdom of glory." This symbol of cosmic hope is supposed to indicate that "creation in the beginning" is an open creation, and that its consummation will be to become the home and dwelling place of God's glory. Human beings already experience the indwellings of God in the Spirit here in history, even if as yet only partially and provisionally. That is why they hope that in the kingdom of glory God will dwell entirely and wholly and for ever in his creation, and will allow all the beings he has created to participate in the fullness of his eternal life.

The embodiment of the messianic promises to the poor and the quintessence of the hopes of the alienated is that the world should be "home." This means being at home in existence—that the relationships between God, human beings, and nature lose their tension and are resolved into peace and repose.

If the creative God himself dwells in his creation, then he is making it his own home, "on earth as it is in heaven." All created beings then find in nearness to him the inexhaustible wellspring of their life, and for their part find home and rest in God.

Then at last the true community of created beings with one another also begins: a community which Jewish and Christian messianic traditions have called "the sympathy of all things." The bond of love, participation, communication, and the whole complex warp and weft of interrelationships determines the life of the one, single creation, united in the cosmic Spirit. A many-faceted community of creation comes into being.

3. THE SABBATH OF CREATION

According to the biblical traditions, creation is aligned towards its redemption from the very beginning; for the creation of the world points forward to the Sabbath, "the feast of creation." On the Sabbath the creation is completed. The Sabbath is the prefiguration of the world to come. So when we present creation in the light of its future—"the glory of God," "existence as home," and the general "sympathy of all things"—then we are developing *a Sabbath doctrine of creation.* What this means, factually and practically, is the aspect and prospect of creation which is perceived on the Sabbath, and only then. The Sabbath is the true hallmark of every biblical—every Jewish and also every Christian—doctrine of creation. The completion of creation through the peace of the Sabbath distinguishes the view of the world as creation from the view of the world as nature; for nature is unremittingly fruitful and, though it has seasons and rhythms, knows no Sabbath. It is the Sabbath which blesses, sanctifies, and reveals the world as God's creation.

Curiously enough, in the theological traditions of the Western churches, creation is generally presented merely as "the six days' work." The seventh day, the Sabbath, was often overlooked. Consequently God was present throughout merely as the creative God: *Deus non est otiosus.* The resting God, the celebrating God, the God who rejoices over his creation, receded into the background. And yet it is only the Sabbath which completes and crowns creation. It is only in his Sabbath rest that the creative God comes to his goal, which means coming to himself and to his glory. When people celebrate the Sabbath they perceive the world as God's creation, for in the Sabbath quiet it is God's creation that they are permitting the world to be.

Israel celebrates the Sabbath in the time and context of her own history. But the Sabbath which is repeated week by week does not merely interrupt the time for work and the time for living. It points beyond itself to the sabbatical year, in which the primordial conditions between human beings, and between human beings and nature, are supposed to be restored, according to the righteousness of the covenant of Israel's God. And the sabbatical year, in its turn, points in history beyond itself to the future of the messianic era. Every Sabbath is a sacred anticipation of the world's redemption. It was with the proclamation of the messianic Sabbath that the public ministry of Jesus of Nazareth began (Luke 4:18ff.). Through his giving of himself to death on the cross, and through his resurrection from the dead, the messianic era which he proclaimed was actually initiated, according to the Christian view. That is why Christians celebrate the first day of the week as the feast of the resurrection: it is the first day of the new creation. They are therefore perceiving creation in the light of the resurrection and discerning reality in the light of its new creation.

The light of the resurrection is a light that fills even times past and the dead with hope for their coming redemption. The light of Christ's resurrection is the light of the Christian Sabbath. But it is more than that. It shines as messianic light on the whole sighing creation, giving it, in its transience, an eternal hope that it will be created anew as the "world without end." . . .

5. CREATION IN THE SPIRIT

According to the Christian interpretation, creation is a trinitarian process: the Father creates through the Son in the Holy Spirit. The created world is therefore created "by God," formed "through God," and exists "in God." Basil wrote in this connection:

> Behold in the creation of these beings the Father as the preceding cause, the Son as the One who createth, and the Spirit as the perfecter; so that the ministering spirits have their beginning in the will of the Father, are brought into being through the efficacy of the Son, and are perfected through the aid of the Spirit.[10]

For a long time theological tradition stressed only the first aspect of this process, so as to place God the Father, as Creator and Lord, over against his creation, in a monotheistic way. Attempts have also continually been made to develop a specifically christological doctrine of creation. Here we shall proceed differently, and shall present the trinitarian understanding of creation by developing the third aspect, creation in the Spirit.

According to the biblical traditions, all divine activity is pneumatic in its efficacy. It is always the Spirit who first brings the activity of the Father and the Son to its goal. It follows that the triune God also unremittingly breathes the Spirit into his creation. Everything that is, exists and lives in the unceasing inflow of the energies and potentialities of the cosmic Spirit. This means that we have to understand every created reality in terms of energy, grasping it as the realized potentiality of the divine Spirit. Through the energies and potentialities of the Spirit, the Creator is himself present in his creation. He does not merely confront it in his transcendence; entering into it, he is also immanent in it.

The biblical foundation for this interpretation of creation in the Spirit is Psalm 104:29-30:

> When thou hidest thy face, they are dismayed;
> when thou takest away their breath, they die and return to their dust.
> When thou sendest forth thy breath, they are created;
> and thou renewest the face of the ground.

From the continual inflow of the divine Spirit (*ruach*) created things are formed (*bara'*). They exist in the Spirit, and they are "renewed" (*hadash*) through the Spirit. This presupposes that God always creates through and in the power of his Spirit, and that the presence of his Spirit therefore conditions the potentiality and realities of his creation. The further assumption is that this Spirit is poured out on everything that exists, and that the Spirit preserves it, makes it live, and renews it. And because, to the Hebrew mind, the Spirit (*ruach*) is feminine, this divine life of creation must be apprehended through feminine metaphors, not merely with masculine ones. . . .

. . . John Calvin was one of the few people to take up and maintain this conception.[11] . . . The Holy Spirit, "the giver of life" of the Nicene Creed, is for Calvin "the fountain of life" (*fons vitae*). If the Holy Spirit is "poured out" on all created beings, "the fountain of life" is present in everything that exists and is alive. Everything that is, and lives, manifests the presence of this divine wellspring.

If the Holy Spirit is "poured out" on the whole creation, then he creates the community of all created things with God and with each other, making it that fellowship of creation in which all created things communicate with one another and with God, each in its own way. The existence, the life, and the warp and weft of interrelationships subsist in the Spirit: "*In him* we live and move and have our being" (Acts 17:28). But that means that the interrelations of the world cannot be traced back to any components, or universal foundations (or whatever name we may give to "elementary particles"). According to the mechanistic theory, things are primary, and their relations to one another are determined secondarily, through "natural laws." But in reality relationships are just as primal as the things themselves. "Thing" and "relation" are complementary modes of appearance, in the same way as particle and wave in the nuclear sector. For nothing in the world exists, lives, and moves *of itself*. Everything exists, lives, and moves *in others*, in one another with one another, for one another, in the cosmic interrelations of the divine Spirit. So it is only the community of creation in the Spirit that can be called "fundamental." For only the Spirit of God exists *ex se*; and it is therefore the Spirit who has to be seen as the sustaining foundation of everything else, which does not exist *ex se* but *ab alio et in aliis*. The patterns and the symmetries, the movements and the rhythms, the fields and the material conglomerations of cosmic energy all come into being out of the community, and in the community, of the divine Spirit. The "essential being" of creation in the Spirit is therefore the co-activity; and the interrelations manifest the presence of the Spirit because they show the "overall consistency." "In the beginning was relation," writes Martin Buber. . . .

. . . Creation in the Spirit is the theological concept which corresponds best to the ecological doctrine of creation which we are looking for and need today. With this concept we are cutting loose the theological doctrine of creation from the age of subjectivity and the mechanistic domination of the world, and are leading it in the direction in which we have to look for the future of an ecological world-community. The progresssive destruction of nature by the industrial nations, and the progressive threat to humanity through the pile-up of nuclear armaments, have brought the age of subjectivity and the mechanistic domination of the world up against their definitive limits. Faced with these limits, we have only one realistic alternative to universal annihilation; the non-violent, peaceful, ecological, worldwide community in solidarity. . . .

6. GOD'S IMMANENCE IN THE WORLD

An ecological doctrine of creation implies a new kind of thinking about God. The center of this thinking is no longer the distinction between God and the world. The center is the recognition of the presence of God *in* the world and the presence of the world *in* God. . . .

. . . The trinitarian doctrine of creation does not start from an antithesis between God and the world, so that it can then go on to define God and the world over against one another ("God is not-worldly and the world is not-divine"). It proceeds differently, starting from an immanent *tension* in God himself: God creates the world, and at the same time enters into it. He calls it into existence and at the same time manifests himself through its being. It lives from his creative power, and yet he lives in it. . . . So in God's creation of the world we can perceive a self-differentiation and a self-identification on God's part.

There are two great concepts which can be used to help us to comprehend this self-differentiation and tension of God's in his creation.

1. The rabbinic and kabbalistic *doctrine of the Shekinah.* "The Shekinah, the descent of God to human beings and his dwelling among them, is conceived of as a division which takes place in God himself. God cuts himself off from himself. He gives himself away to his people. He suffers with their suffering, he goes with them through the misery of the foreign land. . . ." This is the way Franz Rosenzweig describes God's Shekinah among the people of his choice.[12] But the same thing is true in its own degree of the indwelling of God in the creation of his love: he gives himself away to the beings he has created, he suffers with their sufferings, he goes with them through the misery of the foreign land. The God who in the Spirit dwells in his creation is present to every one of his creatures and remains bound to each of them, in joy and sorrow.

2. The Christian *doctrine of the Trinity.* In the free, overflowing rapture of his love the eternal God goes out of himself and makes a creation, a reality, which is there as he is there, and is yet different from himself. Through the Son, God creates, reconciles, and redeems his creation. In the power of the

Spirit, God is himself present in his creation—present in his reconciliation and his redemption of that creation. The overflowing love from which everything comes that is from God, is also the implicit ground for God's readiness to endure the contradictions of the beings he has created. And here too is already the source of his will towards reconciliation and the redemption of the world through the suffering patience of his hope.

The Son, the eternal counterpart within God himself, becomes the Wisdom, the pattern through which creation is made. The Son in whom the world is created becomes flesh, and himself enters into the world in order to redeem it. He suffers the self-destruction of creation in order through his sufferings to heal it. What is not assumed by God in this way in his creation cannot, either, be healed.

God the Spirit is also the Spirit of the universe, its total cohesion, its structure, its information, its energy. The Spirit of the universe is the Spirit who proceeds from the Father and shines forth in the Son. The evolutions and catastrophes of the universe are also the movements and experiences of the Spirit of creation. That is why Paul tells us that the divine Spirit "sighs" in all created things under the power of futility. That is why the divine Spirit transcends himself in all created beings. This is manifested in the self-organization and the self-transcendence of all living things.

7. THE PRINCIPLE OF MUTUAL INTERPENETRATION

The archetype of this dialectical movement is to be found in the Godhead itself. The doctrine of the Trinity is the formulation for the distinctions and the unity in God. Through the concept of *perichoresis*, the social doctrine of the Trinity formulates the mutual indwellings of the Father, the Son, and the Holy Spirit, and the eternal community that is manifested through these indwellings. In God is the eternal community of the different persons, by virtue of their reciprocal indwelling and their mutual interpenetration, as the Johannine Jesus tells us: "I am *in* the Father and the Father is *in* me" (14:11); "I and the Father are one" (10:30). The trinitarian *perichoresis* manifests that highest intensity of living which we call divine life and eternal love; and, conversely, God's infinite intensity of life is manifested in the eternal *perichoresis* of the divine persons. We must not view the trinitarian *perichoresis* as a rigid pattern. We should see it as at once the most intense excitement and the absolute rest of the love which is the wellspring of everything that lives, the keynote of all resonances, and the source of the rhythmically dancing and vibrating worlds.

In God there is no one-sided relationship of superiority and subordination, command and obedience, master and servant, as Karl Barth maintained in his theological doctrine of sovereignty, making this the starting point for his account of all analogously antithetical relationships: God and the world; heaven and earth; soul and body; and, not least, man and woman too.[13] In the triune God is the mutuality and the reciprocity of love.

Our starting point here is that all relationships which are analogous to God reflect the primal, reciprocal indwelling and mutual interpenetration of the trinitarian *perichoresis*: God *in* the world and the world *in* God; heaven and earth *in* the kingdom of God, pervaded by his glory; soul and body united *in* the life-giving Spirit to a human whole; woman and man *in* the kingdom of unconditional and unconditioned love, freed to be true and complete human beings. There is no such thing as solitary life. Contrary to [Gottfried] Leibniz's view, every monad has many windows. In actual fact it consists only of windows. All living things—each in its own specific way—live in one another and with one another, from one another and for one another.

> Everything that lives
> Lives not alone, nor for itself.[14]

It is this trinitarian concept of life as interpenetration or *perichoresis* which will therefore determine this ecological doctrine of creation.

Notes

1. Mircea Eliade, *The Myth of the Eternal Return: Or, Cosmos and History*, trans. Willard R. Trask (London: Routledge, 1955).

2. Rudolf Bultmann, *Glauben und Verstehen* III (Tübingen: J. C. B. Mohr, 1960), 29.

3. Ibid., 26.

4. Gerhard von Rad, *Old Testament Theology*, vol. 1, trans. D. M. G. Stalker (London: SCM Press, 1975).

5. Ludwig Köhler, *Old Testament Theology,* 3d ed., trans. A. S. Todd (London: Lutterworth/ Philadelphia: Westminster, 1957/1958), 88.

6. Ibid., 143.

7. Werner Heisenberg, *The Physicist's Conception of Nature*, trans. Arnold J. Pomerans (New York: Harcourt, Brace and Co., 1958), 29.

8. Karl Marx, *Frühschriften*, ed. Siegfried Landshut (Stuttgart: Kroner, 1953), 237; cf. idem, *Early Writings*, trans. T. B. Bottomore (London: Watts, 1963), 155.

9. The Bucharest consultation of the World Council of Churches on "Science and Technology for Human Development," held in June 1974; see *Anticipation* 18 (August 1974), Department on Church and Society of the WCC, Geneva.

10. Basil, *On the Holy Spirit*, ch. 38 (PG 32, 136b).

11. John Calvin, *Institutes of the Christian Religion*, I, 13, 14.

12. Franz Rosenzweig, *Der Stern der Erlösung*, 3d ed. (Heidelberg: L. Schneider, 1954 [1917]), Pt. III, Book 3, 192.

13. Karl Barth, *Christian Dogmatics* IV/1, 200f.

14. William Blake, "The Book of Thel II," in *Poetry and Prose of William Blake*, The Nonesuch Library, ed. Geoffrey Keynes (London: Nonesuch, 1939), 164.

5

The Way of Jesus Christ

Moltmann devoted the third of his "systematic contributions to theology" to the theme of Christology. He chose as its title The Way of Jesus Christ *because, as he writes, he was trying to grasp Christ dynamically, "in the forward movement of God's history with the world." The symbol of the way "can comprehend Christ's way from his birth in the Spirit and his baptism in the Spirit to his self-surrender on Golgotha. It also makes it possible to understand the path of Christ as the way leading from his resurrection to his parousia." But the way of Jesus Christ is "not merely a christological category. It is an ethical category too, and anyone who really believes in Jesus as the Christ of God will follow him along the way he himself took."[1]*

These words from the book's preface are taken up once more in its final section, "Expectant Creativity": "The expectation of the future of Christ sets the present in the light of the One who will come, and makes bodily life in the power of the resurrection experienceable . . . It becomes a life which is committed to working for the kingdom of God through its commitment to justice and peace in the world."[2]

The Messianic Mission of Christ

Source: Moltmann 1989; ET 1990/1993:136–50.

§8 Jesus—The Messianic Person in His Becoming

Up to now we have looked mainly at Jesus' ministry. We shall now inquire about his person, and shall make a first attempt to find our way from the conceptual angle into the stories about Jesus told by the Synoptic Gospels, so as to understand Jesus himself. Here we shall discover that Jesus' personhood does not exist in isolation, *per se*; nor is it determined and fixed from eternity. It acquires its form in living relationships and reciprocities, and becomes an open identity in the course of Jesus' history. In the traditional Christologies, the *metaphysical concepts of nature* or essence are used to elucidate the constitution of the divine-human person of Christ. But these are not helpful, because they define divinity and humanity by way of mutual negations of the characteristics of the other: finite—infinite, mortal—immortal, passible—impassible, and so forth. The definitions are not drawn from the positive interplay of these attributes. The *concepts of efficacy*, which are summed up in the Protestant doctrine of "Christ's threefold office" as prophet, priest, and king, are also one-sided, because they do not take account of the living relationships and interactions in which Christ acts as prophet, as priest, or as king. In this dogmatic doctrine, the picture of the solitary man and his unique work cuts Jesus off from reality and isolates him from the community of men and women. The more modern (and especially feminist) concepts about Jesus' being as *being-in-relationship* take us a step further.[3] But they do not yet enter into Jesus' being as a *being-in-history*, and the "learning process" of his life and ministry, his experience, and his suffering.

Here we shall try to take up the different christological concepts of person and integrate them, so as to arrive at a fuller, richer portrait of the person of Jesus Christ. We shall look at the divine person, the person in his messianic ministry, the public person commissioned by God, the person in the warp and weft of his relationships, and the person in the emergence and growth of his own life history.

1. The Messianic Person of Jesus

Whether Jesus himself believed that he was Israel's promised messiah and the expected Son of man sent by God is a historical question. The dogmatic question is: Was he, and is he, "the coming one" or not? We are starting here from the historical assumption that Jesus of Nazareth did in fact talk and act messianically; that he put himself in an identifying relationship to the messiah and the Son of man, who were figures of hope; and that the account of Jesus' messianic history is therefore not a projection by the Christian community after Easter on to a human life which in itself provided no grounds for this. Historically speaking, it is inadmissible to assume that on the basis of its experience with the risen and present Christ the Christian community projected anything into the history of Jesus which was inconsistent with the remembrance of him as he was during his lifetime. Historically it is more plausible to assume that the experience of the present Christ and the remembrance of the Christ of the past corresponded, and complemented one another; for the fundamental assertions "Jesus is the Christ" and "Christ is Jesus" identify remembrance and experience, experience and remembrance. . . .

. . . Did Jesus see himself as the messiah, or did the Christian community only declare him messiah after Easter? The reason for the community's acknowledgment that Jesus was the Christ is undoubtedly the Easter event. By this we mean the appearances of Christ in the glory of God after his death, first of all to the women, and then also to the disciples, with the theological conclusion drawn by the people involved that God had raised him from the dead. But this confession of Christ on the basis of the Easter experiences is an acknowledgment of God first of all, and only after that an acknowledgment of Christ (Rom. 10:9). Because of their belief that God has raised him from the dead, believers confess Christ as Lord; and in confessing Christ as Lord, they believe that God has raised him from the dead. This confession says *what* Jesus is, on the basis of his resurrection; but it does not say *who* he is. Only the living remembrance of his life history and his message can say that. That is why the earthly Jesus had also to be brought into "living memory" after Easter. *Easter* determines the *form* of belief in Jesus Christ, but not its content. The *content* is determined by *the history of Jesus' life*.

Does Easter permit anything to be said about Jesus, which does not find support in the remembrance of him and the history of his life as it has been passed down? Can a life that was lived "non-messianically" be declared a messianic one, in a process of hindsight, because of the Easter event? This is historically extremely improbable, and theologically wholly inadmissible. On the other hand, can anything new be known about Jesus after Easter, if everything is really already present and existent in him and with him? Does, in fact, the Easter event say nothing more than that "the cause of Jesus goes on," as Willi Marxsen puts it? This too is historically improbable and theologically inadmissible.

In the patterns it traces, New Testament theology moves between these two extremes, while the extremes themselves become less and less convincing. What is manifested in the Easter confession of faith is in a certain way already implied and prepared for by Jesus himself; he placed himself "indirectly" or "cryptically" in an identifying relationship to the Son of man-Judge of the world. He acted messianically, while himself keeping the messianic secret. Consequently the earthly life and ministry of Jesus contains within itself what [Hans] Conzelmann calls "an implicit Christology," which after Easter led to the explicit Christologies of the Christian congregations. This view of the matter corresponds precisely to the stories about Jesus told in the Gospels, for these present Jesus' life history as a history open to the future, because they look back from its end in his death and resurrection, and make him present in that light. They cannot present him as the completed and finished messiah, or as the Son of man in final form, because his suffering and resurrection are part of the history of his life. They therefore have to conceive of him as the messiah-Son of man "in his becoming." "He is on the way to the one he will be," as Otto Weber says.

The implicit Christology of the Gospels is therefore theologically required. Is it also historically probable? If we judge the matter historically, unprejudiced by dogmatic or humanist postulates, we have to assume that there is a correspondence between the community's remembrance of Jesus, and their Easter experience of the One risen. Inconsistencies would have destroyed either the remembrance of Jesus or the experience of the risen One, and would in either case have broken down the identity involved in the acknowledgment "Jesus—the Christ."

Did Jesus see himself merely as the transcendent Son of man-Judge of the world, or did he also believe himself to be Israel's theo-political messiah? This is one of the "tender spots" in New Testament theology, and not just today; it has been so ever since the early church. Here judgments were always unconsciously apologetic, and are so still. If Jesus indirectly identified himself only with the Son of man of the nations, but not with Israel's messiah, then Pontius Pilate made a mistake, and Jesus was the victim of a regrettable but isolated judicial error. The title written on the cross is wrong. The concern that is behind this way of thinking is obvious: in the Roman empire, so as not to be suspected of being adherents of someone justly executed as a terrorist and a subverter of the *pax Romana* (which would have made them suspect themselves, and open to persecution), Christians from early on allowed Pilate to wash his hands in innocence. By suppressing the political side of Jesus' messiahship, they were able to lay the burden of Jesus' erroneous execution on the Jews instead.

The other concern behind the attempt to strip Jesus of his messiahship is to hand Jesus himself back to Judaism so that on the basis of the kerygma of the death and resurrection of the Son of God, Christianity may be established as a world religion, detached from Judaism altogether.

The intentions behind both these trends are so obvious that they positively provoke the historical conclusion that Jesus must have come forward as Israel's messiah, that the title on the cross is correct, and that the Christian church is the community of the disciples of Israel's crucified messiah. But we must also see that, as his message shows, Jesus evidently had his own interpretation of his messiahship, which was willfully individual compared with the Jewish history of hope; for his life, and the history of his impact, cannot be fitted into the long history of suffering of Israel's disappointed messianic claimants, from Bar Kochba to Shabbetai Zevi.

2. Jesus—the Child of God

In Israel's messianic promises the one who is anointed with God's Spirit is also called "Son of God" (Ps. 2:7). Moreover Israel sees itself collectively as God's first-born son (πρωτότοκος). The special "son of God" is the priestly king on Zion where, in the temple, God will allow his name to dwell. If Jesus of Nazareth is declared Son of God on the basis of his experience of the Spirit at his baptism, this initially means the messianic sonship. It does not yet signify a metaphysical identity of essence with God. Jesus is chosen by God, or "adopted," to take the word used in modern so-called "adoptionist" Christology. But for Matthew and Luke this does not mean that Jesus was not from the very beginning born of the Spirit and filled with the Spirit. The fact that the Spirit "descends" on him in baptism does not for them mean that the Spirit did not already act in him previously. Insofar there is no alternative here between incarnation and adoptionist Christology, as was claimed in the nineteenth century. But at the same time, Jesus' relationship to God as Son, like the sonship and daughterhood of later believers, is defined entirely and wholly pneumatologically (cf. Rom. 8:14, 16). Yahweh's *ruach*/God's Spirit creates the reciprocal relationship in which Jesus calls God "Abba" and understands himself as "child" of this Father.

The special characteristic of Jesus' relationship to God is made clear in the "Abba" prayer.[4] In order to correct later misrepresentations, it is important to come back again and again to the intimacy of this prayer of Jesus'. In Aramaic, "Abba" is baby language. It is the word children use for their original person of reference. Whether it be mother or father, the important point is the sheltering, intimate closeness on which a child's basic trust depends. So when Jesus calls

God "Abba," he is not emphasizing the masculinity of a Father God, or the sovereignty of a Lord God. The stress lies on the unheard-of closeness in which he experiences the divine mystery. God is as close to him in space—as much "at hand"—as the kingdom of God is now, through him, close, or "at hand," in time. The kingdom is so close that God can be called "Abba"; and when God can be called "Abba," then his kingdom has already come. Jesus demonstrates this nearness of God by "having mercy" and "compassion" on the poor and suffering; and by doing so he substantiates God's "feminine" attributes (Isa. 49:15; 66:13).

In his relationship to this Abba God, Jesus experiences himself as God's "child." Again, stress is not on the masculinity of God's Son, but on his "childlike" relationship. The reciprocal intimacy of the Abba and the child is lost the moment that this relationship is depicted as the relationship of God the Father to the Son of God.

The intimacy of this relationship also makes it impossible to see the persons as primary and the relationship as secondary. It is not a matter of "God there" and "Jesus here" first of all, and then the relationship between the two; it is much more that "Abba" and "the child" Jesus discover themselves mutually through one another. In his relationship to Jesus, God becomes "Abba"; and in his relationship to his Abba God Jesus becomes "the child." This exclusive relationship of mutuality is brought out in the revelatory saying in Matt. 11:27. The Gospel of John uses the *perichoresis* idea: "I am in the Father and the Father in me" (14:10, 11). The mutual relationship is a mutual indwelling, and is therefore constitutive for both. Because it stamps the personhood and name of both, it has to be viewed as equally primal. God's being as Abba and Jesus' being as child are in their mutual relationship roles, as it were, into which both grow together in their history from Jesus' baptism until his death on the cross. If this mutual relationship is constitutive for both persons and precedes the history they share, then it is not wrong to consider it to be—in the language of a later dogmatics—*pre-existent.*

The relationship to God described by the name Abba evidently influenced Jesus' understanding of himself quite essentially, for the results of this relationship to God are clearly evident in the scandalous behavior passed down to us by tradition. He leaves "his own people," his mother and his family, and goes to the poor among the people. Mark 3:31–35 par. reports his brusque rebuff to his mother Mary and his brothers:

> And a crowd was sitting about him; and they said to him, "Your mother and your brothers are outside, asking for you." And he

replied, "Who are my mother and my brothers?" And looking around on those who sat about him, he said, "Here are my mother and my brothers! Whoever does the will of God is my brother, and sister, and mother."

His family's opinion about him is like the judgment of the Pharisees: "He is beside himself" (Mark 3:21). This is not merely a dismissal of his mother and his brothers. It is a formal secession from his family. As far as his mother was concerned, this was, and is, unheard of, for it is a Jewish mother that makes a person a Jew. Schalom Ben-Chorin quite rightly sees his as a deliberate breach of the fifth commandment.[5] . . .

. . . What does Jesus put in place of the family bond and the ties with God's chosen covenant with the generations? He recognizes a new community among the people who do the will "of my Father in heaven" (Matt. 12:50). The messianic community which is drawn into Jesus' Abba relationship is made up—in the transferred sense—not merely of "brothers and sisters" but of "mothers" as well. The people who follow him, both women and men, will again find in the messianic community everything they have left behind them in their natural families—brothers, sisters, mothers, children. But there are no longer any fathers! This is often screened out because it is so strange (Mark 10:29-30). But it means nothing less than that "There must no longer be any patriarchal rule in the new family—only motherliness, brotherliness, and the relationship of the child to God the Father." Why no fathers? "Call no man your father on earth, for you have one Father, who is in heaven" (Matt. 23:9). The Abba nearness of God apparently fills and permeates this new messianic community of Jesus to such an extent that the function and authority of earthly fathers disappear. In this respect the messianic community, which Jesus gathers round himself really is at variance with the patriarchal society of that time. But it is not at variance with the mothers, fathers, sisters, and brothers in person. Whoever does the will of the Father in heaven is a member of this new messianic community. That is why later on we find Jesus' mother and his brothers in the community of Christians—not as his mother, and not as his brothers, but as believers (Acts 1:14).

The divine "Abba" secret breaks through Jesus' ties with his origins, aligning him totally towards the future of the messianic kingdom. Under the guidance of this Abba, Jesus enters into the social and religious no-man's-land of a still unknown future: the kingdom of God.

In Rom. 8:15 and Gal. 4:6 Paul cites Jesus' Aramaic address to God in prayer, "Abba, dear Father," as the prayerful cry of the Christian congregation.

It was probably the address used in prayer by the charismatics. Anyone who believes in Jesus the messiah is accepted into this intimate relationship with God: like Jesus and together with him, the believer talks to Abba, the beloved Father. The consequences are analogous. In community with "the first born" among "many brothers and sisters," believers see themselves as "God's children." Like Jesus and in his discipleship, they break with the archaic powers binding them to their origins in family, class, and culture, and now live in the liberty of the Spirit, and out of the future of the messianic kingdom. That is why among the messianic people of God the cry "Abba" becomes the supreme expression of liberty.

The later theological formula about "the father of our Lord Jesus Christ" exactly preserves Jesus' way of speaking about "my Father"; and that way of speaking, in its turn, preserves the "Abba secret," which is the liberating center of Jesus' messianic message. The praxis which this formula makes possible is not the formal address to God the Father, but the confident familiarity and intimacy of the Abba prayer. . . .

3. JESUS—A PERSON IN SOCIAL RELATIONSHIPS

As we have seen, Jesus lived in mutual relationships with the poor and the sick, sinners, and the men and women who had been thrust out of society. It was in these relationships that he spread his gospel. It was in his reciprocal relationships with the faith of the people concerned that the miracles of the messianic era came about. It was in his reciprocal relationships with the men and women disciples who followed him that Jesus discovered his messianic secret. We have to look more closely at his life in the context of these social relationships, for we can only understand the life-histories of men and women in the light of their relations with other people, and the communities to which they belong.

(a) Jesus and his fellowship with women and men

We have already described how a community of people who followed Jesus gathered together, so we shall here look only at the reciprocal relationship between Jesus and the women in this community, and especially the group of women who are known to us. They were the last witnesses of his death and the first witnesses of his resurrection. But these women were close to him not only at the end, but during his lifetime and ministry as well.[6] The woman with the issue of blood (Mark 5:24ff.) exacts from Jesus the healing she needs without his will. The Canaanite woman (Matt. 15:21ff.) convinces Jesus of the generous magnanimity of his God, which does not stop short at the borders of Israel. The poor prostitute (Luke 7:36ff.) is not afraid to force her way into the Pharisee's house, and anoints Jesus' feet. Martha, Lazarus's sister, induces Jesus to raise her dead brother, and confesses him as the Christ of God (John 11:19ff.). Finally, but not least, we must remember the great unknown woman who in Bethany anoints Jesus' head as only kings were else anointed (Mark 14:3ff.). For the Synoptic Gospels, what these women do for Jesus is apparently just as important as what Jesus does for them. At his crucifixion the group of women stand there and see him die, "perceive" his death (θεωρεῖν)—that is, they share in his dying. They do not run away like the men disciples. It is only when they are faced with the empty tomb that "they are afraid." They proclaim the Easter message to the disciples. These women are close to the secret of Jesus' death and resurrection. Without them, the stories wish to say, there would be no authentic witnesses of Jesus' death and resurrection. In Jesus' voluntary "service" (Mark 10:45), which is an alternative to political domination and subjection, the women are again closest to him, for this διακονεῖν is otherwise used only of them (Mark 15:41). In the fellowship of mutual service without domination and without servility, they live out the liberty which Jesus brought into the world.

The closeness of the women to the service, death, and resurrection of Jesus is important not only for the women but for Jesus himself too. Here the fact that Jesus was a man is irrelevant. The community of Jesus and the women manifests the truly human existence which the new creation of all things and all conditions sets free.

(b) Jesus and Israel

Jesus' life and the way he acted was related to community, and it was therefore always a receiving and an acting on the behalf of other people, and in their stead. According to the Gospels, it was just as much related to Israel as was the life and ministry of John the Baptist. For the early Jewish–Christian community, the unity between Jesus and Israel was especially important. Mark 3:14 tells us that "he appointed twelve, to be with him, and to be sent out to preach . . ." According to this passage, Jesus called *twelve* to be special disciples out of the wider circle of those who followed him, passing on to them his own messianic mission (Matt. 10:5ff.). The number twelve represents the twelve tribes of the people of Israel, for the messianic hope was aligned towards the restoration of this people in the era of salvation. According to Ezekiel, this was also to be linked with the re-occupation of the land of Israel. Jesus' choice of twelve disciples is a messianic act: with them the endtime gathering of Israel, as the renewed people of God, is to begin.[7] Consequently, the twelve are also sent to "the whole of Israel," but not to the Gentiles (Matt. 10:5). If the kingdom of God "is near," the gathering of God's people for this kingdom must begin. Then

Israel will become the messianic light of the Gentile nations, and the nations will come to Zion to receive God's righteousness and justice (Isa. 2:1–3). In this order of things, salvation comes "first to the Jews and then to the Gentiles."

Although Jesus turns first of all to Israel, this is not meant exclusively, for in his concern for Israel God is concerned about the Gentile nations and the earth. The appointment of the twelve disciples for Israel's revival is not the same thing as the call to follow Jesus, or identical with the community of women and men who followed him. It has a symbolic meaning for Israel alone. In choosing the twelve, Jesus was not founding any church. He was thinking solely of Israel. Only one person was evidently "co-opted" to this group later on: Matthias took the place of Judas. After that the group did not perpetuate itself. It probably broke up when Christianity spread beyond the bounds of what was open to it among the Jews. For that reason, to trace the church back historically and dogmatically to the calling of the twelve, and the special call to Peter, is untenable, and also pernicious, because it allows the church to push Israel out of salvation history. The church "of Jews and Gentiles" only came into being after the resurrection, and through the experience of the Spirit, and with the rejection of the gospel by "all Israel."

At the same time this early Jewish–Christian hope for the revival of the nation of the twelve tribes binds Jesus into a unity with his people, which Gentile Christians must not destroy. The Synoptics tell the life-history of Jesus in the pattern of the collective remembrance of the history of Israel. The future hope of the people is summed up in their expectation of the messiah. In the gospel to the Gentile nations, the presence of Jesus Christ makes Israel present also, just as, conversely, Gentile Christians through their faith participate in the remembrance, the hope, and also the sufferings of Israel, the people of God.

(c) Jesus and the people

According to the Gospel of Mark, there was originally a particularly close relationship between Jesus and the people (ὄχλος). Mark 3:34 tells us that the people were his true "family," although Matt. 12:46 replaces the people by "the disciples." Wherever Jesus goes in Galilee, the poor who have been reduced to misery gather round him. He teaches them. They bring him their sick. He heals them. They move about with him. The distress of the people awakens in him the divine compassion (Mark 6:34). His call to discipleship is directed to "the multitude with his disciples" (Mark 8:34). The "multitude" are the poor, the homeless, the "non-persons." They have no identity, no voice, no power, and no representative. "The multitude," "the people," is the vocabulary of domination: the plebs, the riff-raff—this is the way the ruling classes define people in the mass, shutting them out into a social no-man's-land. "The people" are also defined and shut out by cultural domination. They are the crowd without "shepherds," without any religious or recognizable ethnic identity. Whereas the word λαός is used for the people of God and ἔθνη is used for the nation, these downtrodden masses are ὄχλος.

In Galilee "the multitude" in this sense were *de facto* the poor Jewish country people. They were not so designated because they were Jewish, but because they were poor. So Jesus' solidarity with these people has a certain universalism, which takes in all the poor who have been reduced to misery. Jesus takes as his family "the damned of this earth," to use [Frantz] Fanon's expression, and discovers among them the dawning future of the kingdom and God's new creation. His "compassion" is not charitable condescension. It is the form which the divine justice takes in an unjust world. These "last" will be "first." Jesus does not merely *go to* the people in the name of God. He is actually their representative, just as the people represent him. He is one of theirs, and they are the least of his brothers and sisters (Matt. 25:40).

4. THE THREE-DIMENSIONAL PERSON OF JESUS CHRIST

Let us sum up what we have discovered.

(a) To confess Jesus as the Christ of God means perceiving him in his *eschatological person.* In him are present Israel's messiah, the Son of man of the nations, and the coming Wisdom of creation itself. He is the kingdom of God in person, and the beginning of the new creation of all things. In this way he is the bearer of hope for the world. In him believers recognize *the messianic human being.*

(b) To confess Jesus as the Christ of God also means perceiving him in his *theological person.* He is the child of God, the God whom he calls Abba, dear Father. As the child of God, he lives wholly in God, and God wholly in him. He opens this unique relationship with God to all who believe him and who, as children of God, like him cry "Abba." They participate in Jesus' joy. In him believers recognize *the childlike human being.*

(c) To confess Jesus as the Christ of God further means perceiving him in his *social person.* He is the brother of the poor, the comrade of the people, the friend of the forsaken, the sympathizer with the sick. He heals through solidarity, and communicates his liberty and his healing power through his fellowship. In him men and women recognize *the brotherly and sisterly human being.*

In each of these three dimensions Jesus as the Christ of God is a public person, not a private one. He is a person publicly commissioned by God, and he personifies the public concerns of the people.

Merely to take account of any single one of these dimensions in Jesus' person as the Christ leads to a one-sidedness that has fatal consequences. Traditional Christology stressed only the *theological* person of the God-man Jesus Christ. Modern eschatological theology stressed the *eschatological* person of Jesus Christ. The most recent contextual Christologies have disclosed the *social* person of Jesus Christ. These last two developments have again begun to take seriously the messianic and social mission of Christ, over against the Christology of the Nicene and Apostles' creeds; for in these creeds there is either nothing at all, or really no more than a comma, between "and was made man, he suffered" or "born" and "suffered . . ." We cannot close this chapter on the messianic mission of Jesus Christ without offering a suggestion for an addition to these two ancient creeds of the church. The intention is not to alter the words of tradition, but one must know what has to be added in thought. After "born of the Virgin Mary" or "and was made man," we should add something along the following lines:

> Baptized by John the Baptist,
> filled with the Holy Spirit:
> to preach the kingdom of God to the poor,
> to heal the sick,
> to receive those who have been cast out,
> to revive Israel for the salvation of the nations, and
> to have mercy upon all people.

The Eschatological Resurrection of Christ

Source: Moltmann 1989; ET 1990/1993:213–27.

"If Christ has not been raised, then our preaching is in vain and your faith is in vain," declared Paul (1 Cor. 15:14). For him and for earliest Christianity as we know it, God's raising of Christ was the foundation for faith in Christ, and thus the foundation of the church of Christ as well. And it is in fact true that the Christian faith stands or falls with Christ's resurrection. At this point faith in God and the acknowledgment of Christ coincide. Faith in the God "who raised Christ from the dead" and the confession that "Jesus Christ is the Lord" are mutually interpretative. . . .

. . . The event which is called "raising" or "resurrection" is an event that happened to the Christ who died on the cross on Golgotha. Where he himself is concerned, the cross and the resurrection are mutually related, and they have to be interpreted in such a way that the one event appears in the light of the other. The cross of Christ is the cross of the Lord who was raised by God and exalted to God. It is only in this correlation that the cross acquires its special saving meaning. The raising by God was experienced by the Christ who "was crucified, dead, and buried." It is only in this interrelation that the raising acquires its special saving meaning.

Christ's death and his resurrection are the two sides of the one single happening which is often termed "the Christ event." But we must notice here how questionable that innocuous "and" is—the "and" which adds together the two happenings which Christ experienced at the end. For these are not two happenings belonging to the same category, which can be listed one after another. On the contrary, here we have an antithesis which could not possibly be more radical. Christ's death on the cross is a historical fact—Christ's resurrection is an apocalyptic happening. Christ's death was brought about by human beings—his raising from the dead is an act on God's part. The cross of Christ stands in the time of this present world of violence and sin—the risen Christ lives in the time of the coming world of the new creation in justice and righteousness. If we look at the christological statements in the creed—"suffered, crucified, dead" and "on the third day he rose again from the dead"—what belongs between them is not an "and" at all. It is a full stop and a pause. For what now begins is something which is qualitatively different: the eschatological statements about Christ.

Anyone who reduces all this to the same level, simply listing the facts of salvation one after another, destroys either the unique character of Christ's death on the cross or the unique character of his resurrection. Anyone who describes Christ's resurrection as "historical," in just the same way as his death on the cross, is overlooking the new creation in which the resurrection begins, and is falling short of the eschatological hope. The cross and the resurrection stand in the same relation to one another as death and eternal life. Since death makes every life historical, death has to be seen as the power of history. Since resurrection brings the dead into eternal life and means the annihilation of death, it breaks the power of history and is itself the end of history. If we keep the two together, than the cross of Christ comes to stand at the apocalyptic end of world history, and the raising of the dead at the beginning of the new creation of the world. That is why we are talking about "the eschatological resurrection of Christ." History and eschatology cannot be added together, for if they are, either history is dissolved into eternity or eschatology is overtaken by history. The two can only be confronted with one another. It is this confrontation which we are talking about when we speak of "the resurrection of the crucified Christ." Paul expressed the incommensurability of Christ's death on the cross and his resurrection by using the phrase "how much more" (Rom. 8:34). In this way he was indicating the eschatological surplus of promise in Christ's resurrection. It is this which echoes through the overflowing Easter jubilation of early Christian and Orthodox worship. . . .

§1 THE GENESIS AND UNIQUE CHARACTER OF THE CHRISTIAN FAITH IN THE RESURRECTION

Jesus was crucified publicly and died publicly. But it was only the women at his tomb in Jerusalem, and the disciples who had fled into Galilee who learnt of his "resurrection." These disciples thereupon returned to Jerusalem, where they openly proclaimed the crucified Jesus as the Lord whom God had raised from the dead.

These are the relatively well-established historical findings.[8] And they are astonishing enough. At the same time, all that is historically provable in these findings is the assertion of the women that at his empty tomb they had heard an angelic message about his resurrection, and the assurance of the disciples that they had seen appearances of Christ in Galilee. After Jesus' death, there were evidently a great many manifestations to a whole number of his disciples, women and men both, manifestations in which Christ allowed himself to be seen as the One eternally alive in God. In the earliest testimony to the resurrection which we possess—the First Epistle to the Corinthians, written in 55 or 56 ce—Paul refers to testimonies that Christ had appeared to Cephas, to the twelve, and then to 5,000 brethren at once. At the end he adds himself, although he had never been one of Jesus' disciples but had actually persecuted the Christians. Paul's account is especially valuable because it is a personal record of his own experience of the way Christ had appeared to him. According to what he says himself, Paul *saw* Christ (1 Cor. 9:1), apparently in the form of an inner experience: "It pleased God through his grace to reveal his Son *in me*" (Gal. 1:15f.). . . . Acts 9 relates this experience of Paul's in the form of a conversion story, on the model of the calling of the Old Testament prophets, with the vision of a blinding light from heaven and an audition: "I am Jesus whom you are persecuting" (9:3, 5).

We ought probably to think of the experiences of the women at the tomb and the disciples in Galilee in terms not very different from these, if we can conceive of exceptional visionary experiences like this at all, and can enter into them imaginatively. The witnesses all agree in reporting that they saw the Jesus who had died as "the living One." They do not say that he had returned to this life. What they say is that he is alive in the glory of God and that it was in this glory that he "appeared" to them in their earthly lives. They had visions of a supernatural light. But of course at this point the interpretations already begin. It is in any case impossible to discover the substance of these experiences in the form of naked facts without the subjective interpretations. The only result would be unhistorical abstractions. Moreover, pure facts are inexpressible. In every perception, what is experienced is interpreted through the ideas which people bring with them. Of course these ideas do not remain what they were; in the process of perception they themselves change. And this is particularly true in the case of revolutionary experiences. Otherwise Saul could not have become Paul. If we perceive something "wholly other," we ourselves are fundamentally changed. If we are not, we have not perceived the wholly other at all; we have merely assimilated it to what we already are and know, repressing its strangeness.

The experiences of Christ which are talked about here were evidently experiences which changed the very existence of the people involved. The disciples had flown from Jerusalem to Galilee out of disappointment and fear, in order to save their own lives. These same disciples are now turned into apostles who return to Jerusalem and risk their lives there in order to preach Christ "boldly" (Acts 9:22, 28). But for the women who had "looked upon" Jesus' execution and death on Golgotha (Mark 15:40f.), the appearances of the risen One were not quite so staggering. They were rather a transition from one kind of beholding to another, in the faithfulness of a reciprocal seeing, knowing, and loving.[9]

According to the Gospel accounts, the presupposition of the visionary phenomena was the disciples' flight into Galilee. This is probably described in such detail in order to exclude any kind of wishful thinking, or any notion of a "projection" prompted by belief: the phenomena, that is, cannot be explained by the faith of the disciples. On the contrary, their faith has to be explained by the phenomena. . . .

. . . The question as to how long the visionary phenomena continued in the early community is hard to answer. The "forty days" which we are told elapsed between Easter and the ascension are symbolic, just like the testimony "raised on the third day . . ." But what is certain is that the appearances of Christ came to an end, and that they were replaced by the proclamation of Christ through the gospel and the experience of Christ's presence in the Spirit. The "seeing" of the risen Christ became faith.

The story of the ascension talks about Christ's absence; but we must not think of the transition from seeing to faith in terms of an unmediated breach. The visionary phenomena were evidently associated with ecstatic experiences of the Spirit, so they will also have passed into the pentecostal experiences of the young church and will have perpetuated themselves in these: from the presence of Christ in his appearances to the presence of Christ in the Spirit. The early Christian faith in the resurrection was not based solely on Christ's appearances. It was just as strongly motivated, at the very least, by the experience of God's Spirit. Paul therefore calls this Spirit "the Spirit" or "power" of the resurrection. Luke makes the end of the appearances with Christ's ascension be followed by the outpouring of the pentecostal Spirit. Believing in the risen Christ means being possessed by the Spirit of the resurrection. In the Spirit, the presence of the living Christ was experienced. Believing in Christ's resurrection therefore does not mean affirming a fact. It means being possessed by the life-giving Spirit and participating in the powers of the age to come (Heb. 6:5). . . .

. . . Paul links these christophany conceptions with the expression αποκάλψις, and by doing so he gives them a special meaning: God unveils something ahead of time which is still hidden and inaccessible to the cognition of the present aeon, or world time. Under the present conditions of knowledge, the secrets of the endtime and God's future new world are still veiled and unknowable, for the present world of sin and violence cannot sustain the new world of God's righteousness and justice. That is why this righteousness of God's is going to create a new world, and will be manifested only at the end of the time of this world, and in the daybreak of the new creation. Only then will "the glory of the Lord appear." But even in the history of this world there are already revelations of the new world to come, revelations ahead of time. In the Old Testament, these revelations of God's future are linked with the callings of his prophets, and these calls are often founded on the vision of this coming divine glory (Isaiah 6). The people who experienced the christophanies became apostles, both women and men—Mary Magdalene and Paul and the rest. The anticipatory beholding of the glory of God in the face of Jesus Christ led directly to the call to the apostolate and to service in this transitory world for what is to come. The christophanies were not interpreted as mystical translations into a world beyond. They were viewed as radiance thrown ahead of itself, the radiance of God's coming glory on the first day of the new world's creation. And these christophanies are daylight visions, not phantasms of the night.

If we look at the way these christophanies and the Easter seeing of the men and women concerned were interpretatively perceived, we can discover three dimensions in their structure:

The first is *prospective:* they saw the crucified Christ as the living One in the splendor cast ahead by the coming glory of God.

The second is *retrospective:* they recognized him from the marks of the nails and in the breaking of bread: the One who will come is the One crucified on Golgotha.

The third is *reflexive:* in this seeing they perceived their own call to the apostolate: "As the Father has sent me, even so I send you" (John 20:21). . . .

. . . The texts about the resurrection are the oldest Christian texts and the most widespread. If we ask why, we are compelled to come back to the premises on which the men and women concerned based their interpretation. They had gone with Jesus to Galilee and Jerusalem. They had believed his message about the imminent coming of the kingdom of God, and had seen the signs and wonders which testified to its nearness. In one way or another they had experienced his helplessness in Gethsemane and his forsakenness on Golgotha. And they had drawn their own conclusions from their experiences with Jesus. This was the immediate, personal framework for their interpretation. The further interpretative background—the prophetic and apocalyptic tradition of the Judaism of the time—comes only after that. These men and women also lived and thought in the context of Jewish apocalyptic—the framework of its expectation and the world of its images. These became especially important when they tried to communicate their newly acquired faith in Christ to their fellow-countrymen and contemporaries by pointing out that Christ had been raised from the dead "in accordance with the scriptures" (1 Cor. 15:4). But it seems obvious that Christ's appearances, viewed as advance reflections of God's coming glory, should have been explained by his rising from the dead as "the first fruits of those who have fallen asleep" (1 Cor. 15:20), because the imminent eschatological expectation which this reflects so entirely corresponds to Jesus' proclamation of the imminent coming of the kingdom. If he has appeared as "the first fruits of those who have fallen asleep" and as "the leader of life," then "the last days" before the end of this time have dawned. But this means that with Christ the general resurrection of the dead has already begun. The annihilation of death through the coming of eternal life is already in process. New creation is beginning in Christ in the very midst of this world of violence and death.

The eschatological symbol of the raising of the dead is an interpretative category well suited to comprehend the contradictory experiences of the men and women disciples with Jesus: crucified in weakness—living in glory. No more can be said about the verification in Jesus himself. What happened to him between his death on Golgotha and his appearances no one saw, and no one claims to have seen. . . . Only "the empty tomb" gave ambiguous tidings of what had happened there. That Jesus' tomb was empty seems to be an extremely well attested fact, because both Jews and Christians knew of it. The message of the resurrection brought by the disciples on their return to Jerusalem could hardly have lasted a single hour in the city if it had been possible to show that Jesus' body was lying in the grave. But this does not prove who emptied the tomb—whether it was the disciples, as the Jews claimed, or God, as the apostles said. The proclamation that Jesus had been raised from the dead is not an interpretation of the empty tomb. The empty tomb was passed down by tradition only as an external sign of "Jesus' resurrection." The resurrection itself is the interpretation of the experience of Christ's appearances. . . .

Is this eschatological symbol an appropriate way of describing the experiences with Jesus? Is it an arbitrary way of expressing them, or does it offer itself with an inward and inevitable cogency? It apparently grew up out of the apocalyptic structure of the "seeing" of Christ. But does it also fit the experience of his death on the cross? The answer is "yes," inasmuch as raising presupposes death, and the eschatological raising of the dead does not mean a revivification; nor does it mean a return to this life, which leads to death. The resurrection is not a revival, as in the case of Jairus's daughter, or Lazarus, whom Jesus brought back to this life but who later died once more. "The raising of the dead" at the end of days means a qualitatively new life which no longer knows death and is not a continuation of this mortal life. Cosmically, the eschatological raising of the dead has been linked since time immemorial with the hope for the elimination of death from God's creation (Isa. 25:8; 26:19). The symbol of "the raising of the dead" also excludes ideas about a "life after death," the immortality of the soul, or the transmigration of souls; or that the cause of Jesus will continue in his spirit. All these notions can co-exist with death. They accept it by transcending it. But if "the raising of the dead" means "the annihilation of death," then the hope of resurrection is a hope against death, and a contradiction in the name of the living God of this most intransigent confutation of life. The expression "resurrection from the dead" does not deny the deadliness of death or the totality of death. Jesus did not just seemingly die. He died truly, not merely physically but wholly, not merely for human beings but for God too. "Raising from the dead" is the term for a new creative act of God's, an act with which the new creation of all mortal and transitory being begins. This eschatological symbol is appropriate for the contradictory experiences with Jesus because it denies neither the deadliness of his death nor his livingness in his appearances.

And yet to apply the eschatological symbol of the resurrection of the dead to the experiences with Jesus is to transform its very essence. The formula "Christ was raised from the dead" says that he alone was raised, but not the other dead, and that he was raised ahead of all the other dead. According to prophetic ideas, God will raise the dead "on his Day." There was no mention of the earlier raising of an individual before time, not even if he was the messiah. All the same, we ought not to think merely of "the Last Judgment." The events of the end can also extend over a certain period of time, as talk about "the last days" shows. The transformation of the universal eschatological symbol of "the raising of the dead" into the christological symbol "raising from the dead" is only justified as long as that universal expectation is still joined with the perception of the raising of Christ.[10] If the general "raising of the dead" is left out, the testimony about "the raising of Christ from the dead" becomes increasingly feeble, and finally loses its meaning. The Christian belief in the resurrection remains dependent on its verification through the eschatological raising of all the dead. As long as this has not been manifested, the belief is still only hope. But in this eschatological context the raising of Jesus speaks for itself. It speaks its own language of promise and well-founded hope, but it is not yet the language of accomplished fact. As long as the facts that determine this world are the facts of violence and suffering, the world is not able to furnish proof of the resurrection of life and the annihilation of death. In this "unredeemed world" the resurrection of Christ is still dependent on its eschatological verification through the new creation of the world.

Once this transformed symbol of the resurrection of the dead was applied to the crucified Jesus, the content of the old prophetic expectation changed. According to the Torah, the "raising to eternal life" was promised only to the just, while the unjust had to expect "resurrection to everlasting contempt" (Dan. 12:2). This makes it clear that in Israel the expectation of resurrection was not an anthropological symbol, nor was it a soteriological one. It was not aligned towards endless life, or towards celestial bliss. It was a theological symbol for faith in the victory of God's righteousness and justice at the end of history, through the glorification of the Torah in the just and the unjust. Righteousness has to triumph in the end because it is God's righteousness. Because even death can lay down no limits for God, the dead will be raised for God's final judgment. It is not the desire for eternal life that dominates the prophetic expectation of the resurrection of the dead; it is the thirst for righteousness.[11]

If this eschatological symbol is applied in its transformed Christian form to the condemned, forsaken, and crucified Jesus, the question about God's justice and righteousness is the result. If God raised Jesus, he puts all those who condemned, abandoned, and crucified him in the wrong. Then the raising of the One crucified is the divine justification of Jesus of Nazareth and his message, for which he was put to death (Acts 2:22ff.). With the raising of the condemned and executed Jesus, God himself re-opens the trial of Jesus, and in this theodicy trial of Jesus Christ the apostles are the witnesses. If in this context the raising of Jesus means the justification of Jesus as the Christ of God, then the resurrection endorses Jesus' proclamation of the compassionate justice of God, which sets everything to rights; and the double event of his surrender to death and his raising becomes the revelation of the messianic righteousness of God—which is to say his justifying righteousness.

This is how Paul saw it when he interpreted this double event as "delivered up for our trespasses, raised for our justification" (Rom. 4:25). The God who calls into being the things that are not, who makes the dead live, is also the God who makes the Godless just. In the framework of eschatological symbolism this can only be interpreted to mean that in his death on the cross Christ has vicariously anticipated the final judgment of God for all the Godless and the unjust, so that as a result his raising from this death manifests to everyone the righteousness and justice of God which puts everything to rights and makes the unjust just. His own raising from the dead was not a raising for judgment, such as Daniel 12 envisages for all the dead; it was a raising into the glory of God and eternal life. And the Christian resurrection hope which is grounded on the remembrance of Christ's sufferings and resurrection is therefore an unequivocally "joyful hope" for the resurrection and the life of the world to come. It is not a fearful expectation of a Last Judgment whose outcome for the human beings concerned is uncertain.

It is true that in the history of Christian theology and art the rapturous joy of Easter jubilation has continually been subdued, if not stifled, by fear of the final judgment; but wrongly so, and less in the Christian than in the apocalyptic sense. If at the Last Judgment the crucified One himself is the judge, the justice that will prevail is his merciful and justifying righteousness, and none other.

This impression becomes stronger still if we do not concentrate solely on the symbol "raising from the dead" but also enter into the other symbol, "risen from the dead." The first phrase talks about God's own exclusive act in and for the dead Jesus. The second phrase designates "an act of Christ performed in his own power." The first formula joins Jesus with the common fate of all the dead. The second stresses the special divine power in him. If God really was "in Christ," as Paul says, then Christ was crucified in the weakness of God and rose in the power of God. God did not merely act on him from heaven; he also acted in him and out of him. Of course the two ideas dovetail, and are therefore not treated as alternatives. The one whom God wakens from sleep must rise himself; and the one who has to rise must first of all be wakened. In considering Christ's history with God his Father we have to draw on both ideas if we are to grasp the mutual relationship of the Father and the Son: the raised Son rose in the power of the life-giving Spirit.

For the first Christian community this idea about Christ's resurrection was also important as a way of describing the special position of the messiah in relation to the living and the dead. Just like all other human beings before him, Jesus "died" and "was buried"; but *the fullness and wholeness of his bodily nature* was preserved through his resurrection ahead of time "on the third day." He rose with *an uncorrupted body*. Peter's address in Acts 2:27 cites Psalm 16:10: "Thou wilt not let thy Holy One see corruption." God "raised him up, having loosed the pangs of death, because it was not possible for him to be held by it" (Acts 2:24). . . .

Finally, we come to the astonishing transition from the "seeing" of Christ in his appearances to "faith" in Christ's gospel. Many hypotheses have been pressed into service to explain the early Christian christophanies. Proposals range from fraudulent deception to projection by the unconscious, and from the supposition of subjective visions to the assumption of objective ones. All these hypotheses are really superfluous, because there is nothing comparable which could provide the analogies on which to base an understanding. Wilhelm Hermann rightly said that we cannot talk about those Easter experiences in the way that we talk about our own. Nor did the early Christian apostles ever try to bring other people to similar visions of Christ. Paul did not proclaim his experience on the road to Damascus as a conversion experience that was open to everyone. Nor, probably, did he ever make it the subject of his preaching. The real problem is to be found in the transition from seeing to believing; for one day the christophanies came to an end. So why did the Christian community not come to an end too? Apparently this question was taken seriously and was answered by: "blessed are those who have not seen and yet believe" (John

20:29). But then what is the relation of faith to sight? The people to whom Christ "appeared" were so overwhelmed that they apparently had no choice. But among the people who had not seen, some believed the apostles and others did not. The transition from seeing to believing must have been made even in the Easter witnesses themselves. They did not remain in a "seeing" relationship to the Lord; but when the seeing stopped, they believed. They testified to the Lord whom they had "seen" through the proclamation of the gospel, and their preaching awakened faith without sight in other people. Whereas the seeing of Christ allowed those involved no freedom of choice, the word of the proclamation brings men and women face to face with the decision of faith. Faith of this kind—faith in response to the Word that a person has heard—is possible only when Christ's "appearances" cease. It is only by returning to the hidden safe-keeping of God that Christ makes this faith possible. Yet because faith in the gospel of Christ came into being from the seeing of Christ in his appearances, this faith, in its turn, waits and hopes for the seeing of Christ "face to face" (1 Cor. 13:12), and in doing so it waits also for that "coming again" of Christ in visible, universal glory which we call his parousia.

The history of the proclamation of faith goes back to its foundational beginnings in the seeing of Christ's appearances. It is therefore aligned towards Christ's parousia in visible glory. The *successio apostolica* is nothing other than the *successio evangelii* and is a true historical *processio*—a moving forward in expectation of the universal future of Christ at the end of history.

If the gospel takes the place of Christ's appearances, then it has to exhibit the same structures as these appearances: (1) The gospel is *retrospectively* "the Word of the cross." It makes the crucified Christ present. (2) The gospel is *prospectively* the anticipation in the Word of Christ's parousia, and therefore has itself a promissory character. (3) The gospel which proclaims the one crucified as the one to come, the one humiliated as the one who is exalted, and the one dead as the one who is alive is *the present call* into the liberty of faith. Accordingly the Christian faith is a life lived out of Christ, a life lived with Christ, and a life lived in expectation of Christ. And in being these things it is also a life of new creation in the midst of the shadows of the transient world.

The Parousia of Christ

Source: Moltmann 1989; ET 1990/1993:338–41.

§6 EXPECTANT CREATIVITY: THE EXPECTATION OF THE PAROUSIA AND AFFIRMED EMBODIMENT

When it is talking about Christ's parousia, the New Testament hardly talks about it in speculative terms at all. The context is always eucharistic and parenetic. The practical testimony to the eschatological expectation of Christ is the celebration of the eucharistic feast through which "the Lord's death is proclaimed till he comes" (1 Cor. 11:26). In act and in the Word of promise, the shared meal calls to remembrance Christ's death and anticipates his coming in glory. The feast itself is celebrated in expectation of the parousia. That is why the cry "*maranatha*" probably has its origin in the celebration of the Lord's Supper. The congregation begs the Christ who is present in the Spirit of God for the coming of his kingdom. The fellowship of the eucharistic feast is therefore understood as a gift given in advance, and in anticipatory presentation of the great banquet of the nations at which all human beings will be satisfied.

On the one hand the Christian ethic expressed in the New Testament paranesis takes its impress from the Eucharist: those who have shared the supper of the Lord should live in the fellowship of Christ and lead their whole life in his Spirit. But on the other hand its orientation is eschatological. The expectation of Christ's parousia directs all the senses towards his future, and makes them receptive here and now for the experience of history.

Where the expectation of the parousia is strongly apocalyptic in character, the paranesis stresses the need to "endure" in faith until the end: "Be patient. Strengthen your hearts, for the coming of the Lord is at hand" (James 5:8). "He who endures to the end will be saved" (Matt. 10:22; 24:13). Experience of life here is always determined by assailments and hostilities. The danger of falling away from faith is obvious. But the person who hopes for Christ's impending parousia will stand fast and will not run away. The people who stand fast are the true believers, for at this coming Christ will find them to be the men and women who have hoped for him. The people who run away show that they are unbelievers, because they have not had this hope. So *perseverantia usque ad finem*—endurance to the end—always counted as the sign and testimony of true faith, and as the effect in personal life of hope for the parousia. "The patience of hope" (1 Thessalonians 3) is part of the fundamental structure of new life in the community of Christ. Faith is not a matter of continually new decision. It means faithfulness to the decision which God made for men and women in

Christ. Those who believe in Christ will become "sharers in the tribulation and the kingdom and the patient endurance of Christ" (Rev. 1:9).

Where expectation of the parousia is more strongly marked by awareness of the presence of Christ, it calls men and women to reshape their lives in the community of Christ. The "day" is at hand, so believers can already "rise" now, in this life. "Awake, O sleeper, and arise from the dead, and Christ shall give you light" (Eph. 5:24; Rom. 13:11). Believers are "children of light" (Eph. 5:8f.) and as children of light they should give their lives the appropriate form, casting away "the works of darkness" and laying hold of "the weapons of light" (Rom. 13:12). It is in this light symbolism that the kingdom of Christ and the new creation are described. Although in this world-time of violence and injustice it is still dark, believers can anticipate the light of the new creation and can already live here and now from the future of Christ.

In the parousia parenesis *the body* of human beings evidently acquires a special importance: "Put on the Lord Jesus Christ and keep your bodies in such a way that no desires arise" (Rom. 13:14). Here, in my view, Paul is talking about destructive dependencies and obsessions which are the enemy of life; the idea is not that lust should give way to a general listlessness. In 1 Corinthians 6 too all attention is devoted to the body. "The body belongs to the Lord and the Lord to the body," says 1 Cor. 6:13, stressing the reciprocity between the body and the Lord in an astounding way. The reason is the resurrection: "God raised the Lord and will also raise us up by his power" (v. 14); the experience is an experience in the Spirit, for: "Your body is a temple of the Holy Spirit" (v. 19); and the conclusion is: "Glorify God in your body" (v. 20). So the Holy Spirit is experienced in the body, for the body is already pervaded by the life-giving powers of the future world. Because Christ came for the sake of the bodily resurrection, and on his day will complete the redemption of the body from the destructive power of death, God is not experienced merely in the soul. Paul stresses that he is experienced in the body too, and is therefore praised in the body. This, finally, is what Paul's hope for the parousia also has to say: "From there we expect a Savior, the Lord Jesus Christ, who will change our lowly body to be like his glorious body" (Phil. 3:20, 21). The expected real transformation of the body there, corresponds to the bodily quickening in the Spirit here. The hope for the parousia is not a flight from the world. Nor does it provide any foundation for hostility towards the body. On the contrary, it makes people prepared to remain true to the earth, and to honor the body.

Life in hope for the parousia is not a matter of mere "waiting," guarding oneself, and holding fast to the faith. It goes far beyond that, reaching out to the active shaping of life. It is *life in anticipation* of the coming One, life in "expectant creativity."[12] People do not live merely from traditions. They live from expectations too. In their fears and hopes they anticipate their still unknown future and adapt their present to it, shaping their lives accordingly. The expectation of the future of Christ sets the present in the light of the One who will come, and makes bodily life in the power of the resurrection experienceable. In this power it becomes life lived "with raised heads" (Luke 21:28) and with what Ernst Bloch called "an upright walk." It becomes a life which is committed to working for the kingdom of God through its commitment to justice and peace in this world.

It was to this life in anticipation that the World Council of Churches called at its assembly in Uppsala in 1968. The message of Uppsala brings out the creative hope for the parousia and is more relevant today than ever:

"We ask you, trusting in God's renewing power, to join in the anticipation of God's kingdom, showing *now* something of the newness which Christ will complete on his day."

Notes

1. Moltmann 1989; ET 1990/1993:xiiif.

2. Ibid., 340f.

3. Cf. Carter Heyward, *The Redemption of God: A Theology of Mutual Relation* (Washington, DC: University Press of America, 1982); Elisabeth Moltmann-Wendel, *A Land Flowing with Milk and Honey*, trans. John Bowden (London: SCM Press/New York: Crossroad, 1986).

4. Joachim Jeremias, *The Prayers of Jesus*, trans. John Bowden (London: SCM Press/ Naperville, IL: Alec R. Allenson, 1967).

5. Schalom Ben-Chorin, *Mirjam–Mutter Jesu: Maria in Jüdischer Sicht* (Munich: List, 1971), 99ff.

6. Cf. Moltmann-Wendel, *Land Flowing*, 117ff.

7. Gerhard Lohfink writes, "With the constitution of the twelve and with their proclamation of the kingdom of God, the existence of the Israel of the endtime already begins," in *Jesus and Community: The Social Dimension of the Christian Faith*, ET (Philadelphia: Fortress Press/ London: SPCK, 1985), 21.

8. The study by Peter Carnley, *The Structure of Resurrection Belief* (Oxford: Clarendon, 1987), is quite excellent.

9. It is disastrous to exclude this feminine apostolate from the present discussion about the ordination of women. It is wrong to maintain that Jesus only called male disciples and apostles, and to make this a reason for rejecting the ordination of women, as Pope John Paul II does in his encyclical *Mulieris Dignitatem* of 1988.

10. Cf. Wolfhart Pannenberg, *Revelation as History*, trans. Edward Quinn (London: Sheed and Ward/New York: Macmillan, 1969).

11. Thus rightly Ernst Bloch, *The Principle of Hope,* 3 vols., trans. Neville Plaice, Stephen Plaice, and Paul Knight (Oxford: Basil Blackwell, 1986).

12. Cf. Vincent J. Genovesi, *Expectant Creativity: The Action of Hope in Christian Ethics* (Philadelphia: St. Joseph's University Press, 1982), who pursues the line of my theology of hope in the field of ethics.

6

The Spirit of Life

Moltmann published his book on the Holy Spirit in 1991. Its subtitle, A Universal Affirmation, *expresses the book's main concern: that the workings of the Spirit should not be viewed solely as spiritual in the usual sense of the word, but that the Spirit is indeed "the Lord and giver of life," as the Nicene Creed says—life meaning life in all its fullness, physical as well as spiritual. In his autobiography, Moltmann says that in presenting "life in the Spirit" of God he wishes to bring out "the liberation, the justification, the rebirth, the sanctification, and the mystical experience of life." And speaking of the fellowship of the Holy Spirit, following V. Taylor, he calls the Spirit "The Go-between God, the Deity who is sociality."[1] This doctrine of the Spirit therefore belongs intrinsically within Moltmann's social doctrine of the Trinity as whole.*

APPROACHES IN PNEUMATOLOGY TODAY

Source: Moltmann 1991; ET 1992:1–14.

About twenty years ago it was usual to introduce studies on the Holy Spirit with a complaint about "forgetfulness of the Spirit" at the present day generally, and in Protestant theology in particular. The Holy Spirit was said to be the Cinderella of Western theology. So it had to be specially cherished and coaxed into a growth of its own. This was undoubtedly a reaction against a particular kind of "neo-orthodoxy" in the Protestant churches, as well as a counterweight to the christocentricism of Karl Barth's theology, and the theology of the 1934 Barmen Declaration of the Confessing Church. So one of Barth's own last words was always quoted: he dreamed, he said, of a new theology which would begin with the third article of the creed and would realize in a new way the real concern of his old opponent, [Friedrich] Schleiermacher.

This criticism of contemporary theology, and this reminder of the master's blessing, initiated a whole flood of writings about the Holy Spirit and its special efficacies.[2] "Forgetfulness of the Spirit" gave way to a positive obsession with the Spirit. But if we look critically at the actual results, we are bound to conclude that in sober fact, although light has been thrown on a whole number of individual aspects, a new paradigm in pneumatology has not yet emerged. Most studies are no more than prolongations of the traditional doctrines, either pursuing further the Catholic doctrine of grace, or expanding the Protestant pattern "Word and Spirit." It is only hesitantly that the very foundation of the Western church's pneumatology is even put forward for discussion—by which I mean the doctrine about the Spirit's origin *a patre filioque,* the doctrine which led to the division of the church in 1054.[3] No less hesitant is recognition of the new pentecostal and charismatic movements, and reflection about their special experiences of the Spirit.[4]

Between the patristic pneumatology of the Orthodox church on the one hand, and the pentecostal experiences of the young churches on the other, there are also the still unsettled questions of modern European times—the age of "subjectivity" and "experience." Fired by Joachimite expectation, the classic German philosophers, [G. E.] Lessing, [Immanuel] Kant, [J. G.] Fichte, and [G. W. F.] Hegel, interpreted "Enlightenment" as "the third age"—that is to say, "the age of the Spirit." So there can be no question of the Spirit's "being forgotten" in modern times. On the contrary: the rationalism and pietism of the Enlightenment was every bit as Enthusiastic as pentecostal Christianity today.

It was the established churches' fear of the religious, as well as the irreligious, "free thinking" of the modern world which led to more and more reserve in the doctrine of the Holy Spirit. In reaction against the spirit of the new liberty—freedom of belief, freedom of religion, freedom of conscience, and free churches—the only Spirit that was declared holy was the Spirit that is bound to the ecclesiastical institution for mediating grace, and to the preaching of the official "spiritual pastors and teachers." The Spirit which people experience personally in their own decision of faith, in believers' baptism, in the inner experience of faith in which "they feel their hearts strangely warmed" (as John Wesley put it), and in their own charismatic endowment, was declared "unholy" and "enthusiastic." Even today, in ecclesiastical discussions about the Holy Spirit, people like to turn first and foremost to "the criterion for discerning the spirits"—even when there do not seem to be any spirits to hand.

On the other hand, the continual assertion that God's Spirit is bound to the church, its word and sacraments, its authority, its institutions and ministries, impoverishes the congregations. It empties the churches, while the Spirit emigrates to the spontaneous groups and personal experience. Men and women are not being taken seriously as independent people if they are only supposed to be "in the Spirit" when they are recipients of the church's ministerial acts and its proclamation. God's Spirit is more than merely the being-revealed of his revelation in human beings, and more than simply the finding of faith in the heart through the proclaimed word. For the Spirit actually brings men and women to the beginning of a new life, and makes them the determining subjects of that new life in the fellowship of Christ. People do not only experience the Holy Spirit outwardly in the community of their church. They experience it to a much greater degree inwardly, in self-encounter—as the experience that "God's love has been poured into our hearts through the Holy Spirit" (Rom. 5:5). Many people express this personal experience of the Spirit in the simple words: "God loves me." In this experience of God they also experience their own indestructible and inalienable dignity, so that they can get up out of the dust. They find themselves, and no longer have to try despairingly to be themselves—or despairingly not to be themselves. Don't the words of the Bible which have come down to us over the centuries, and the words of proclamation which we hear from Christians today, spring from experiences of the Spirit like this?

There are no words of God without human experiences of God's Spirit. So the words of proclamation spoken by the Bible and the church must also be related to the experiences of people today, so that they are not—as Karl Rahner said—merely "hearers of the Word" but become spokesmen of the Word too.

But this is only possible if Word and Spirit are seen as existing in a *mutual relationship,* not as a one-way street. The Spirit is the subject determining the

Word, not just the operation of that Word. The efficacies of the Spirit reach beyond the Word. Nor do the experiences of the Spirit find expression in words alone. They are as multifarious and protean as sensory reality itself. The Spirit has its non-verbal expressions too. The indwelling of the Spirit "in our hearts" goes deeper than the conscious level in us. It rouses all our senses, permeates the unconscious too, and quickens the body, giving it new life (1 Cor. 6:19f.). A new energy for living proceeds from the Spirit. To bind the experience of the Spirit solely to the Word is one-sided, and represses these dimensions. The non-verbal dimensions for their part show that the Word is bound to the Spirit, but that the Spirit is not bound to the Word, and that Spirit and Word belong in a mutual relationship which must not be conceived exclusively, or in merely intellectual terms.

1. THE ECUMENICAL AND PENTECOSTAL INVITATION TO THE FELLOWSHIP OF THE HOLY SPIRIT

The ecumenical movement has come up against questions of pneumatology in different ways: (*a*) in the motivation to ecumenical fellowship; (*b*) in the encounter of churches with differing experiences and theologies of the Holy Spirit.

(*a*) The motivation towards ecumenical fellowship with the other churches, the overcoming of painful divisions between churches, and the prospect of a conciliar union of divided churches was often ascribed by the pioneers of the movement to God's Spirit. After centuries of Western division in matters of belief, and following generations of denominational absolutism, the ecumenical movement is without doubt the most important Christian event of the twentieth century. For the first time, there is a revolution of feeling. The other churches are no longer viewed as opponents or competitors. They are taken seriously as partners on a shared path. But this is possible only if we see "the fellowship of the Holy Spirit" as something that transcends the denominational frontiers, and throws them open, so that we view Christians belonging to other churches as members of this great community of God. At the moment people are no longer interested in laying down demarcation lines, as a way of safeguarding their own territory. Their concern is to discover mutual complementariness, as a means of arriving at a greater unity. This ecumenical experience of the Spirit seems to me more important than the highly-charged expectations which some theologians . . . have brought to the ecumenical movement, interpreting it in the context of salvation history as a transition to the epoch of the Spirit, or as entry into the third age of "the Johannine church"—which is to say the church of the Spirit.

(*b*) If we encounter the other churches as partners, parallel to our own church in the all-embracing "fellowship of the Holy Spirit," we inevitably enter once more into the disputes which once led to church division. In the context of pneumatology, there are two points to be mentioned here: (1) The question of the *filioque*, with the canon-law and symbolic significance of this Western interpolation into the 381 version of the Nicene Creed, as well as the consequences for trinitarian theology of the subordination of the Spirit to the Son, which was the practical result; (2) The question about the charismatic experiences of God's Spirit and their importance for personal, shared, and political life, and for the life of nature. In 1961 the Orthodox churches joined the ecumenical movement, and a number of pentecostal churches came in later. So it is in these two problem complexes that ecumenical ventures in pneumatology are being made. The successful growth of pentecostal churches outside the ecumenical movement is also a serious challenge to all the old, mainstream churches. And not least, return to the common confession of faith in the words of the Nicene Creed led to theological work on its third article in the Commission on Faith and Order, and at congresses in Rome. With or without the addition of the *filioque*, this article leaves so many questions open that it is essential to work towards common answers, which will take us beyond the solutions of the church Fathers.

2. OVERCOMING THE FALSE ALTERNATIVE BETWEEN DIVINE REVELATION AND HUMAN EXPERIENCE OF THE HOLY SPIRIT

The dialectical theology of [Karl] Barth, [Emil] Brunner, [Rudolf] Bultmann, and [Friedrich] Gogarten led to an alternative which today is proving to be unfruitful. The dialectical theologians began by reproaching nineteenth-century liberal and pietistic theology with starting from human consciousness of God, not from the divine Word to men and women; this, they said, was theology "from below," not theology "from above." In the German tradition, Friedrich Schleiermacher was regarded as the founder of the modern theology of consciousness and experience. If God-consciousness is always already inherent in a human being's immediate self-consciousness (since he knows that he is "simply dependent"), then there is continuity between the human spirit and the Spirit of God. But if God-consciousness only comes into being at all because the Wholly Other God reveals himself, then the Spirit of God is the being-revealed of this self-revelation of God in us; and it remains for us just as inexperienceable, hidden, and "other" as God himself. In this case there is a permanent discontinuity between God's Spirit and the spirit of human beings. For then the Holy Spirit is not a modality of our experience of God;

it is a modality of God's revelation to us. If the Spirit is a modality of our own experience, then human experience of God is the foundation of human theology. But this can be at the cost of the qualitative difference between God and human beings. If the Spirit is viewed as a modality of the divine revelation, then the foundation of theology is God's revelation of himself. But in this case the qualitative difference between God and human beings makes every immediate relation of human beings to God impossible. And so there can be no natural human theology either.

Hendrik Berkhof and Alasdair Heron believe that this alternative is the main problem in pneumatology today. Berkhof even thinks that it is "the determining question in the whole history of the Western church." I do not myself see this question as a problem, because I cannot see that there is any fundamental alternative between God's revelation to human beings, and human experience of God. How is a man or woman supposed to be able to talk about God if God does not reveal himself? How are men and women supposed to be able to talk about a God of whom there is no human experience? It is only in the narrow concepts of modern philosophy that "revelation" and "experience" are antitheses. But theology ought not simply to take over modern epistemological and scientific conceptualizations of experience, and then look round for alternatives. It ought to determine these conceptions themselves. God's revelation is always the revelation of God to others, and is therefore a making–itself–experienceable through others. The experience of God is always a suffering of the God who is Other, and the experience of fundamental change in the relationship to that Other.

In 1929, in his lecture "The Holy Spirit and Christian Life," Karl Barth settled accounts with Idealist notions about the continuity between the Spirit of God and the spirit of human beings.[5] He employed three arguments: (1) God's Spirit is not the spirit of human beings, because there is no continuity between Creator and what he has created, not even in the soul's remembrance of its divine origin (as Augustine had once said). The relationship between Creator and creature in the Holy Spirit is conferred by the Creator alone. (2) The human being does not simply *differ* from the Creator because of his "creatureliness." He is actually at variance with God much more fundamentally than that, because he is a sinner. So the "Holy" Spirit encounters him in utter contradiction to his own sinful spirit. It is the Holy Spirit as reconciler who contravenes this human enmity towards God, and in that very way is on the true side of human beings, in the name of God's grace contraverting human hostility towards grace. Sanctification through the Holy Spirit therefore coincides with the justification of the sinner through God's grace. Sinful men and women remain dependent on this "alien," external grace. Christian life is nothing other than "a receiving of God's revelation." Finally (3), the Holy Spirit is holy because "it is *eschatologically* present to the human spirit in God's revelation, and in no other way." But "the Holy Spirit as redeemer" is "eschatological" because it belongs to eternity, and therefore to God, whereas human beings exist here in time and in the shadow of death.

Barth undoubtedly thinks that by saying this he has formulated the Spirit's "true continuity to the human spirit." But his eschatology is not linked with the future of the new creation of all things; it is related to God's eternity, over against the temporality of human beings. Consequently the Holy Spirit reveals nothing to human beings which they could see, hear, smell, or taste, and so experience through their senses; on the contrary, it reveals something which human beings can never experience: God's eternity and the life which lies beyond the frontier of death, as eternal life. Barth therefore calls the Holy Spirit "the Spirit of promise," because it places human beings in expectation of the "Wholly Other," and can hence never be experienced. As the subjective reality of God's self-revelation, the Holy Spirit remains entirely on God's side, so it can never be experienced by human beings at all. Even the faith which the Spirit effects does not know itself. It remains hidden and inexperienceable to itself so that the believer has to believe in his belief.

By setting up this antithesis between revelation and experience, Barth merely replaced the theological immanentism which he complained about by a theological transcendentalism. But the real phenomenon is to be found neither in the Spirit's immanence nor in its transcendence, neither in the continuity nor in the discontinuity. It is to be found in God's *immanence* in human experience, and in the *transcendence* of human beings in God. Because God's Spirit is present in human beings, the human spirit is self-transcendently aligned towards God. Anyone who stylizes revelation and experience into alternatives ends up with revelations that cannot be experienced, and experiences without revelation. The new foundation of the eschatology, which takes its bearings from the future by way of the "theology of hope," does away with the Platonic time-eternity pattern, which Barth and his brother, the philosopher Heinrich Barth, maintained in 1930. The new approach now develops eschatology as the horizon of expectation for the historical experience of the divine Spirit. The Holy Spirit is not simply the subjective side of God's revelation of himself, and faith is not merely the echo of the Word of God in the human heart. The Holy Spirit is much more than that. It is the power that raises the dead, the power of the new creation of all things; and faith is the beginning of the rebirth of human beings to new life.

But this means that the Holy Spirit is by no means merely a matter of revelation. It has to do with life and its source.[6] The Holy Spirit is called "holy" because it sanctifies life and renews the face of the earth.

3. THE DISCOVERY OF THE COSMIC BREADTH OF THE DIVINE SPIRIT

In both Protestant and Catholic theology and devotion, there is a tendency to view the Holy Spirit solely as *the Spirit of redemption*. Its place is the church, and it gives men and women the assurance of the eternal blessedness of their souls. This redemptive Spirit is cut off both from bodily life and from the life of nature. It makes people turn away from "this world" and hope for a better world beyond. They then seek and experience in the Spirit of Christ a power that is different from the divine energy of life, which according to the Old Testament ideas interpenetrates all the living. The theological textbooks therefore talk about the Holy Spirit in connection with God, faith, the Christian life, the church, and prayer, but seldom in connection with the body and nature. In Yves Congar's great book on the Holy Spirit, he has almost nothing to say about the Spirit of creation, or the Spirit of the new creation of all things. It would seem as if the Spirit of God is simply and solely the Spirit of the church, and the Spirit of faith. But this would restrict "the fellowship of the Holy Spirit," and make it impossible for the church to communicate its experience of the Spirit to the world. Some theologians have discovered a new love for the charismatic movements; but this can also be an escape, a flight from the politics and ecology of the Spirit in the world of today.

What is behind this trend, which must undoubtedly be termed purely individualistic? One reason is certainly the continuing Platonization of Christianity. Even today this still puts its mark on what is termed "spirituality" in the church and religious groups. It takes the form of a kind of hostility to the body, a kind of remoteness from the world, and a preference for the inner experiences of the soul rather than the sensory experiences of sociality and nature.

Another reason, I believe, is the far-reaching decision in favor of the *filioque*. This has meant that the Holy Spirit has come to be understood solely as "the Spirit of Christ," and not at the same time as "the Spirit of the Father." As *the Spirit of Christ* it is *the redemptive Spirit*. But the work of creation too is ascribed to the Father, so *the Spirit of the Father* is also *the Spirit of creation*. If redemption is placed in radical discontinuity to creation, then "the Spirit of Christ" has no longer anything to do with Yahweh's *ruach*. According to this notion, the soul is saved from this vale of tears, and from this frail husk of the body, and is carried up into the heaven of the blessed spirits. But these notions of redemption are not Christian. They are Gnostic. It was in order to contravert them that the ancient church introduced "*the resurrection of the body*" into the third article of the Apostles' Creed, and confessed the Spirit "who spake by the prophets," as the Nicene Creed puts it. But if redemption is the resurrection of the body and the new creation of all things, then the redeeming Spirit of Christ cannot be any Spirit other than Yahweh's creative *ruach*. If Christ is confessed as the reconciler and head of the whole cosmos, as he is in the Epistle to the Colossians, then the Spirit is present wherever Christ is present, and has to be understood as the divine energy of life animating the new creation of all things.

But this brings us up against the question about the continuity and discontinuity of the redemptive and the newly creating Spirit on the one hand and the creative and all-animating Spirit on the other—the relation between the *Spiritus sanctficans* and the *Spiritus vivificans*. This is not a special problem of pneumatology, however. It is the question about the unity of God's work in the creation, redemption, and the sanctification of all things. In both the Old and the New Testaments, the words used for the divine act of *creating* are also used for God's liberating and redeeming acts (e.g., Isa. 43:19). Redemption is the final new creation of all things out of their sin, transitoriness, and mortality, for everlasting life, enduring continuance, and eternal glory. The new creation is not without any presuppositions, like creation-in-the-beginning. It presupposes what is old, and is therefore seen pre-eminently in *the raising of the dead* (Ezekiel 37; 1 Corinthians 15). But if the redeeming Spirit is the Spirit of the resurrection and new creation of all things, then to employ Platonic and Gnostic conceptions is simply to misunderstand it. To experience the power of the resurrection, and to have to do with this divine energy, does not lead to a non-sensuous and inward-turned spirituality, hostile to the body and detached from the world. It brings the new vitality of a love for life.

The new approaches to an "ecological theology,"[7] "cosmic Christology,"[8] and the rediscovery of the body,[9] start from the Hebrew understanding of the divine Spirit and presuppose that the redeeming Spirit of Christ and the creative and life-giving Spirit of God are one and the same. So experience of the life-giving Spirit in the faith of the heart and in the sociality of love leads of itself beyond the limits of the church to the rediscovery of the same Spirit in nature, in plants, in animals, and in the ecosystems of the earth.

To experience the fellowship of the Spirit inevitably carries Christianity beyond itself into the greater fellowship of all God's creatures. For *the community of creation*, in which all created things exist with one another, for one another and in one another, is also *the fellowship of the Holy Spirit*. Both experiences of the Spirit bring the church today into solidarity with the cosmos, which is so mortally threatened. Faced with "the end of nature," the churches will either discover the cosmic significance of Christ and the Spirit, or they will share the guilt for the annihilation of God's earthly creation. In earlier times, contempt for life, hostility towards the body, and detachment from the world was merely an inward attitude of mind. Now it has become an everyday reality in the cynicism of the progressive destruction of nature. Discovery of the cosmic breadth of God's Spirit leads in the opposite direction—to respect for the dignity of all created things, in which God is present through his Spirit. In the present situation this discovery is not romantic poetry or speculative vision. It is the essential premise for the survival of humanity on God's one, unique earth.

4. THE QUESTION ABOUT THE PERSONHOOD OF THE HOLY SPIRIT

From the very beginning, the personhood of the Holy Spirit was an unsolved problem, and the problem is as difficult as it is fascinating. To start from the *experience* of the Spirit meant finding largely non-personal words and phrases to describe it: the Spirit is a divine energy, it is wind and fire, light and a wide space, inward assurance and mutual love. Because of what the Spirit effects, its nature was often described through analogies of this kind, drawn from other experiences. Yet in prayer, direct address has to take the place of paraphrases like these. But addresses to the Holy Spirit in prayer are rare, compared with the many ways of addressing God the Father, and the appeals to Christ the Lord and to Jesus. Prayers to the Holy Spirit are always *epikleses*—pleas for the coming of the Spirit: *veni Creator Spiritus.* They seldom include thanksgiving or cries for help.

Theological assertions about the personhood of the Holy Spirit were made in the patristic church in the dispute with the Pneumatomachi. These people interpreted the general Christian subordinationism to mean that the Spirit is subordinated to the Son as the Son is subordinated to the Father. "The Spirit of the Son" then means the Son's mode of efficacy—a way in which the Son exercises his power—but not an independent divine person, over against the Son; just as "the Spirit of the Father" means the Father's efficacy, but not an independent divine person, over against the Father. Tertullian's famous trinitarian formula, *una substantia—tres personae,* asserts the divine personhood of the Holy Spirit, and puts it on the same level as the personhood of the Father and the Son. It secures for the Holy Spirit the same worship and glorification as that given to the Father and the Son; and it is this that is stated in the third article of the creed. This divine personhood of the Spirit is really only asserted, however, not demonstrated. But for all that, to assert the personhood of the Spirit in the theology of the Trinity leads in a different direction from statements based on the experience of the Spirit. What the Spirit *effects* allows its subjectivity to be discerned (as the effector of a work), but not its personhood. Its personhood becomes comprehensible only from that which the Spirit *is*, in relation to the Father and the Son. For personhood is always being-in-relationship. But the relationships which constitute the personhood of the Spirit must be looked for within the Trinity itself, not in the Spirit's outward efficacies.

If we proceed from the experience of the Spirit, then we must not start with a hard and fast definition of experience, but must keep the concept open for the transcendent origin of experiences. People call what they "experience" about God "the power of God" or "the Spirit of God." Do they mean by this a *characteristic* of the eternal God's essential being? Then it would have to be "the powerful God, the spiritual God." By making the power or Spirit of God a substantive, more is evidently meant than merely a divine attribute. This is a reality in which God himself is present according to his will. So "Yahweh's *ruach*" is described as "confronting event of the efficacious presence of God."[10] It is not a characteristic of God's being. It is *a mode of his presence* in his creation and in human history. But if we were to term this "God in action," we should be rashly setting bounds to the perception of the Holy Spirit. The mode of God's presence in human history comprehends not merely God in action but God in passion too; and this touches both God's suffering with his people, in whom he desires to be present, and also "the descent of the Spirit." If we take up later Jewish insights into the nature of the Shekinah, when we talk about the Holy Spirit we can talk about "God's indwellings." It is characteristic of these divine indwellings to be hidden, secret, and silent. In everyday life they are perceived as God's inexpressible closeness. They are experienced as God's companionship. In experiences of suffering they often lead to the assurance of God's nearness.

Because of these modes of descent, self-emptying, and participation in the situation of men and women, some theologians have talked about an "anonymity of the Spirit,"[11] about an "unknown" or "unacknowledged God,"[12] or about "the shy member of the Trinity." So when experience of the Spirit leads us to talk about "the power" of God, about wind, fire, light, or a wide space, we are talking about the *kenotic forms* of the Spirit, forms of his self-emptying. They are not objectifications of the Spirit, but as kenotic forms actually presuppose the personhood of the Spirit, as the determining subject of these forms.

The subjectivity of the Spirit becomes more clearly discernible still if we see God's Shekinah not only as a *mode of his presence*, but also as *God's counterpart in God himself*. According to late Jewish writings, the Shekinah in its earthly history of suffering turns to God himself; and it is in the same way that in his descent the indwelling and co-suffering Spirit of God also turns to God himself (Rom. 8:23; Rev. 22:17). Just as in the Wisdom literature, Wisdom is by no means merely thought of as "one of God's attributes," but is also seen as "God's daughter," so the Holy Spirit too has to be understood as a counterpart of God in God himself.

I have deliberately avoided the terms "hypostasis" and "person" at this point, because I do not wish to blur the differences between the personhood of the Father, and the personhood of the Son, and the personhood of the Spirit, by using a term for person common to them all. The Holy Spirit has a wholly unique personhood, not only in the form in which it is experienced, but also in its relationships to the Father and the Son. We should be losing sight of this if we expected the Spirit to have the same kind of personhood as the Father. We should be losing sight of it if we presupposed that the Spirit has a personhood like that of the Son. In praying to the Father, to Christ, and to the Spirit, these differences can immediately be noticed in the different form of intercession, invocation, and adoration.

Among more recent outlines of pneumatology, the work of Hendrik Berkhof and Heribert Mühlen may be mentioned, as opposite poles.

In his brief *Theology of the Holy Spirit* (1964), Berkhof puts forward a modalist pneumatology. He takes up Karl Barth's early modalistic trinitarian doctrine about the "One God in three different modes of existence" and uses the three modes of God's existence for three ways of divine movement (*modi motus*): a unified creative movement proceeds to the world from God the Father through Christ in the energies of the Holy Spirit. "Spirit" is to be interpreted as a predicate of the subjects "God" and "Christ," and is simply the name for "the efficacious God." The Spirit of the Father means the efficacious Father, the Spirit of the Son the efficacious Christ. This means that, unlike Barth, Berkhof surrenders the three divine modes of existence. Instead of a Trinity, he asserts a binity of Father and Son. The Spirit is nothing other than their efficacy. It is then only possible to talk about a "personhood" of the Spirit to the extent in which this divine efficacy has "person-like features," and can make itself felt, for example, in "personal encounter." But this is determined by our human personhood, not by personhood in its divine form. In his dogmatics (ET *Christian Faith,* 1979), Berkhof then drew the appropriate conclusions, and went over to a unitarian pneumatology. Like Israel, Jesus Christ is God's partner in the covenant, and the Holy Spirit is the divine bond in this covenant between God and human beings. As the perfect partner to the covenant, Christ is both the work of the Spirit and the sender of the Spirit into the world. For Berkhof,

God the Father is "the One God, who is Person." The Holy Spirit is the mode of efficacy of the one God, who creates his human partner to the covenant in the Spirit-imbued Christ, and through Christ's mediation draws human beings into this divine covenant.

Berkhof's sequence of ideas is consistent, and makes it clear that to surrender the personhood of the Holy Spirit does not result merely in the dissolution of the doctrine of the Trinity. It leads to the dissolution of Christology as well. Trinity turns into binity, and binity becomes monism. All that is left is the divine monarch of the world.

We have to thank Heribert Mühlen, on the Catholic side, for his endeavors to find a new foundation for the personhood of the Spirit.[13] After Karl Barth, Karl Rahner too, in German Catholic theology, had departed from the concept of person in the doctrine of the Trinity, on the grounds that in modern times this term has become open to misunderstanding. He talked instead about "One God in three distinct modes of subsistence."[14] But both Barth and Rahner misunderstood the modern concept of person because they interpreted it individualistically. The modern philosophical personalism of [J. C. F.] Hölderlin, [Ludwig] Feuerbach, [Martin] Buber, [Ferdinand] Ebner, and others defines person as "primal distance and relationship" (Buber's phrase). To be a person means "being-in-relationship." These thinkers did not see even "subjectivity" in isolation, but viewed it in the social network of "intersubjectivity." Mühlen is one of the first to draw on these conceptual possibilities in order to develop a "personalist" doctrine of the Trinity in which "person," "relation," and "sociality" are used as complementary terms. If the Father is the divine "I," then the Son is the divine "THOU," and the Holy Spirit, as the bond of love and peace between the two, is the divine "WE."

This is an interesting conceptual attempt, but it has limitations. For the divine "WE" has no inward relation such as the divine "I" and "THOU" have to one another; it merely represents the community of the two outwardly. It therefore still has to look for its personal counterpart. What exists in God is really a binity, which merely appears outwardly as a unity, thus representing a trinity. This is a modern personalistic variant of the Western doctrine of the Trinity, according to which the Spirit "proceeds from the Father and the Son." It does not yet provide a new starting point for trinitarian doctrine itself. Like the Western trinitarian doctrine that follows Augustine, this attempt too shows its weakness in its pneumatology.

Over against Berkhof's modalism and Mühlen's personalism, I shall try here to develop *a trinitarian pneumatology* out of the experience and theology of the Holy Spirit.

The Personhood of the Spirit

Source: Moltmann 1991; ET 1992:268–309.

A more precise discernment of the personhood of the Holy Spirit is the most difficult problem in pneumatology in particular, and in the doctrine of the Trinity generally. If we take the experience of faith as our starting point, then even in the New Testament it is already an open question whether God's Spirit was thought of as a person or a force. If we make the doctrine of the Trinity our point of departure, then the personhood of the Spirit is asserted rather than proved if, with Tertullian's principle *una substantia—tres personae,* the concept of person derived from God the Father is simply transferred to the Spirit, or if, for doxological reasons, the Spirit—as the Nicaeno-Constantinapolitan Creed declares—"together with the Father and the Son is worshiped and glorified." Simply to transfer like this a concept of person acquired elsewhere, obscures rather than makes apprehensible the special personhood of the Spirit. Consequently we have to reject any generalizing talk about the "three persons" of the Trinity. The Spirit is different from the Father and the Son. Recent feminist analysis of the anthropological model for the trinitarian concept of person has shown the androcentric impress of the "person" concept employed by Augustine, and then by Aquinas in the wake of Boethius. To define person as *rationalis naturae individua substantia* ("an individual substance rational in nature") certainly yields a concept reflecting the separated, no-further-divisible, self-sufficient masculine self of our Greek and Roman cultural history. But applied to the Trinity, it is at best applicable to "the origin of the Godhead who is himself without origin"—that is, the Father. But the Son and the Spirit exist *from* the Father, and even "the origin without origin" can ultimately be called "Father" only in his relation to the eternal Son.

It is true that in its later development of trinitarian doctrine, Christian theology has replaced this interpretation of "person" in terms of substance by a relational and perichoretic understanding, and has hence, in the anthropological correspondence too, prepared the way for a self rich in relation and sociality. But even this development has not yet arrived at the unique personhood of the Holy Spirit; it has merely socialized the Spirit relationally, so to speak, as "the third in the bond." Emphasis is then no longer on the divine Persons in themselves but on their relationality and their unique community. But then how are we to understand the person of the Spirit?

In this chapter we shall approach the personhood of the Holy Spirit without a previous concept of person, and we shall do so from two angles.

First we shall draw on the help of the metaphors with which experiences of the Spirit have been described; second, we shall try to think through once more the relations of the Spirit in its origin, and in the consummated Trinity. We shall start from what the Spirit *effects*, and shall combine this with that which the Holy Spirit *is*, in his constitutive relations to the Father and the Son.

§1 METAPHORS FOR THE EXPERIENCE OF THE SPIRIT

[Earlier] we used a whole series of metaphorical ways of describing the operation of the Spirit. We shall now try to sum up these systematically, in order to relate them to one another in such a way that they complement and deepen one another, though without excluding new and different experiences, and still other metaphors. For this, the dual complementarity for which models already exist would seem to suggest itself. But I shall try instead to arrive at a triadic complementarity, and shall gather together four groups, each comprising three different metaphors:

1. the personal metaphors: the Spirit as lord, as mother, and as judge;
2. the formative metaphors: the Spirit as energy, as space, and as Gestalt;
3. the movement metaphors: the Spirit as tempest, as fire, and as love;
4. the mystical metaphors: the Spirit as source of light, as water, and as fertility.

After that I shall try to discover the inner relationships in these metaphors—the relations between subject and force, origin and field of energy, force and space, presence and counterpart. I should like to find patterns for the realities and experiences of life which are expressed in the astounding and still wholly uncomprehended assertion that "God the Holy Spirit" is "poured out" on all flesh.

It is hardly necessary to stress that this is not an attempt to arrive at a systematic structure. No limits are set to the power of the imagination to discover metaphors and to devise ways of expressing experience. But we should remember that nowadays the nature images employed—air, light, water, fire, and the rest—are images taken from an impaired life. Ever since Chernobyl, human confidence in nature too has been shaken. In many places the air and the water are poisoned. If we then still take these images to express the operation of the creating, preserving, and life-giving Spirit of God, our intention is not romantic; it is critical and therapeutical. When we draw on images taken from biblical and Christian traditions, we are using metaphors derived from the pre-industrial era. We hardly ever choose metaphors drawn from technopolis and the experiences of "the media landscape" deriving from it. That too is not romantically meant. It expresses the search for primal experiences, and for authentic and personal experiences of life in which the presence of eternity meets us.

1. PERSONAL METAPHORS: LORD—MOTHER—JUDGE

The third article of the Creed calls the Spirit "the Lord who gives life" (the German version) or (in the more accurate English rendering) "the Lord and giver of life (*dominum et vivificantem*). Two metaphors springing from the experience of the Spirit are bound together so that they complement one another: the experience of liberation, and the experience of new life.

Behind the name "Lord" is the idea of freedom, which we find in 2 Cor. 3:17: "The Lord is the Spirit; but where the Spirit of the Lord is, there is freedom." Paul means the Spirit of the resurrection, which takes possession of believers here and now, freeing them from the compulsion of sin and the power of death because it now already mediates to them eternal and imperishable life. In this Spirit they find direct and impregnable access to God, and begin to live with God, and in God. So the name "Lord" has nothing to do with enslavement. Its context is liberation. This can only be explained from the first commandment: it is the exodus experience which is Israel's revelation of God. When the Spirit is given the name Lord, Christian experience of the Spirit is being set within Israel's history with Yahweh. The endtime outpouring of the Spirit at "Pentecost" is understood as a messianic exodus experience. In the Nicene Creed, this continuity is brought out by saying that it is the Holy Spirit "who spake by the prophets." According to the messianic understanding of Christians, Israel's "Lord" is the Holy Spirit, and "the Old Testament" is the testimony of the history of the Spirit for the future of the kingdom of God; and as this testimony, it is present here and now, and must be heard as determinative for the present. There is nothing "old" about it, as the name falsely suggests. If "Lord" is the name for the experience of liberation and for free life, then the name is misunderstood and brought into disrepute if it is interpreted in terms of masculine notions of rule. So it was good that this name should be complemented by the name of the One who gives and quickens life.

For Paul, it is the raised Christ who has become the "life-giving Spirit" (1 Cor. 15:45). For John, it is the Paraclete, who comforts as a mother comforts and from whom believers are "born anew" (John 3:3-6). With the Syrian Fathers and [Nicolaus] Zinzendorf, we have apprehended these experiences through the metaphor of the Mother of life. Human life is born, nurtured, and accompanied by the life of the mother. So it is useful to use feminine metaphors for corresponding experiences of the Spirit. The medieval expressions for the life-giving Spirit, *fons vitae* and *vita vivificans*, clearly point to this. The rebirth to life corresponds to the conquest of sin, with its separation, and death, with its lack of relation. Freedom and life are the two key facts in experiences of the divine Spirit. Freedom without new life is empty. Life without freedom is dead.

But living freedom and free life can endure only in justice and righteousness. In justice, human freedom ministers to life—the life shared by all living beings. In justice, human life struggles for the freedom of everything that lives, and resists oppression. So justice brings the two key factors freedom and life down to a common denominator, just as, conversely, freedom and life prepare the broad place which the divine justice is to fill, so as to waken the hunger and thirst for righteousness and justice in all created beings. Only justice puts life to rights, and defines the content of liberty through "the covenant of life." It is only in justice that life can endure. The experiences of liberation and rebirth through the Spirit are joined by an inward necessity to the experience of the righteousness and justice of God which itself creates justice, justifies, and rectifies.[15] The Spirit whom we are told "convicts the world of its sins" (John 16:8), does not come to condemn but to save (John 3:17). That is why "to convict of sin" becomes at the same time the conviction of sin's forgiveness.

Because the Spirit is also called "the Spirit of truth," sin is thought of pre-eminently as the lie, the obscuring of reality, and the deception of other people which is also a self-deception. It is only in truth that life comes to rest on a firm foundation and becomes dependable. This is true for the victims in one way and for the perpetrators in another—it applies to the people who have been deceived in a different way from the deceivers. That is why we distinguished the victims' experience of God's righteousness and justice which creates justice, from the perpetrators' experience of God's atoning and justifying righteousness and justice, although the two things cannot be separated. The two facets of the rectifying justice belong together, just as perpetrators and victims were brought together by the lie, the deception, and the act of violence.

According to Old Testament ideas, to establish justice and to rectify are active functions performed by the judge, and this "judging with righteousness" is expected to be a final and universal act on the part of the Messiah (Isaiah 11), on whom "the Spirit of the Lord rests"; so it is appropriate to call the Holy Spirit "judge." In the New Testament the word used for the Spirit is the "Paraclete"—that is, the advocate and intercessor; but according to the Old Testament idea, the judge is the "savior" too, and his justice is a saving justice. In this sense the Spirit of God is invoked as "Savior."

These three experiences, then—the experiences of "being set free," of "coming alive," and of being made "just"—belong together and complement one another, making up the fullness of life in the experience of God; and in the same way the three names given to the source of these experiences also belong together and complement one another: the Spirit as lord, as mother, and as judge. Every countercheck will at once discover how one-sided the viewpoint becomes if any one of these facets is left out, or if one term is reduced to something different.[16] This reduction already appears in the German translation of the third article of the Creed: ". . . and in the Lord, the Holy Spirit, who gives life." The "Lord" becomes the subject of "giving life" whereas the Greek and Latin texts distinguish *between* the lordship and the giving of life. The German reduction robs the coming alive from the Spirit of its own special character, and suppresses the Spirit's motherhood. On the other hand, the opposite way of linking the designations is worth consideration: the Holy Spirit—the mother who liberates. Rebirth from the eternal divine life is also liberation from the separations of sin and from the fate of death. According to the logic of the metaphor, only female life is capable of communicating physical life in the literal sense, not a "lord" conceived of in masculine terms. The mother who gives life also frees the child for its own independent existence, and keeps that freedom alive through her nurturing commitment. The freedom of "the liberating lord," on the other hand, as the exodus motif tells us, is rather freedom from extraneous rule and self-imposed immaturity.

The use of masculine and feminine metaphors for these experiences of the divine Spirit open up different ways of access to human life. . . .

. . . Finally, it is striking that these three metaphors should trace back experience of the operation of the divine Spirit to determining subjects who are thought of in personal terms. It is true that "lord," "mother," and "judge" are functions, not personal names, but in each of them a transcendent subject is named for the efficacies, which are immanently experienced. Because the experiences are contingent and cannot be "acquired" or "made," the Spirit is ascribed subjective freedom: "The Spirit blows were it wills." The metaphors are always born out of inferences drawn from these experiences – inferences about the things which allow themselves to be experienced in these particular ways. The experience of freedom, which we have not "acquired" for ourselves, but which has "befallen" us, lets us infer the transcendent power of liberation. The experience of the new life given to us lets us infer the womb or source of life from which that new life has come. The righteousness which puts us right lets us infer the just Judge who has acted on us. But this means that these descriptions for the divine Spirit apply only to his subjective relation to what he effects; they are not applicable to the interpersonal relations in which he himself exists.

2. FORMATIVE METAPHORS: ENERGY—SPACE—GESTALT

I am giving the name "formative metaphors" to the descriptions of the divine Spirit as energy, as space, and as Gestalt, because these images are not talking about agents and their acts. They describe forces which impose a profound impress. We can observe these in nature too. Because they only express particular aspects of the experience of the Spirit in any given case, it is important to relate them to one another as complements. In themselves, they are even less able than the individual personal metaphors to express the operation of the divine Spirit adequately.

The experience of the divine Spirit as an *energy* and *vital power* goes back to the Hebrew *ruach* concept. This experience of the Spirit does not release those who are touched by it from this earth and their own earthly bodies, so that their souls can soar into the realms of spirits. It fills them with a new vitality entirely and wholly, body and soul. We sense in ourselves the personal dynamic given to us, and then perceive it in everything else that lives. The experience of this vital power is as protean as living things themselves; and yet for all that it is a *single* vital power, which has gathered everything living into a great community of life, and sustains it there. The community of Christ's people can be a model for this, since it lives in the diversity of its different charismata and energies, and is united in the fellowship of the one energy of the Spirit—it *can,* that is, be such a model, provided that it relates itself to the diversity and the unity of everything living in the cosmos, and does not separate itself, withdraw into itself, and make itself poorer than it is.

We are mentioning the image of the charismatic community of Christ here so that we may ask about the forms and configurations assumed by the divine Spirit's torrent of energy. Neither in physics nor in love does energy exist as a pure thrust towards life. Through their frequencies, the electromagnetic fields acquire symmetrical structures which transpose their times and spaces into vibrations. There is no such thing as formless matter. Electrons, atoms, molecules, and the higher structures are arranged in open systems. Open systems exist from the fluctuating exchange of energy. This does not mean that a calculable cosmos determines everything. There is chaos in nature too. Cosmos and chaos are evidently not merely destructively related to one another; they are creatively related as well. If we think about the personal levels, we find—in spite of all the dissimilarity—analogous energizing rhythms and fields of force in what goes on in relationships. What is "between" people on the emotional level is like a field of attraction and repulsion—an order that soothes us and does us good, and a deranging chaos. The reciprocity of an energizing stimulus and an irritating sense of derangement frees new energies and awakens unguessed-of vitality; and this inspires life with new forms of expression. Joy in other people can be "infectious." That is the *vita vivificans*, and ultimately speaking all human beings lead a *vita vivificata*, since life is stimulated life *and* stimulating life, in living community. The countercheck is easy. If in the dynamic field between people only repulsion is conveyed and only rejection is experienced, then life is diminished and impaired, because it is thrown back on itself. The vital impulses then turn against themselves or wither away.

The experience of God is closely bound up with the experience of life between human beings, because the one is mediated through the other, because most of the images for experience of God are taken from the sphere of human relations and, finally but not least important, because experience of God is given in, with, and beneath experience with other people.[17] To feel the closeness of the living God is to experience new vitality. To believe and sense the closeness of the risen Christ means that body and soul are lifted up by "the power of the resurrection." The mystics—especially the women mystics—have repeatedly described this closeness of God as illuminating and flowing waves of energy. Surrounded, flooded, and interpenetrated by divine streams of energy, body and soul awaken like flowers in the spring and become fruitful—that is, they themselves become life that gives life.[18] Jeremiah and John already described the experience of the Spirit in just this way: God is "the fountain of living water" (Jer. 17:13; John 4:14). If a person believes "out of his heart [KJV: out of his belly] shall flow rivers of living water" (John 7:38)—that is to say, people touched by the Spirit will pass on the energies of the life that gives life, and apparently not only from soul to soul, but through their bodies too. The bodily zones that radiate energy are the glowing face, the shining eyes, the speaking mouth, the play of features, and the gestures which show affection and commitment. It is these which supply and charge the metaphors for the life-giving, stimulating, and electrifying closeness of God in the Spirit.

If it is to develop, every life needs its corresponding *living space*. Vital power and energy are not enough by themselves. That is why the creation story already tells us that spaces for living were prepared first of all, before living things were created and put into them—the spaces of heaven and earth, air, land, and water. The living spaces are the outward sides. They provide the spheres and "elbow-room" for the different living things, and are just as important as the living things themselves. Indeed living things can even be viewed as the inner side of the spaces, and as the bodies that move in them—their embodiment, as it were. Modern, atomizing, and individualizing thinking has viewed these living spaces as subsidiary, or has disregarded them, the intention being to integrate other living things into our own living space—the space of human beings—so that they can be utilized for human purposes. But anyone who destroys the living spaces of other living things destroys these things themselves, by destroying their chances for living. The progressive destruction of nature by modern society makes this as obvious as the "burnt earth" strategy used in modern warfare. Economic competition too can mean disposing of people by "cutting the ground" from under their feet. These negative examples show the importance of living space for the existence and development of the living thing. Between people it is essential to concede personal liberty. This liberty is given to children when parents withdraw—it is given through the trust which links affection with respect—it is given in the love whose desire is to set free, not to possess. In the warp and weft of social relationships we find the freedom to move freely, and in these free spaces we discover our potentiality for development. The free spaces sustain our freedom, and invite us to our full unfolding. In a merely competitive society, which guarantees personal liberty but offers no free spaces, personal liberty degenerates into a wolf-like, predatory liberty, and into the "liberty" of the unemployed and homeless. That is the misery of a "free world" which doubtless respects subjective liberties, but not the free spaces in social life.

Experience of God is bound up with these experiences between people in many different ways. According to Israel's seminal experience, experience of God means experiencing liberation from slavery in the exodus, and experiencing the promised land into which it entered: "Now the Lord has made room for us, and we shall be fruitful in the land" (Gen. 26:22). There is no liberation without the land of liberty. There is no liberation without the day of liberty, which is the Sabbath. Even the personal experience of God uttered in the Psalms embraces freedom from these two sides: "Thou hast set my feet in a broad place" (Ps. 31:8). The divine Spirit is experienced as the Lord who sets free, and as the free space in which "there is no more cramping." That is why it can also be said that "Thou encompasseth me from every side" (Ps. 139:5); and people who have this experience know that they are kept safe and set free in the broad place of the Spirit in which they can breathe deeply and unfurl their potentialities.

Out of the energies of life, and in the free spaces of life, the multifarious *configurations of life* come into being. A configuration or Gestalt is "minted form which takes shape as it lives," to use a phrase of Goethe's. In its Gestalt, the inward and the outward sides of a living being arrive at equilibrium. The contours of a Gestalt restrict, but its frontiers are open, communicative frontiers. That is why the individual configurations of life build communities for living with other living things, through an exchange of energy that sustains the life of them all. The wealth of species in nature, and the wealth of configurations in the species, show the wealth of possibilities in life itself.

In the human sphere, the individual Gestalt is made possible and given its impress by inner genetic conditions and by the frame of reference imposed by ecology and cultural history. Defined more closely, it is social conditions, and in particular the individual biography, which form the configuration of our lives. In the personal sphere, the important thing is always the way in which we mediate between our expectations of life and our experiences of life. The configuration or Gestalt of our body, soul, and character is an expression of all the conditions we have mentioned, and yet in all these things the Gestalt is something unmistakably individual, and undeducible from the factors that contribute to it.

Experience of life in the experience of God also gives us form or Gestalt. If the experience of God is linked with life in the community of Christ, then it is never a general religious feeling or merely what Schleiermacher called "a feeling and taste for the infinite." The discipleship of Christ is a practical, personal way of living. On this path of discipleship we are "formed" by God's Spirit—that is we are "made like in form" to Christ, the "first-born" of God's children (Rom. 8:29). We are "conformed" to his messianic life and his healing, radiating, and loving way of living. We are conformed to his path of suffering in our conflicts with the powers of destruction. In his Spirit we already participate here and now in his resurrection, "as dying, and behold we live" (2 Cor. 6:9), and expect one day to be made "like in form to his glorious body" (Phil. 3:21). Dietrich Bonhoeffer called this "Christ's taking form in us."[19] We would add: it comes about through the operation and guidance of the Holy Spirit.

Experience of the Spirit is experience of the divine life, which makes our human life something truly living. That is why when we talk about the Spirit as vital energy, as living space, and as the Gestalt of every community for living, these metaphors belong together. No one of them is enough by itself, but taken together they tell us something about the mystery of life—created life, life-giving life, and holy life. We can only talk about this life in metaphors such as these, because we are in it, and it is in us, and it is inexhaustible as long as we are here.

3. MOVEMENT METAPHORS: TEMPEST—FIRE—LOVE

The early Christian experience of Pentecost is presented with metaphors about the rushing of a great wind, and a flaming fire: "And suddenly a sound came from heaven like the rushing of a mighty wind, and it filled all the house, and there appeared to them tongues as of fire . . . and they were all filled with the Holy Spirit and began to proclaim in other tongues, as the Spirit gave them utterance" (Acts 2:2-4). I am calling these metaphors *movement metaphors* because they express the feeling of being seized and possessed by something overwhelmingly powerful, and the beginning of a new movement in ourselves. They describe a movement that sweeps people off their feet, which possesses and excites not only the conscious levels but the unconscious depths too, and sets the men and women affected themselves on the move towards unsuspected new things. Deeply moved, we ourselves move, and go out of ourselves. The primal image is the Pentecost story, which tells how the experience of the Spirit turns a crowd of Jesus' intimidated disciples into free witnesses to Jesus Christ, apostles of the gospel who carry the tidings "to the ends of the earth" (Acts 1:8). I am relating the movement metaphors of tempest and fire to the experience of the life-affirming, life-giving love of God—that is, to the presence of the Holy Spirit.

The image of the *tempest* picks up once more the original meaning of Yahweh's *ruach*. The divine is the living compared with the dead, and what is moving compared with the things that are petrified and rigid. God's Spirit is the breath of God's life, which gives life to human beings and animals. In the Old Testament, experiences of God are often presented with pictures of the rushing of wind or water. "Thou makest the winds thy messengers, fire and flame thy ministers" (Ps. 104:4). "And behold, the glory of the God of Israel came from the east; and the sound of his coming was like the sound of many waters; and the earth shone with his glory" (Ezek. 43:2). Elijah's experience of God on Mount Horeb is described in 1 Kings 19:11ff. with the help of all the natural elements: a mighty wind went before the Lord, tearing apart the mountains and breaking the rocks asunder. Then came earthquake and fire "but the Lord was not in them." After the fire came "the voice of a hovering silence" (Buber's translation). When Elijah heard that, he covered his face and came forward and the Lord spoke to him. It is a comparable experience of God, which the early Christian Pentecost story describes with "the sound from heaven like the rushing of a mighty wind."

From time immemorial, *fire* has been associated in many religions with the experience of God. It is especially central in Zoroaster. In the Old Testament, fire often accompanies the supernatural visions of God's glory. People experience the divine light like a devouring fire. For Moses, the burning bush which was not consumed was the sign of the presence of the holy God (Exod. 3:2). God went before the wandering people in a cloud by day and in a pillar of fire by night (Num. 9:15). The cloud in the form of fire covered the tabernacle, which was God's presence in the exodus. If we are eager about something we say that we are "fired" with enthusiasm. Like fire, enthusiasm "kindles" enthusiasm. Fire warms us, and we pass on the warmth. It lights us up, and we begin to shine. It consumes us, and we become a consuming flame for other people.

God's essential nature itself is described as a "devouring fire" (Deut. 4:24), for he is a *passionate God*.[20] His "jealous wrath" is like fire (Ps. 79:5; Ps. 89:46; Zeph. 1:18; Heb. 12:29). The awesome and mysterious God is graphically described in Ps. 18:8: "Smoke went up from his nostrils, and devouring fire from his mouth; glowing coals flamed forth from him." The God personified in these tremendous terms is the One who frees men and women from the fetters of hell and death. When the fire is called a "devouring fire," it is describing *God's wrath*. But this wrath of God's is not the antithesis of his love. It is nothing other than his love itself, repulsed and wounded. It is not that the passionate love for the life of what he has created, and for his human children, is now transformed into deadly anger. On the contrary, this love assumes the form of such anger so that it may remain love. Only the withdrawal of God from his creation would be deadly. But his anger contains within itself his persevering and enduring love, and in his judgment is his grace. That is why in "the devouring fire" of his anger the ardor of his love is manifested and experienced.

According to the Pentecost experience, the "flaming fire" of the Holy Spirit makes those it touches incandescent in the presence of God. According to Luke 12:49, Jesus came "to cast fire upon the earth"; but this does not mean the apocalyptic fire that consumes the world. It means the dawn of the kingdom of God, through the outpouring of the Holy Spirit on all flesh. This is what the messianic promise put into the mouth of John the Baptist is talking about too: "He will baptize you with the Holy Spirit and with fire" (Matt. 3:11; Luke 3:16, following Mal. 3:2-3). It is the fire of purification in which everything is reforged: an image for the new creation of the world.

The images of the tempest and the raging fire are also images for the experience of the *eternal love* which creates life and energizes it from within, so that life can live. Why is love "strong as death"? Because "its embers are fiery" and it can itself be called "a flame of the Lord" (Song of Sol. 8:6). If human love can become an experience of God, then the experience of God can be described as the experience of the divine love. Joy in one's own existence awakens in the experience of being loved. Human love and divine love are not identical, but the one can happen and confront us in the other. That is why human love becomes the "real" symbol for eternal love—real in the sense that symbol and the thing symbolized partake of the same essence. The pentecostal hymns beseech the Holy Spirit to "kindle a flame of sacred love"[21] in us. This shows how close the fire metaphor is to love, and to the Holy Spirit. Hildegard of Bingen wrote:

> Fire thou and Comforter,
> Life of all creation's life,
> Holy art thou, quickening all forms of being. . . .

She also directly called the Holy Spirit "fire Spirit" and "firebrand of love."

4. MYSTICAL METAPHORS: LIGHT—WATER—FERTILITY

The divine Spirit can be described as "flowing light," "living water," and "fertility," and I am calling these descriptions *mystical metaphors*, because they are concepts charged by mystical experience, and because they express so intimate a union between the divine Spirit and what is human, and between the human spirit and what is divine, that it is hardly possible to distinguish the two. We shall again relate these images to each other, so that they complement one another in a meaningful way. The simplest prototype for this meaningful interplay is the plant, which builds up its life and becomes fruitful from the light of the sun and the water of the earth, through its leaves and through its roots.

The *light* metaphor for the divine Being is age-old. It is especially stressed in the biblical writings, although the sun is never turned into a deity. "God is my light" (Ps. 27:1; Mic. 7:8; John 1:5). He is "the Father of light" (Jas. 1:17). Light is "the garment" that he wears (Ps. 104:2). "He dwells in unapproachable light" (1 Tim. 6:16). This tells us that the radiance of the divine glory is for creaturely being unendurable, and yet that all creatures reflect it, and that "the light of God's countenance" shining on them (Ps. 4:6), is their salvation. It is just this shining radiance of God's glory, which is said to have shone on the face of Christ (2 Cor. 4:6; John 1:9; 8:12). But the same is said of the gospel too, and of the people who witness to it through their lives (Matt. 5:14). And it is this same radiance that is attributed to the Holy Spirit, who illuminates believers so that they are "in the light," "walk in the light," and "abide in the light" (Eph. 5:8; 1 John 1:7; 2:9f.). Of course "light" means the enlightenment of the eyes, for it is with the eyes that we see. But what we see is only that which shows itself to us. That is why in our experience God is both the object of our knowing and its source: "In thy light do we see light" (Ps. 36:9). Because both the knowing and the knowledge proceed from God, in this context he is also called a "living fountain" (Ps. 36:9). This divine fountain of light illuminates the whole of creation, so that in its light we perceive what things are, and who we ourselves truly are. According to the medieval view, when the Creator floods his creation with his light, it appears as it is in his eyes, and we again see it in such a light that we can affirm and love it.

To say the same thing without metaphors: reality is characterized by a divine rationality, for it is created according to God's *ratio*, and his Spirit is within it. Our human rationality is capable of perceiving reality as far as this is intelligible. In the context of the created world, this means that created beings are able to know one another within their limits with their own rationality, because a divine rationality precedes them. If there were no congruences, however fragmentary, between the perceiving reason and the perceived reality, there could be no perceptions. But for finite human rationality, the reality of the world is of transcendent depth, since for human rationality the divine rationality is like "a light that can never be drained to the lees."[22] We have called this the concept of immanent transcendence.

But the divine light means more than merely perception through the eyes. It also means the streams of energy which we cannot see but sense, and which flood through us, transposing our life into vibrations and resonances. The divine light of the Spirit is not merely the cold light of rational knowledge. It is also the warm light of loving perception. According to Mechthild of Magdeburg, the experience of "the flowing light of the Godhead" is the beatific experience of the love of God. The divine love draws the Deity out of itself, so to speak, so that the energies of the divine life brim over from the Godhead on to created beings, to transfigure them and make them eternally alive. In this light and this love, the divine Spirit is so entirely all-embracing presence that he cannot be perceived as counterpart at all: we are in the Spirit, and the Spirit is in us.

The special thing about the metaphor of light for the experience of the Spirit is the fluid transition from the source of light to the emanating beam, and then to the radiance shed. It is one and the same light in the source, in the beam, and in the shining. The difference is in the emanation. It would take us no further to reintroduce at this point the distinction between Creator and creature, eternity and time, infinity and finitude. In pneumatology we have to take up the concept of emanation, which has been falsely denigrated as neo-Platonic; for through emanation, created being will be "deified,"[23] and God is glorified in what he has created.

The *water* metaphor is generally associated with the images of source, fountain, and well. What is meant is the water which comes out of the earth. Whereas the light metaphor describes the operation of the Spirit "from above," the metaphor of the source, spring, fountain, or well sees it as coming "from below." The union of light and water is a necessity of life. Where light, water, and warmth come together, the meadows become green and the trees blossom and bear fruit. In the Old Testament God himself is called "the fountains of living waters" (Jer. 2:13; 17:13), or "the fountain of life" (Ps. 36:9). "The voice of the Father speaks in the song of praise: 'I am an overflowing well which no one can drain dry,'" wrote Mechthild of Magdeburg. In the Greek doctrine of the Trinity, God the Father was called "the wellspring of the Godhead." Out of God, blessing and the energies of life spill over on to the whole of creation (Ps. 65:9); from this fountain people receive "grace upon grace" (John 1:16). In his conversation with the Samaritan woman, Jesus talks about the "living water," using the remarkable turn of phrase: "The water that I shall give him will become in him a spring of water welling up to eternal life" (4:14). The "well of life" is not in the next world, and not in the church's font: it is in human beings themselves. If they receive the life-giving water, they themselves become the wellspring of this water for other people. With this as background, Meister Eckhart painted the picture of God—the Spirit of life—as a great underground river which rises to the surface in the springs and fountainheads. The image of the spring of water has two other important aspects as well: the water of life comes "for nothing," and it is there "for all" who are thirsty (Isa. 55:1ff.; Rev. 21:6).

The bond between the image and the Holy Spirit is symbolized by baptism. People are born again "from water and Spirit" so that they may see the kingdom of God (John 3.5). If we do not take the birth "out of the water" to be a merely fortuitous, outward sign of the inward new birth, then the water of baptism surely means not merely well-water, but also the nurturing waters out of which the new-born child comes. The symbolism of the fonts used in the ancient church frequently shows this motherhood of the life-giving Spirit. But this certainly does not exhaust the symbolism of the well-water. It reveals its meaning to us in the degree to which we "thirst" for life and righteousness (Matt. 5:6).

There are many links in our language between light and water. We talk about sources of light and floodlight; about light streaming from a door or window; about light waves and ocean waves; and so forth. So it is just as appropriate to experience the operation of the divine Spirit as a "flowing" or a "flooding" light as it is to talk about the "outpouring" of the Spirit on all flesh. In this metaphor too, it is one and the same water, which wells up out of its source, allowing created being to live and be fertile. From time immemorial, the Roman fountain, which spills its water from basin to basin, has been an image for the doctrine of emanation.

Finally, the image of *fertility* emerges with inner logic from the link between the light and the water metaphors. As an image for the experience of God, it comes from the Old Testament: "I am like an evergreen cypress, from me comes all your fruit" (Hos. 14:8). The "tree of life" is a favorite expression in Hebrew. The divine Wisdom is a "tree of life" (Prov. 3:18). Hope that has been fulfilled and "a gentle tongue" are called "a tree of life" (Prov. 13:12; 15:4). According to the Yahwist's creation account, a single "tree of life" stood in the middle of paradise (Gen. 2:9). We meet this tree again at the end, as "the tree of life" which will stand in God's paradise (Rev. 2:7) and in the city of Jerusalem which is to come down from heaven (Rev. 22:2)—an evergreen and uninterruptedly fruitful tree which gives eternal life. In John 15, Christ is compared with the vine, and believers with its grapes: "He who abides in me, and I in him, he it is that bears much fruit" (15:5). According to Gal. 5:22, it is the Spirit whose "fruits" are "love, joy, peace, patience, kindness, goodness, faithfulness. . . ." Because life is conceived by other life, and because it is life that makes life living, fertility is the quintessence of life in all its livingness.

Hildegard of Bingen chose "fertility" as a way of expressing her experience of God, and she believed that the primal creation was always green and vital. It was only with the coming of sin that a kind of winter descended on creation, making it freeze and dry up. But when the Spirit of flowing light and living water is experienced, the eschatological springtime of the new creation begins, and the rebirth of the whole of life. So experience of the Spirit is the experience of a new vitality which finds its truth in community with the living God. In the experience of the Spirit, men and women sense the creative breath of God and wake up, like nature in the spring. What is eternal life? Meister Eckhart tells us that one of the attributes of eternity is "that in it Being and being-young are one."[24]

In the mystical metaphors, the distance between a transcendent subject and its immanent work is ended. The distinctions between causes and effects disappear. In the metaphors of light, water, and fertility, the divine and the human are joined in an organic cohesion. The result is a perichoretic interpenetration: you in me—I in you. The divine becomes the all-embracing presence in which what is human can fruitfully unfold. This implies a still closer relationship than the one suggested by the concept of emanation.

§2 THE STREAMING PERSONHOOD OF THE DIVINE SPIRIT

Starting from the metaphors used to express the operation of the Spirit and human experience of the Spirit, we shall now try to deduce the contours of his personhood. This is only a deductive knowing, derived from the operation experienced, not a direct knowing face to face. But neither is it a speculative intrusion into the depths of the triune Deity in an attempt to understand the primordial relationships of the Spirit who proceeds from the Father and radiates from the Son. In the primordial trinitarian relationships, the Spirit must appear simply as he is. There, it is of course true that only the Father knows the Spirit whom he breathes out, and only the Son knows the Spirit whom he receives. But in the efficacies experienced and in the energies perceived, this primal personhood of the Spirit is concealed from us, and we paraphrase the mystery of his life with many metaphors. And yet the operation of the Spirit is different from the acts of creation which we ascribe to the Father, and different from the reconciling sufferings which we ascribe to the Son; and from this difference in kind of his efficacy and his energies, the unique character of his personhood is revealed. If all God's activity in the world is pneumatic, and hence every human experience of God too (since according to the ancient "trinitarian order" the Father always acts through the Son/Logos in the Spirit, and the Son too acts in the name of the Father through the Spirit who rests on him), then in the operation of the Spirit we experience the operation of God himself, and all the metaphors used for the Holy Spirit are metaphors for God in his coming to us, and in his presence with us. An understanding of the unique personhood of the Spirit is therefore decisive for the understanding of God in general.

When we call the Holy Spirit Lord, Mother, or Judge, we are distinguishing between a determining subject and the acts which proceed from that subject. The subject remains transcendent to his acts. This means that he is also free in what he does, and his acts in their efficacies are experienced by us as contingent.

But then we of course have to differentiate. The "Lord" is truly transcendent. As the exodus happening from which he takes his name shows, he intervenes in Israel's history from outside, marvelously and "with a strong arm," saving his people from their persecutors. The "Mother" acts differently. She does not act outwards. She carries her child within herself, communicates her life to it, and gives birth to it with pain, so that she may hold it on her lap with joy. She is the archetypal image for the *vita vivificans*. The child's life grows in her, and then emerges from her. It is a giving of life in closest personal participation, with pain and with joy. The life that is born is life of her life and flesh of her flesh. It is a life differentiated from hers, a life of its own which grows up to autonomy; but the relationships are quite different from the relation between an author and his book, or an artist and his work. After it has been born, a life remains in life's relationships, whereas the work has to be able to exist on its own. Even in the case of the Judge who "establishes justice" for the wretched and "justifies" sinners through atonement, we found a profound inward participation through his solidarity and his atoning intervention; for it is out of the surrender of his own life that the justice emerges which gives new life to those without rights. Here the reciprocal operation of act and suffering can be clearly seen. The judge justifies by suffering the injustice. From this a shared life comes into being which becomes the source of inexhaustible vital energies. That, at least, is the way Paul experienced it: "If God is for us, who can be against us? . . . Nothing can separate us from the love of God which is in Christ Jesus" (Rom. 8:31, 39). The notion of the determining subject and the act is complemented by the concepts of the one who gives birth to life, and the one who puts life right.

The formative metaphors and the mystical images paraphrase the experiences of the Spirit with ideas of emanation and *perichoresis* because they stress the immanence of God and attach no great importance to the aloofness of his transcendence. They describe a presence of God in which God as counterpart is not yet—or is no longer—discernible. The experience of "flowing light" of course does not deny the transcendent source of light, and the experience of the "living water" does not forget the inexhaustible wellspring; but the important thing is not the distinction between source and river. The whole weight lies on the connection. In this experience of God, the Spirit is known as a "broad place" and a "flooding light" in which those touched by it can discover themselves and develop. But we cannot make whatever encompasses us an object without moving out of it. We do not see the eyes we see with. We cannot perceive the place where we are standing unless we leave it. The same is true of experience of the Spirit. The Spirit is in us and round about us, and we are in him. In the Spirit, God is for us pure presence. In order to perceive him as "object," we have to distance ourselves from his presence. But in the presence of the Spirit, can we perceive the Spirit as counterpart? Apparently the Spirit allows himself to be known as presence *and* counterpart, so that it is *only* in his presence that we can perceive him as counterpart at all: "In thy light do we see light."

There are analogies in the relations between people. A child grows *in* its mother and only become a counterpart *outside* the mother once it has been born and its umbilical cord has been cut. It experiences the mother first of all as "encompassing presence,"[25] before she becomes a "person" and a recognizable counterpart, and thus a finite human individual. Lovers experience each other as counterpart and presence. Their subjectivity "becomes soluble" in their relationships, and concentrates itself once again in their own individual being, and it is in this rhythm that their intersubjective shared life emerges. In mutual love they arrive at one another and themselves. They mutually come close to one another and to themselves. These experiences of personhood are different from the experiences of the solitary subject acting on objects, or from "the individual and his property" as Max Stirner puts it. In the flow between counterpart and presence, a personhood comes into being with permeable frontiers, in energy-charged relationships. Selfhood is not arrived at by way of demarcations and differentiations. It comes to its full flowering through the power of life-giving relationships. "Self-sufficiency" and "self-dispersion" are simply frontier marks. Between "closed" and "open" lie the wide fields in which impressions are absorbed and processed, and expressions are found for experiences.

If we take up this analogy as a way of understanding the experience of God, we then perceive the personhood of the divine Spirit in the flow between his presence and his counterpart, his energies and his essential nature. It is therefore no wonder that the people affected should talk about the Spirit as power and as person, as energy and as space, as wellspring and as light. This is not cloudiness in human thinking, or "anonymity" on the divine side; it is wholly appropriate.

When the Spirit himself "is poured out" on all flesh, this is a self-emptying through which he becomes present to all flesh in the force of his energies. Once men and women enter into his presence, in his light they perceive God, the fountain of light. According to the prophetic promise, the Spirit does not merely bring life and righteousness. He also brings the knowledge of God to all flesh. In the practice of Christian experience of the Spirit, this has led to a threefold prayer addressed to the Holy Spirit himself:

1. The *epikleses:* like most of the Pentecost hymns, these are simply prayers for "the coming of the Holy Spirit"—that is, they are pleas for his parousia, his all-comprehending presence: "*Veni Creator Spiritus.*" They are "Maranatha" prayers. In this plea for the presence of the Spirit, the petitioners open themselves for the influence of his energies, for a new heart, and for the renewal of the face of the earth (Ps. 51:10f.; Ps. 104:30). The cry from the depths for the life-giving Spirit is already a sigh of the Spirit itself, and is one of his first signs of life.

2. According to the ancient Christian order, it is in the Spirit that the Father is invoked through the Son, so that in this ancient Christian conception the Spirit carries prayers through the Son to the Father. What is important about this idea is that when people cry out in pain or in gratitude, they are then not just invoking a far-off God in heaven. Their cries are uttered in the presence of God on earth, and in their own situation. They cry to God, and experience that

it is the Spirit of God himself who cries out in them and who, when they fall dumb, intercedes for them with groans that cannot be uttered.

3. In the experienced presence of the Spirit, individual and particular petitions to the Holy Spirit are then uttered too—prayers for the outpouring of his gifts, and for his charismatic endowment of life. This too is expressed in the ancient Whitsun hymn: "Come down O Love divine . . ."

Boethius defined "person" as "*rationalis naturae individua substantia.*" According to what we have said here, we have to find a different definition for the personhood of the Holy Spirit, as it is experienced by men and women in its efficacies:

(*a*) It is not indivisible; it is self-communicating.

(*b*) It is not a "self-existence" (*substantia*), cut off from all relationships; it is a social being, rich in relation and capable of relation.

(*c*) It does not manifest rational nature alone; it is also the disclosure of the eternal divine life, as wellspring of the life of all created being.

This brings us to the following definition: *The personhood of God the Holy Spirit is the loving, self-communicating, out-fanning, and out-pouring presence of the eternal divine life of the triune God.*

§3 THE TRINITARIAN PERSONHOOD OF THE HOLY SPIRIT

. . . The nature of the Holy Spirit is perceived only in his relationships to the other persons of the Trinity, who are "of like nature." His trinitarian inter-subjectivity illuminates his subjectivity, because his subjectivity is constituted by his inter-subjectivity. In his trinitarian inter-personhood he is person, in that as person he stands over against the other persons, and as person acts on them. With this we enter a different level from the level of experience, efficacy, and the inference about the primordial Trinity drawn from the economic Trinity in its work for salvation. But can we enter upon this level at all? Do not all our attempts to explore even the very depths of the Godhead remain fettered by our existence and our modes of experience, and therefore bound to the revelations of God? But what then actually happens when we forget ourselves and in doxological ecstasy praise and glorify the triune God for his own sake? Are we not then departing from his operations and adoring his essential nature? What we revere and love for itself, rests for us in itself and exists in itself even without us.

Let us try to approach the inner-trinitarian personhood of the Spirit with all due caution about speculation and over-hasty dogmatizations. . . . We shall abandon the conceptual framework used hitherto—the pattern of essence and revelation, being and act, immanent and economic Trinity—because these dualities prove to be too wide-meshed a grid. Instead we shall work with the patterns of the *monarchical Trinity*, the *historical Trinity*, the *eucharistic Trinity*, and the *doxological Trinity*.[26]

1. THE MONARCHICAL CONCEPT OF THE TRINITY

The monarchical concept of the Trinity was developed preeminently in the West. It is meant to be applied to the economy of salvation, not to be used in an inner-trinitarian sense, as in the East. The starting point here is the event of the self-revelation (Barth's phrase) or self-communication (Rahner) of the One God: the unity of God precedes the triunity. It is a single movement in which the One God reveals himself through himself and communicates himself to men and women. This movement proceeds from the Father through the Son in the Spirit, and spreads out in creation though the manifold energies of the Spirit. The monarchical structure can be seen in all God's works: the Father always acts through the Son in the Spirit. The Father creates, reconciles, and redeems the world through the Son in the power of the Spirit. All activity proceeds from the Father, the Son is always its mediator, and the Holy Spirit the mediation. The Father is the revealer, the Son the revelation, and the Spirit God's revealedness, The Son is God's self-revelation and also his self-communication. As the Father's other Self, he is wholly related to the Father, and the same is correspondingly true of the Spirit. In this unified divine movement, the Spirit appears directly as "Spirit of the Son" and mediates through the Son as "Spirit of the Father." But he himself is nothing other than the efficacy of the Son and Father. The Spirit is gift, not giver. Consequently everything that happens from God's side happens in the Spirit, every divine efficacy is effected by the Spirit. The divine energies flow from the Spirit into the world. Understood, then, as "God's efficacious presence," no independent personhood can be perceived in the Spirit over against the Father or the Son.

According to the monarchical pattern for the Trinity, the "economic Trinity" (as is always stressed) is bound to correspond to the "immanent Trinity"—indeed must be identical with it; for if God is truth, then God corresponds to himself in his revelation, thereby making his revelation dependable. How else are people to trust God's promises unless God himself promises his faithfulness in history and unless he is in his essential nature "the faithful one"? For the sake of the dependability of revelation, we have to assume theologically that God is in himself as he appears to us: "God remains faithful for he cannot deny himself" (2 Tim. 2:13).

It follows from this that the "trinitarian deduction"[27] from the revelation which is experienced and believed finds just that in God which revelation presupposes. God is "beforehand in himself" (Barth's phrase; the English translation of Barth's [*Christian Dogmatics*] uses the phrase "antecedently in himself") what he is afterwards in his revelation. But what precedes revelation as its foundation is not "the immanent Trinity." If the doctrine of the Trinity describes only "the transcendent primordial ground of salvation history," then it must infer the transcendent "primordial ground" from the historical operations, and can naturally find nothing in the "primordial ground" that fails to correspond to salvation history. This, however, means that "the immanent Trinity" is related to "the economic Trinity," and identified with it. But if this is the conclusion, then there is in actual fact no "immanent Trinity" at all which could exist independently in itself. There is only a Trinity open and prepared for revelation and salvation. I am calling this the "primordial Trinity."

If in the history of salvation the Holy Spirit after Christ's cross and resurrection proceeds from the Father and the Son, or from the Father through the Son, then this cannot be any different in God as he was "beforehand in himself," or in "the transcendent primordial ground" of this event. If we infer the primordial *processio* from the *missio* of the Spirit that has been experienced, we find only the correspondence; but then we have not yet talked about the Holy Spirit as he exists in himself in his relation to the Father and the Son; we have viewed him only as he shows himself to be as "primordial ground" for salvation. But this means that the trinitarian inference does not take us outside the economy of salvation at all. We can infer the transcendent primordial ground, or God "as he is beforehand in himself" but this still does not bring us within reach of what is called the "immanent Trinity"; we still invariably arrive only at the Trinity which destines itself, and opens itself, for the economy of salvation. We always reach only the "God for us" and discern nothing of "God in himself."

In this monarchical divine movement we cannot know God directly in his essential nature, as God knows himself in his Word, and as the Son knows the Father. This is not due to God's inaccessibility. It is due to the power of the divine movement into which we are impelled or drawn when we experience God's self-communication. In this divine movement we have God at our back, as it were, and in front of us the world, as field for the proclamation and for acts performed in God's Spirit. God is the one, single, mighty subject. He is sovereign in his revelation. Even our knowledge of his self-revelation is determined by him, that is, through his Spirit—since he *permits* himself to be known to us, *gives* himself to be known, as German puts it. We might also call this monarchical trinitarian pattern the "identity model," because it stresses the experience of identity; God's essential nature *in* his operations, God's Being *in* his revelation, God's revelation *in* our perception of it, God's Spirit *in* us. But this is the model of a functional doctrine of the Trinity.

It was therefore quite logical that the monarchical concept of the Trinity should lead to the introduction of the *filioque* into the Nicene Creed. The Holy Spirit proceeds "from the Father and the Son" because in salvation history he is sent by the Father and the Son, and is experienced in this way by human beings; and his eternal *processio* in the "immanent" Trinity as transcendent primordial ground *must* correspond to his mission in the economic Trinity as this is experienced.[28]

At this point we shall not as yet criticize the logic of the trinitarian inference, but shall first of all, with its help, remove the *filioque* from the Nicene Creed again. For with the *filioque*, the Holy Spirit is once and for all put in the third place in the Trinity, and subordinated to the Son. But this makes it impossible to comprehend salvation history adequately. It is true that this order applies to the sending of the Spirit through Christ on the foundation of the resurrection, but it does not apply to Christ's own history in the Spirit. If Christ was conceived by the Holy Spirit, baptized with the Spirit, and ministered by virtue of the energies given him by the Spirit, then he presupposes the Spirit, and the Spirit precedes him. Christ comes from the Father in the Spirit. That is the truth of the synoptic Spirit Christology which in the course of history was driven out by the christological pneumatology of Paul and John. The relations in Israel's history with God cannot be seen in any other way either: it is through the liberating and guiding operation of the Spirit that Israel becomes God's first-born son.[29] . . .

. . . . The doctrine of the Trinity traditionally held in the Western church can also be interpreted as a doctrine about *the Trinity in the sending*, since for this doctrine "sending" is the quintessence of the relationships of the divine persons to one another and of their shared relationship to the world. "The Father is always only the sender, sending both the Son and the Holy Spirit. The Son can be sent, but only by the Father, whereas he for his part can also send, but only the Holy Spirit. The Holy Spirit, finally, cannot send in any way at all, but can only be sent—and sent both by the Father and by the Son."[30] From the discerned sending of the Son Jesus Christ, and of the Holy Spirit through Christ, the eternal origin of these temporal sendings is inferred. Just because the eternal origin is the origin of just these particular temporal sendings, the economic Trinity always reveals merely an eternal Trinity which is already turned in commitment towards the world. . . .

. . . . The history of the life of God, which communicates itself inexhaustibly and in unfathomable depth, is disclosed through the "sending" Trinity. But for that very reason, this "sending" Trinity cannot be the sole trinitarian concept of God to emerge from the contemplation of the history of Christ and from the experience of the Holy Spirit.

2. THE HISTORICAL CONCEPT OF THE TRINITY

The historical concept of the Trinity links on to the monarchical concept, transposing it from the vertical eternity-time relation to the sequence of the times of the Father, the Son, and the Holy Spirit in salvation history. It is only possible to talk about an "economic Trinity" if this is taken to mean the inner cohesion and dynamic thrust of all works of the Trinity in the economy of salvation. Although according to Augustine the *opera trinitatis ad extra sunt indivisa*, from earliest times the work of creating the world has been ascribed to the Father, the work of reconciling the world to the Son, and the work of sanctifying the world to the Holy Spirit. These "trinitarian works" do not stand side by side, without any relation to one another. They belong within the context of salvation history, for the work of sanctification presupposes the work of reconciliation, and both have the work of creation as premise. The sense of time in salvation history is aligned towards the future of that history—that is to say, towards the eternal Sabbath of the world in the kingdom of glory of the triune God: the work of creation is aligned towards the work of reconciliation, and the work of reconciliation is aligned towards the work of sanctification. The one thrusts forward to the other without supplanting it, and together they are all directed eschatologically towards the new creation of all things in the eternal kingdom.

We are indebted to Joachim of Fiore for the historical interpretation of the doctrine of the Trinity in its bearing on the economy of salvation.[31] His historical periodization of salvation history, and his eschatological vision of its perfecting shaped the Western interpretation of history, particularly its modern form. The modern faith in progress grew out of the messianic form Joachim gave to salvation history. Ever since [G. E.] Lessing, "modern times" have been viewed as the fulfillment of the "third kingdom of the Spirit" which history had prepared and heralded. This was the emotional thrust behind the Enlightenment. It knew itself to be the goal of history, and the revelation and solution of history's riddle. . . .

. . . Lessing was convinced that with the age of Enlightenment this future had come, and that he himself was its prophet. In the history of salvation, the law of the Old Covenant was succeeded by the gospel of the New Covenant, and this will be fulfilled in the kingdom of the Spirit, in which no one will have to teach the other because all will perceive the truth for themselves, and do what is good simply because it is good. . . .

. . . Joachim's vision of the movement of the Spirit which thrusts forward in salvation history grew up out of his study of the relationship between the New Testament and the Old. He discovered that the Old Testament outlines a history of promise which the New Testament neither fulfills nor abrogates, but endorses and expands. In this way he arrived at the conviction that in salvation history there was not only the one transition from "the old law" of Moses to "the new law" of Christ, as Aquinas taught, but that a further transition from the *nova lex Christi* to the *intelligentia Spiritus Sancti* was to be expected: "the knowledge of all truth." He associated with this expectation the apocalyptic hope for the coming of the *evangelium aeternum* before Christ's parousia; this, he believed, would bring Christians and Jews into the eternal kingdom. . . .

. . . The monarchical concept of the Trinity, according to which the Father always acts through the Son in the Spirit, and through the Spirit in the Son, describes *synchronically* what the salvation-history sequence of the kingdoms of the Father, the Son, and the Spirit depicts *diachronically*. History begins with creation and ends with the transfiguration of the world. It begins in the Father and is consummated in the Spirit.

3. THE EUCHARISTIC CONCEPT OF THE TRINITY

The eucharistic concept of the Trinity is the logical consequence of the monarchical form of the Trinity, for the experience of grace arouses gratitude, and where God is known in his works, creation's song of praise awakens. Thanksgiving, prayer, adoration, praise, and the silent sinking into wonder, proceed from the energies of the Spirit who gives life, are directed towards the Son, and go with the Son to the Father. Here all activities proceed from the indwelling Spirit, all mediation takes place through the Son, and the Father is purely the recipient of the thanksgiving and songs of praise of his creatures. . . . The monarchical concept of the Trinity has its place in *the sending*, for the proclamation of the gospel and the accomplishment of Christian obedience in the world; but the situation in human life for this other concept of the Trinity—its *Sitz im Leben*—is *the celebration of the Eucharist* and the life which itself becomes a feast because it has been filled with grace and happiness. . . .

If we look at the experiences of God which men and women find in his works, then the monarchical "sending" Trinity precedes the eucharistic Trinity. . . . But if we ask about God's intention in his work of creation, reconciliation, and redemption, then it is only in eucharistic form that the monarchical form of the Trinity arrives at its goal. For the intention of God's works is not that they should happen, but that they should awaken joy and thanksgiving, and the song of praise that returns to God. According to the first chapter of Genesis the completion of the works of creation, and hence their goal too, is the Sabbath of creation and God's rest; and in the same way the end of all God's works in salvation history is the eternal Sabbath in the kingdom glory—what Athanasius described as "the feast without end.". . . .

4. THE TRINITARIAN DOXOLOGY

The trinitarian doxology leads beyond these three conceptions of the Trinity. This doxology is touched on in the Nicene Creed in the clause about the Holy Spirit "who with the Father and the Son together is worshiped and glorified." Anyone who is glorified "together with" others cannot be subordinated to these others. He is their equal. "Worship and glorification" go beyond the salvation that has been experienced and the thanksgiving that has been expressed. The triune God is worshiped and glorified *for his own sake.* The trinitarian doxology is the only place in Christian practice in which—at least in intention—our gaze passes beyond salvation history to the eternal essence of God himself, so that here we can talk about a doctrine of the Trinity in which the "economic" themes play no part. . . .

. . . [T]he trinitarian doxology is the beginning of the seeing itself, for the seeing of God's glory is the goal of salvation history, and the trinitarian doxology anticipates this goal in the very midst of salvation history. . . .

In trinitarian doxology the linear movements end and the *circular* movements begin. This is objectively expressed in the co-equality axiom of the Nicene Creed: if the Holy Spirit "together with" the Father and Son is "at the same time (*simul*) worshiped and glorified," then the Spirit is seen in the perichoretic fellowship he shares with the Father and the Son, and this puts an end to his position as "third Person" in the Trinity; for "at the same time" permits no "pre" and no "post." Spirit—Father—Son are now no longer in the linear monarchical movement of God's self-communication to human beings, nor are they any more in the eucharistic movement of the self-communication of human beings to God; this is now the self-circling and self-reposing movement of *perichoresis.* . . .

. . . Trinitarian doxology does not put an end to the monarchical Trinity, the historical and the eucharistic Trinity; it completes their movements. That is why it can also be viewed as presupposition for the origin of these divine movements. Its underlying conception of the "immanent Trinity" must preserve the ideas in the other trinitarian conceptions. Even if it excels these, nothing can emerge in its own concepts which could contradict any of the other movements of the Trinity. . . .

5. IS THE FILIOQUE ADDITION TO THE NICENE CREED NECESSARY OR SUPERFLUOUS?

. . . Finally, *the trinitarian doxology* is paralleled by *the social analogy* of the triune God. The perichoretic unity of the divine persons who ek-sist with one another, for one another, and in one another, finds its correspondence in the true human communities which we can experience—experience in love, in friendship, in the community of Christ's people which is filled by the Spirit, and in the just society. The correspondences are called to life through the fascinating attraction of the triune God who rests in himself and revolves in himself. In the monarchical Trinity the unity of the three persons comes into being through the unified movement of *God's sovereign rule*. In the historical Trinity the unity comes into being through the direction of time, which thrusts towards *the future*. In the eucharistic Trinity the unity of the divine persons comes into being through the unified movement of *thanksgiving*. It is through the trinitarian doxology that we first perceive the immanent Trinity as it rests and revolves in itself, and whose unity lies in the eternal *community* of the divine Persons. The essential nature of the triune God *is* this community. The unity of God also appears as the community of the three Persons who exist with one another, for one another, and in one another. The Spirit who is glorified "together with" the Father and the Son is also the wellspring of the energy which draws people to one another, so that they come together, rejoice in one another, and praise the God who is himself a God in community:

> Let's get together and be alright,
> One love, one heart.
> Give thanks and praise to the Lord
> And be alright.[32]

Notes

1. Jürgen Moltmann, *A Broad Place: An Autobiography*, trans. Margaret Kohl (Minneapolis: Fortress Press/London: SCM Press, 2008), 347.

2. For literature in English, cf. Alasdair I. C. Heron, *The Holy Spirit: The Holy Spirit in the Bible, in the History of Christian Thought and in Recent Theology* (Philadelphia: Westminster/ London: Marshall, Morgan & Scott, 1983).

3. The first thrust in this direction can be found in Lukas Vischer, ed., *Spirit of God, Spirit of Christ: Ecumenical Reflections on the Filioque Controversy*, Faith and Order Paper No. 103 (Geneva: World Council of Churches, 1981).

4. Cf. Walter J. Hollenweger, *The Pentecostals*, trans. R. A. Wilson (London: SCM Press/ Minneapolis: Augsburg, 1972), which is still a standard work. Also Stanley M. Burgess and Gary B. McGee, eds., *Dictionary of Pentecostal and Charismatic Movements* (Grand Rapids: Zondervan, 1988).

5. Karl Barth and Heinrich Barth, *Zur Lehre vom Heiligen Geist*, Beiheft 1, Zwischen den Zeiten (Munich: Chr. Kaiser Verlag, 1930).

6. Paul Tillich is correct in this. Cf. his *Systematic Theology*, vol. 3: *Life and the Spirit* (Chicago: University of Chicago Press, 1963), 11ff.

7. Günter Altner, ed., *Ökologische Theologie. Perspektiven zur Orientierung* (Stuttgart: Kreuz Verlag, 1989); Philip N. Joranson and Ken Butigan, eds., *Cry of the Environment: Rebuilding the Christus Creation Tradition* (Santa Fe: Bear, 1984).

8. Cf. Allan D. Galloway, *The Cosmic Christ* (New York: Nisbet, 1951); Pierre Teilhard de Chardin, "Christology and Evolution," in his *Christianity and Evolution: Reflections on Science and Religion*, trans. René Hague (New York: Harcourt Brace Jovanovich, 1971), 76–95.

9. Elisabeth Moltmann-Wendel, *Wenn Gott und Korper sich begegnen: Feministische Perspektiven zur Leiblichkeit* (Gütersloh: Gütersloher Verlagshaus, 1989), following Dietmar Kamper and Christoph Wulf, *Die Wiederkehr des Korpers* (Frankfurt: Suhrkamp, 1982).

10. Thus Hans-Joachim Kraus, *Systematische Theologie im Kontext biblischer Geschichte und Eschatologie* (Neukirchen-Vluyn: Neukirchener, 1983), 449.

11. Vladimir Lossky, *In the Image and Likeness of God* (London: Faith, 1974), 92.

12. Yves Congar, *I Believe in the Holy Spirit*, trans. David Smith (New York: Crossroad/ London: Geoffrey Chapman, 1983).

13. Heribert Mühlen, *Der Heilige Geist als Person. In der Trinität, bei den Inkarnation und im Gnadenbund: Ich-Du-Wir* (Münster: Aschendorff, 1963).

14. Karl Rahner, "Der dreifaltige Gott als transzendenter Urgrund der Heilsgeschichte," in *Mysterium Salutis* II (Einsiedeln: Benziger, 1967), 317–401.

15. Cf. Moltmann 1985; ET 1985/1993:140ff. (ch. 6: "The Space of Creation").

16. Philip Rosato, *The Spirit as Lord: The Pneumatology of Karl Barth* (Edinburgh: T&T Clark, 1981).

17. John V. Taylor stresses this particularly emphatically in *The Go-Between God: The Holy Spirit and the Christian Mission* (London: SCM Press/Philadelphia: Fortress Press, 1972).

18. For Hildegard of Bingen the power of the Holy Spirit is *viriditas*, the power of greening. She called God "purest springtime."

19. Dietrich Bonhoeffer, *Ethik* (Munich: Chr. Kaiser Verlag, 1949), 23ff. (ET: *Ethics*, trans. N. H. Smith [London: SCM Press, 1955]).

20. Cf. Abraham Heschel, *The Prophets* (New York: Harper & Row, 1962), 247ff., who talks about the pathos of God.

21. Charles Wesley.

22. Josef Pieper, *Das unaustrinkbare Licht. Das negative Element in der Weltansicht des Thomas von Aquin* (Munich: Kösel, 1953).

23. I understand "deification" here in the sense of Orthodox theology. Cf. Dumitru Staniloae, *Orthodoxe Dogmatik* I (Gutersloh: Gütersloher Verlagshaus, 1985), 291ff.: "The world is destined to be deified."

24. Meister Eckhart, *Schriften und Predigten* I (Leipzig: Diederichs, 1903), 164.

25. Thus Dorothy Dinnerstein, following Catherine Keller, *From a Broken Web: Separation, Sexism and Self* (Boston: Beacon, 1986), 118ff. I have derived suggestions from Catherine Keller for the following passage. On the concept of feminine personhood, cf. Carol Gilligan, *In a Different Voice: Women's Conception of the Self and of Morality* (Cambridge, MA: Harvard University Press, 1982).

26. See also Jürgen Moltmann, *History and the Triune God: Contributions to Trinitarian Theology*, trans. John Bowden (London: SCM Press/New York: Harper & Row, 1991), 68ff.

27. Karl Barth, *Christian Dogmatics* I, summary headings to §§10-12.

28. George S. Hendry, *The Holy Spirit in Christian Theology* (London: SCM Press, 1965), 42ff., in criticism of Barth.

29. *Wisdom of Solomon*, chs. 9–11.

30. Joseph Pohle and Josef Gummersbach, *Lehrbuch der Dogmatik* I (Paderborn: Schöningh, 1952), 464.

31. Cf. Moltmann, *History and the Triune God*, 91ff.

32. Bob Marley, "One Love."

7

The Coming of God

In his earlier, profoundly influential book Theology of Hope *(1964), Moltmann already made eschatology his theme. In this fifth of what he calls his "systematic contributions to theology," he turns to it once more. In his preface, he indicates the theme: that "the Last Things" are also the first, and are therefore the embodiment of God's promise—the promise of the resurrection of the dead and of the new creation of all things. This vista is behind the book's title: what we are looking toward is not an "Endgame," but the coming of God. The Last Things open up the vista of what is promised us in Rev. 21:1: the new heaven and the new earth. In his preface, he writes: "In God's creative future, the end will become the beginning, and the true creation is still to come and is ahead of us."*[1]

PREFACE TO *THE COMING OF GOD*

Source: Moltmann 1995; ET 1996:x–xvii.

In the end is the beginning: Eschatology is generally held to be the doctrine of "the Last Things," or of "the end of all things." To think this is to think in good apocalyptic terms, but it is not understanding eschatology in the Christian sense. To think apocalyptically means thinking things through to their end: the ambiguities of history must sometime become unambiguous; the time of transience must sometime pass away; the unanswerable questions of existence must sometime cease. The question about the end bursts out of the torment of history and the intolerableness of historical existence. To echo a German proverb: better a terrifying end than this endless terror.

Eschatology seems to search for the "final solution" of all the insoluble problems, as Isaiah Berlin indignantly remarked, playing on the phrase used at the Wannsee conference in 1942, where the SS decided for a "final solution" of the Jewish question in the camps of mass annihilation. Theological eschatology seems to present the "Endgame" of the theodrama World History. This was Hans Urs von Balthasar's view, when he took over this title as a legacy from Samuel Beckett. If we look back to the history of eschatology, we see it pictorially represented as God's great final judgment of the good and the wicked, with heaven for the one and hell for the other. Is the Last Judgment God's final solution for human history? Other people have dreamed about Armageddon, the final duel in the struggle between Christ and Antichrist, or God and the Devil—whether the duel be fought out with divine fire or with modern nuclear armaments.

Eschatology is always thought to deal with the end, the last day, the last word, the last act: God has the last word. But if eschatology were that and only that, it would be better to turn one's back on it altogether; for "the last things" spoil one's taste for the penultimate ones, and the dreamed of, or hoped for, end of history robs us of our freedom among history's many possibilities, and our tolerance for all the things in history that are unfinished and provisional. We can no longer put up with earthly, limited, and vulnerable life, and in our eschatological finality we destroy life's fragile beauty. The person who presses forward to the end of life misses life itself. If eschatology were no more than religion's "final solution" to all the questions, a solution allowing it to have the last word, it would undoubtedly be a particularly unpleasant form of theological dogmatism, if not psychological terrorism. And it has in fact been used in just this way by a number of apocalyptic arm-twisters among our contemporaries.

But *Christian* eschatology has nothing to do with apocalyptic "final solutions" of this kind, for its subject is not "the end" at all. On the contrary, what it is about is the new creation of all things. Christian eschatology is the remembered hope of the raising of the crucified Christ, so it talks about beginning afresh in the deadly end. "The end of Christ—after all that was his true beginning," said Ernst Bloch. Christian eschatology follows this christological pattern in all its personal, historical, and cosmic dimensions: *in the end is the beginning.*

That is how Dietrich Bonhoeffer took leave of his fellow prisoner, Payne Best, in Flossenbürg concentration camp, as he went to his execution: "This is the end—for me the beginning of life." That is how John on Patmos saw the Last Judgment of the world—not as annihilation, a universal conflagration, or death in a cosmic winter. He saw it as the first day of the new creation of all things: "See, I am making all things new" (Rev. 21:5). If we perceive it in remembrance of the hope of Christ, what is called the end of history is also simply the end of temporal history and the beginning of the eternal history of life. Christ can only be called "the end of history" in the sense that he is the pioneer and leader of the life that lives eternally. Wherever life is perceived and lived in community and fellowship with Christ, a new beginning is discovered hidden in every end. What it is I do not know, but I have confidence that the new beginning will find me and raise me up.

Because of this, I have deliberately avoided calling this book about Christian eschatology "The Last Things" or "The End of All Things," but have given it the title: *The Coming of God.* In God's creative future, the end will become the beginning, and the true creation is still to come and is ahead of us.

This eschatology, written thirty years after the *Theology of Hope* (1964; ET 1967), is entirely in line with that doctrine of hope. . . .

. . . . *The Adventure of Theological Ideas:* At that time I was trying to find a new fundamental category for theology in general: the theology of love in the Middle Ages and the theology of faith at the Reformation was to be followed in modern times by the theology of hope. My present concern is the doctrine of hope in a special sense—i.e., the horizons of expectation for personal life, for political and historical life, and for the life of the cosmos: What *is* hope for eternal life, and what is its effect? What is hope for the kingdom of God, and what is its effect? What is hope for the new heaven and the new earth, and what is its effect? What is the hope of glory for God himself, and what is its effect? In accord with the new fundamental theological category, I said then, with the young Karl Barth: "Christianity is wholly and entirely eschatology, not just in an appendix. It is hope, a vista, and a forward direction, and it is hence a new departure and a transformation of the present." Now I am concerned with the content of that vista and that forward direction.

In the last thirty years I have traveled a long theological road, a road with many surprises and many bends. Very little that actually happened was planned. But since the beginning of the "systematic contributions to theology" which I began in 1980 with *The Trinity and the Kingdom of God* (ET 1981), and continued most recently with the fourth volume on *The Spirit of Life* (1991; ET 1992), a certain program has emerged. I have followed up particular lines. For me these lines point, first, to a trinitarian thinking about God; secondly, to an ecological thinking about the community of creation; and thirdly, to an eschatological thinking about the indwellings of God in his people, in his Christ, and in our hearts through his life-giving Spirit. In this book on eschatology, the different horizons of eternal life, the eternal kingdom, and the eternal creation draw together to a single focus: *the cosmic Shekinah of God.* God desires to come to his "dwelling" in his creation, the home of his identity in the world, and in it to his "rest," his perfected, eternal joy. In 1985, in the doctrine of God (*God in Creation*), the goal and culminating point was God's Sabbath; in this doctrine about the future I am focusing attention on the goal of God's eschatological Shekinah, in which the whole creation will be new and eternally living, and every created thing will with unveiled face arrive at its own self. In my Christology, *The Way of Jesus Christ*, I used messianic dimensions, and in my pneumatology, *The Spirit of Life*, I came back to the vitality of Yahweh's *ruach*; so it is easy to see how much Israelite and present Jewish thinking has influenced me, and how profoundly. For this I should like to mention with particular gratitude Ernst Bloch and Franz Rosenzweig.

None of us are given hope just for ourselves. The hope of Christians is always hope for Israel too; the hope of Jews and Christians is always hope for the peoples of the world as well; the hope of the peoples of the world is always also hope for this earth and everything that lives in it. And hope for the whole community of creation is ultimately hope that its Creator and Redeemer will arrive at his goal, and may find in creation his home.

Theological Method: Suggestions in a Community: I am often asked about my theological method, and seldom provide an answer. At a time when so many colleagues are concerned solely with questions of method, what interests me are theological ideas, and their revision and innovation. There is a personal reason for this, among other things. As a child I underwent no very profound Christian socialization, but grew up with the poets and philosophers of German Idealism. When I was forced to become a most unhappy soldier, at the end of 1944, I took with me Goethe's poems and his *Faust*, and Nietzsche's *Zarathustra*.

I only acquired a Bible when one was given me by an American chaplain, in a prisoner-of-war camp in Belgium, and it was there that I began to read it for the first time. Since the moment when I began to study theology (first in England, in the prisoner-of-war camp at Norton, near Nottingham, and then, from 1948, in Göttingen) everything theological has been for me marvelously new. I have first to discover everything for myself, and understand it, and make it my own. Right down to the present day, theology has continued to be for me a tremendous adventure, a journey of discovery into a, for me, unknown country, a voyage without the certainty of a return, a path into the unknown with many surprises and not without disappointments. If I have a theological virtue at all, then it is one that has never hitherto been recognized as such: curiosity.

I have never done theology in the form of a defense of ancient doctrines or ecclesiastical dogmas. It has always been a journey of exploration. Consequently my way of thinking is experimental—an adventure of ideas—and my style of communication is to suggest. I do not defend any impersonal dogmas, but nor do I merely express my own personal opinion. I make suggestions within a community. So I write without any built-in safeguards, recklessly as some people think. My own propositions are intended to be a challenge to other people to think for themselves—and of course they are a challenge to objective refutation too. Theologians also belong to the *communio sanctorum*, the communion of saints, provided that the true saints are not merely justified sinners but accepted doubters too, thus belonging just as much to the world as to God.

Theology is a community affair. Consequently theological truth takes the form of dialogue, and does so *essentially,* not just for the purposes of entertainment. There are theological systems which are not only designed to be non-contradictory in themselves, but aim to remain undisputed from outside too. They are like fortresses which cannot be taken, but which no one can break out of either, and which are therefore starved out. I have no desire to build any such fortress for myself. My image is the exodus of the people, and I await theological Reed Sea miracles. For me theology is not church dogmatics, and not a doctrine of faith. It is *imagination for the kingdom of God* in the world, and for the world in God's kingdom. This means that it is always and everywhere *public* theology, and never, ever, a religious ideology of civil and political society—not even so-called Christian society. Some people think that I say too much theologically, and more about God than we can know. I feel profoundly humble in the face of the mystery that we cannot know, so I say everything I think I know.

The Aim: Integrating Eschatology: With this eschatology, I am aiming at an integration of perspectives which so often diverge: the perspectives of "individual" and universal eschatology, the eschatology of history and the eschatology of nature too. The traditional medieval, Protestant, and modern eschatologies concentrated on the individual hope with which the questions of personal living and dying were answered. What is going to happen to me when I die, at the Last Judgment and afterwards? Where can I find enduring certainty in my living and my dying? The salvation of the individual and, in the individual, the salvation of the soul, was so much at the center of things that the salvation of the body, human society, and the cosmos were pushed out on to the sidelines, or did not receive any attention at all. But if the Christian hope is reduced to the salvation of the soul in a heaven beyond death, it loses its power to renew life and change the world, and its flame is quenched; it dies away into no more than a Gnostic yearning for redemption from this world's vale of tears.

Ever since Augustine, "God and the soul" have gone together and, following his lead, people have put the fate of the soul at the center of the ultimate questions. There are two reasons for this. On the one hand, we have the well-known condemnation of the millenarian historical hope by the mainline churches. If there is no longer any historical future worth hoping for, all that is left is the vista of eternity, an eternity equally close to every time, and equally far off. But on the other hand, the Constantinian imperial churches condemned early Christian millenarianism only because they saw themselves in the Christian imperium as "the holy rule" of Christ's Thousand Years' empire. So every future hope for a different, alternative kingdom of Christ was feared and condemned as heresy. The completion of history was pushed out by the completion of the individual life in death. Universal eschatology lost all its relevance. If the church as the kingdom of Christ is the last thing in history, then all that can come after the church is the end itself. So universal eschatology was found only as an apocalyptic expectation of the end directed to the era after that symbolic thousand years of the church's holy rule. In order to bring individual and universal eschatology into a living relation to one another, therefore, the presentative millenarianism of the holy rule, the holy empire, and "the Christian era" must be dispelled. Hope as the embracing theological category has to be freed from the wreckage of Christian history.

We shall only be able to overcome the unfruitful and paralyzing confrontation between the personal and the cosmic hope, individual and universal eschatology, if we neither pietistically put the soul at the center, nor secularistically the world. The center has to be *God*, God's kingdom and God's glory. The first three petitions in the Lord's Prayer make this clear. What do we really and truly hope for? We hope for the *kingdom of God.* That is first and foremost a hope for God, the hope that God will arrive at his rights in his creation, at his peace in his Sabbath, and at his eternal joy in his image, human beings. The fundamental question of biblical eschatology is: When will God show himself in his divinity to heaven and earth? And the answer is to be found in the promise of the coming God: "the whole earth is full of his glory" (Isa. 6:3).

This glorifying of God in the world embraces the *salvation* and eternal life of human beings, the *deliverance* of all created things, and the *peace* of the new creation.

Christian eschatology has four horizons:

1. It is hope in God for God's glory.
2. It is hope in God for the new creation of the world.
3. It is hope in God for the history of human beings with the earth.
4. It is hope in God for the resurrection and eternal life of human people.

That is the *ontic* order of the different horizons of Christian eschatology. But because the *noetic* order is always the reverse of the ontic order of things, our perception has to begin, not with the cause, but with the effect. So in eschatology it makes sense to begin with the personal hope, then to advance to the historical hope, and finally to pass on to the cosmic hope, so as to end with God's glory for God's sake. The first effect of eschatology is personal faith. New life in this world follows. And out of that springs the hope for the redemption of the body and the expectation of the transformation of this whole world into God's kingdom. . . .

. . . Earlier, when I was writing on other subjects, I had a picture before me on my writing desk. And during my work on this eschatology of "the coming of God" I have again had a picture in front of me: It is the Angel of the Annunciation, by Simone Martini, painted in 1315 and now in the Galleria Uffizi in Florence. The angel is not looking back to the wreckage of history, as does Paul Klee's "Angelus Novus," which Walter Benjamin called the Angel of History. This angel of the future is gazing with great eyes towards the messianic Child of the coming God, and with the green branches in his hair and in Mary's hand proclaims the Child's birth. The tempest of the divine Spirit is blowing in the angel's garments and wings, as if it had blown him into history. And its meaning is the birth of the future from the Spirit of promise.

The Kingdom of God: Historical Eschatology

Source: Moltmann 1995; ET 1996:235–55.

§11 The Restoration of All Things

1. "The Last Judgment" and Its Ambivalent Outcome

The expectation of a Last Judgment has always had a particular fascination for the imaginations of Christians. In medieval churches, we see the final judgment represented on the outside portals and in pictures inside: on the right-hand side, angels carry the righteous away to the heaven of everlasting bliss; on the left devils drag the wicked into the hell of everlasting damnation; in the middle Christ sits on the judgment seat with the two-edged sword between his lips. In this great reckoning there are only two verdicts: eternal life or eternal death. Originally, hope for the Last Judgment was a hope cherished by the victims of world history, a hope that the divine justice would triumph over their oppressors and murderers. It was only after Constantine that Judgment—now orientated solely towards the perpetrators—was interpreted as a divine criminal tribunal where evildoers were tried, and was understood as the prototype of imperial judicial power.

The medieval pictures of judgment disseminated fear and terror in order that tempted men and women should seek comfort and salvation in the means of grace provided by the church. The Reformers disseminated distress of conscience in order to awaken justifying faith through the gospel. Is there any grace except that of the judge? Who expected of the Last Judgment the final redemption of the world from evil? The expectation of judgment was a threatening and intimidating message, not a joyful and liberating one. Because psychologically it has done so much to poison the idea of God. It is high time to discover *the gospel of God's judgment* and to awaken joy *in God's coming righteousness and justice.*[2]

> *Dies irae, dies illa*
> solvet saeclum in favilla.

Until 1969 this twelfth-century Latin sequence from the requiem Mass was sung during the liturgy for the dead between Reading and Gospel, and it can therefore still be heard in many famous requiems. It is probably "the most representative, the most culturally influential, and hence the most famous poem of the Latin middle ages."[3] The cathedral scene in Goethe's *Faust* is built up round it, its first, sixth, and seventh verses being interspersed there with an organ accompaniment. In books of Catholic dogmatics up to about 1960 the treatise on eschatology is constructed according to the sequence of ideas in this poem, and therefore treats first "the eschatology of the individual," with death, judgment, purgatory, and hell, and then "the eschatology of the human race, with the Last Day, the resurrection of the dead, and final Judgment."[4]

Protestant dogmatics really always inquire merely about the outcome of the Last Judgment. Is there a "double outcome"—believers into heavenly bliss, unbelievers into the torments of hell? Or are all in the end redeemed, all saved, and all things brought into the new creation? Behind this question is the question about God. Does God, as their creator, go with all his created beings into life, death, and resurrection—or does God as judge stand over against those he has created, detached and uninvolved, to pardon or condemn? How can the God who loves what he has created condemn not just what is evil, destructive, and godless in created beings but these beings themselves?

The question: "double outcome of judgment or universalism" is generally discussed as if it were already clear what judgment is, who the Judge is, and what the justice and righteousness is, according to which judgment is passed. But if Jesus is the judge, can he judge according to any other righteousness than the law which he himself manifested—the law of love for our enemies, and the acceptance of the poor, the sick, and sinners? Can the righteousness which the Last Judgment serves be any righteousness other than the righteousness of God which creates justice and redeems, the righteousness to which the law and the prophets testify, and which the apostle Paul proclaimed in his gospel as justifying righteousness? Does theology not involve the Christian faith in inward contradictions if what is expected of the great Judgment is something different from what God has revealed in Israel's history and the history of Jesus Christ? And what is the ultimate purpose of the Last Judgment? If Judgment is just God's great final reckoning with the sinners and the saints, then this Judgment would indeed be "the Last." Or does it serve revelation and the establishment of God's righteousness and justice among all people and all things, so that God can build his "new world" on lasting justice, and can therefore create for eternal peace? In that case the Last Judgment would not at all be "the last" that can be expected of God; it would only be "the last but one." "The last" would then be his kingdom, and the new creation of all things. Just as the first thing was not sin but the primal blessing given to creation, so judgment would then not be the last thing either. What would come last would be the final blessing of the new creation in which righteousness and justice dwells.

In this chapter we shall first discuss the biblical and theological arguments for and against universalism, and shall try to solve a problem in eschatology which has been unsolved ever since Origen and Augustine. We shall then inquire about the person of the Judge, and about the righteousness and justice which he is to create. Finally we shall ask about the history of his own sufferings, and shall discover in Christ's descent into hell on the cross of godforsakenness the most profound reason for the "confession of hope" for the restoration of all things.

2. THE RETURN OF THE DOCTRINE OF UNIVERSAL SALVATION

"Universalism," "apokatastasis panton," "universal salvation," or "the restorations of all things" are all terms for the most disputed question in Christian eschatology. It is an eschatological question. But theologically it can be decided only in the framework of Christology. The theologians of the mainline churches have always rejected these universalist doctrines and have condemned those who supported them. In his doctrine of salvation as an educative process, Origen wanted to see even the Devil ultimately redeemed; but he was unable to prevail. His doctrine was condemned in the patristic church, at the emperor's command. Augustine won the day with his idea that out of all the lost—the massa perditionis of human beings—only a limited number of the elect (numerus electorum) would be redeemed. For the Lutheran churches, Article XVII of the Augsburg Confession declared: "It is also taught among us that our Lord Jesus Christ will return on the last day for judgment and will raise up all the dead, to give eternal life and everlasting joy to believers and the elect but to condemn ungodly men and the devil to hell and eternal punishment. Rejected, therefore, are the Anabaptists who teach that the devil and condemned men will not suffer eternal pain and torment" (in the Latin version: "hominibus damnatis ac diabolis finem poenarum futurem esse"). The Confessio Helvetica posterior, Article XI, made a similar statement for the Calvinist churches. The Heidelberg Catechism, in answer to Question 52, adds a personal thought: ". . . to throw all his and mine enemies into everlasting pains, but to translate me with all his chosen unto himself, into celestial joys and everlasting glory."

It was only in the seventeenth and eighteenth centuries that the rejected doctrine appeared once more in Protestantism, and when it emerged it was neither out of the humanism of the Enlightenment, nor from the Anabaptist sects, but—together with the millenarianism that had been equally rejected—out of early Pietism. It was his own biblicism, not secular humanism, that convinced the influential Württemberg theologian Johann Albrecht Bengel (1687–1752) of the truth of the doctrine of apokatastasis. There is certainly final judgment, and heaven and hell, but everything serves only the consummation of God's universal kingdom. Consequently the torments of hell are not everlasting; they are aeonically limited. Once God is "all in all," there will be no more hells. Bengel's most important pupil, F. C. Oetinger (1702–1782), went on to develop both doctrines, millenarianism and "the restoration of all things," making the whole of eschatology subject to God's resolve in Christ "to unite all things in him, things in heaven and things on earth" (Ephesians 1; Colossians 1). If election is the beginning of all God's ways, then the restoration of all things is its goal and end.[5] In the Hahn Community in Württemberg "the restoration of all things" was held as "central doctrine." In the revival movement associated with Johann Christoph Blumhardt (1805–1880) and Christoph Blumhardt (1842–1919), universalism became "the confession of hope." The expectation of Christ's imminent parousia, experiences of the present powers of the Spirit in healings of the sick, and hope for the whole world: all these belonged together here.[6] The Blumhardt movement in Württemberg inspired the "religious socialists" Hermann Kutter and Leonhard Ragaz to combine hope for Christ's coming kingdom of peace on earth with active participation in the democratic, socialist, anti-colonial, and peace movements of the years before the First World War. They not only expected the final redemption of all human beings; they also looked for the restoration of all the things of nature in the new creation.

Karl Barth took the futurist orientation of his early theology from the preaching of the Blumhardts,[7] as well as his later trend towards universalism. It was the dispute which Barth's old adversary, Emil Brunner, waged with him about universal salvation or a double outcome of judgment which brought the discussion into modern German theology: "Barth goes far beyond all historical universalists. Scripture does not talk about universal reconciliation. On the contrary, it talks about judgment, and a double outcome of judgment: salvation or damnation. So the doctrine of universalism is the denial of judgment."[8] Paul Althaus tried to mediate between the viewpoints: "Christian eschatology cannot dispense with the idea of a possible double outcome of humanity's history, for Christ's sake and for the sake of conscience." "God's purpose with non-believers is a mystery." Theologically it is therefore necessary, said Althaus, to preserve: first the idea and fear of being eternally lost; second, trust in the providence of God which will put everything to rights. There follows from this, thirdly, that "We must think both thoughts, the idea of the double outcome and the idea of *apokatastasis*."[9] Gerhard Ebeling again follows Brunner when he says: "The Bible speaks unanimously about a double outcome of the final event, using the symbols of heaven and hell. . . . The idea of universal redemption, the *apokatastasis panton*, goes beyond what can be specifically said in the light of the situation before God, in favor of a harmonizing theory. What the end of evil will be is as hidden from us as is the explanation of its origin."[10]

Before we discuss this question biblically and theologically, we must be clear about the general doubts and objections on both sides:

If *universalism* is proclaimed, is the result not the light-minded recklessness that says: Why should I believe, and bother to lead a good and righteous life, if I and everyone else are going to be redeemed in any case? If we preach the redemption of all human beings, does the proclamation not really annul itself? Why is it necessary to preach what is going to happen anyway?

If *the double outcome of judgment* is proclaimed, the question is then: Why did God create human beings if he is going to damn most of them in the end, and will only redeem the least part of them? Can God hate what he himself has created without hating himself? If salvation or damnation depends on a person's faith and righteousness, is God not then making his Judgment dependent on the will of human beings, thus really making himself dispensable?

3. THE DISPUTE ABOUT THE BIBLE: PRO AND CONTRA UNIVERSALISM

In their dispute with Barth, Brunner and Ebeling appealed purely and simply to "the scriptures" or "the Bible," going on to reject the doctrine of universal salvation as speculative theology. Evangelical and fundamentalist theologians still argue in just the same way today. We shall first follow this argumentation, which claims to be "true to the Bible," in order to see more precisely what it is saying, though without differentiating historically between the testimonies of scripture.

The expression *apokatastasis panton* is used only in Acts 3:21, where it describes "the time for establishing all that God spoke by the mouth of his holy prophets from of old." What is meant is the fulfillment of God's promises, but not universal salvation. Over against this, Eph. 1:10 says: ". . . to unite all things in Christ, things in heaven and things on earth," and with it Col. 1:20: ". . . to reconcile to himself all things, whether on earth or in heaven, making peace by the blood of his cross." In the cosmic Christology of the Epistles to the Ephesians and the Colossians, not only all human beings and earthly creatures but the angels too—evidently the disobedient ones, since for the others it is unnecessary—will be reconciled through Christ. As reconciled, they will be gathered together under their head, Christ (who must here be understood as the personified Wisdom of Creation), and will thus be perfected. What is meant is nothing other than the restoration of all things, the homecoming of the universe in the form of what Irenaeus called the *recapitulatio mundi.*

The hymn extolling Christ in Philippians 2 also ends with the vision of the glorified universe in its peace and concord: ". . . that at the name of Jesus every knee should bow, in heaven and on earth and under the earth, and every tongue confess that Jesus Christ is Lord, to the glory of God the Father" (2:10f.). If Christ is made Pantocrator, nothing in his kingdom can be lost, all his enemies will be put under his feet (1 Cor. 15:25), so that he can hand over to God the rule now consummated as his kingdom, that God may be "all in all" (1 Cor. 15:28). The great chapter on the resurrection, 1 Corinthians 15, makes no mention at all of a judgment with a double outcome. Paul builds up his Adam-Christ typology on the same pattern: "As one man's trespass led to condemnation for all men, so one man's act of righteousness leads to acquittal and life for all men" (Rom. 5:18), and consequently: "As in Adam all die, so also in Christ shall all be made alive" (1 Cor. 15:22). This universalism embraces "Jews and Gentiles" without abolishing the difference between them, or reducing it to uniformity: "God has consigned all men to disobedience, that he may have mercy upon all" (Rom. 11:32).

On the other hand the passages that talk about faith and disbelief do talk about a *double outcome of judgment*, especially in Matthew's Gospel: Matt. 7:13f. distinguishes "the way that leads to life" from "the way that leads to destruction." Matt. 12:32 says that "the sin against the Holy Spirit" will not be forgiven, "either in this age or in the age to come." In Mark 16:16 we are told that he who believes and is baptized will be saved; but he who does not believe will be condemned." Matthew 25 tells the parable of "the wise and foolish virgins" and then presents the vision of the great Judgment of the Son of man (vv. 31-46). To those on his left, the Son of man–Judge of the world says: "Depart from me, you cursed, into the eternal fire prepared for the devil and his angels." To those on his right he says: "Come, O blessed of my Father, inherit the kingdom prepared for you from the foundation of the world." The decision is made on the basis of what they have done for the poor and the hungry, for, says the Judge of the world: "What you did to one of the least of these my brethren, you did to me." Mark 9:45 also talks about "hell," and Mark 9:48 speaks of the everlasting fire that "is not quenched." According to Luke 16:23, the rich man, Dives, goes to "Hades, torment," whereas the poor man Lazarus is "in Abraham's bosom." The Gospel of John identifies faith with eternal life and disbelief with damnation: "He who believes in the Son has eternal life: he who does not believe in the Son shall not see life, but the wrath of God rests upon him" (3:36). The person who does not believe "will perish" (3:16). Paul also talks about a state of "being lost" (*apoleia*) in Phil. 3:19; 1 Cor. 1:18; 2 Cor. 2:15; and elsewhere.

Universal salvation *and* a double outcome of judgment are therefore both well attested biblically. So the decision for the one or the other cannot be made on the ground of "scripture." If one presupposes that scripture does not contradict itself, because the word of God to which it testifies is inerrant, one can then try to resolve the contradiction in the sense of the one side or the other.

Let us begin with the *resolution in the sense of the first side,* or postulate: There is indeed damnation, but is it eternal? The Greek word *aionios,* like the Hebrew word *olam,* means time without a fixed end, a long time, but not time that is "eternal" in the absolute, timeless sense of Greek metaphysics. Consequently there are plurals *olamim* or *aiones,* which there cannot be for timeless eternity, because timeless eternity exists only in the singular. If damnation and the torments of hell are "eternal," they are then aeonic, long-lasting, or endtime states. Only God himself is "eternal" in the absolute sense, and "unending" in the qualitative sense. According to Mark 9:49, hell-fire is a purifying fire—a corrective punishment. Salvation and damnation are a-symmetrical, according to Matthew 25: for the blessed, the kingdom has been prepared "from the foundation of the world"; but fire has not been prepared for the damned "from the foundation of the world," so it does not have to last until the end of the world either. Paul and John talk about "being lost" only in the present tense, never in the future. So unbelievers are "given up for lost" temporally and for the endtime, but not to all eternity. This being so, we can conclude with Walter Michaelis that what is said about judgment, damnation, and "everlasting death" is aeonic, and belongs to the endtime; it is not meant in an "eternal" sense. For eschatologically, against the horizon of the ultimate, it is penultimate. The ultimate, the last thing is: "Behold, I make *all things* new" (Rev. 21:5). In the new creation of heaven and earth there will be no more death, neither "natural" death, nor "the death of sin," nor "everlasting death." "However strong or weak the testimony to universalism may be, it is the sole information which scripture offers us about the ultimate goal of God's salvific plan."[11]

Let us try to find *the resolution in the sense of the second side,* or postulate. God certainly wants all human beings to be helped, but do they all really want to let themselves be helped? The biblical message is the proclamation of the gospel, with the goal of faith, but it is not a theory about the divine plan of salvation in world history and its possible end. We are supposed to decide, not to speculate. But if we speculate, we have to ask whether God's grace is still free grace if at the end all human beings are bound to be saved. Does this not make the decision for faith superfluous? Universalism makes God's grace cheap grace. It imposes bounds on God's freedom. It dissipates the finality of faith's decision.

But "it is appointed for men to die once, and after that comes judgment" (Heb. 9:27). If salvation is tied to faith, then all the universal statements in the New Testament must be related to God's good salvific intention, but not to the outcome of history. What is meant is the possibility of redemption, not its inevitable actuality. It is true that the word *aionios* does not mean the absolute eternity of God, but it does mean the irrevocability of the decision for faith or unbelief. Faith's experience that in the presence of the call to decision one is standing before God has as its corollary the finality of human decision. Consequently "the double outcome" is the last word of the Last Judgment.

4. THE THEOLOGICAL ARGUMENT ABOUT UNIVERSAL SALVATION OR THE DOUBLE OUTCOME OF JUDGMENT

Following a second train of thought let us ask about the theological arguments for the one side and the other.

What speaks against a double outcome of Judgment is the experience that God's grace is more powerful than human sin. "But where sin increased, grace abounded all the more" (Rom. 5:20). In God himself love outbalances wrath, for God is angered by human sin not *although he* loves human beings but *because* he loves them. He says No to sin because he says Yes to the sinner. He says a temporal No because in eternity he has said Yes to human beings, as the beings he has created, and his image. He judges the sins of the world so as to save the world. "The Lord kills in order to bring to life. He brings down to hell and out again" (1 Sam. 2:6). It is not his anger, which is everlasting; it is his grace: "His anger is but for a moment, and his favor is for a lifetime" (Ps. 30:5). God hates the sin, not the sinner; he loves the sinner, not the sin, said Augustine. God's judgment separates the sin from the person, condemns the sin and gives the person of the sinner a free pardon. The anger with which the righteous God condemns the unrighteousness, which makes people cast themselves and this world into misery, is nothing other than an expression of his passionate love.

For our problem, this means that the historical particularism of the divine election and rejection must serve the universalism of salvation. His "Last Judgment" has no "double outcome," but serves the universal establishment of the divine righteousness and justice, for the new creation of all things. The preponderance of God's grace over his anger, which is experienced in faith, means that Judgment and the reconciliation of the universe are not antitheses. The reconciliation of the universe comes about through the Judgment in which God reveals the righteousness that creates justice and puts things to rights, in order that he may gather all and everything into the realm of his glory.

What speaks against universalism is that—however he may deal with other creatures—the reconciling and righteous God desires to save human beings, at least, through faith. The surpassing power of God's grace is not a force of destiny, nor is it a compulsive power, which disposes over people without asking them. It is the power of love, which calls men and women to faith through the gospel, and entices them to free decision. God saves human beings not by overpowering them but by convincing them. In Christ and through the gospel he apparently descends to human beings to the very point of making his will to salvation dependent on their decision for faith. He lowers himself so much that he puts his glory in the hands of men and women. He is apparently dependent on mutuality, for he respects the free decision of human beings, their faith and their unfaith too, and gives to each of them in "the Last Judgment" as they have believed—or not believed. That has nothing to do with vengeance or sadism: "to each his own," the own that he or she has chosen—to believers salvation, to non-believers doom and disaster. The doctrine of universal salvation does not take the decision of faith as seriously as God does, when he wants to save men and women through "the preaching of the foolishness of the cross." Whereas universalism stresses the all-embracing totality of divine salvation, the doctrine of the double outcome of Judgment stresses the mutuality of God's salvation and human faith.

This really brings the question "universalism or a double outcome of Judgment" down to the relationship between divine and human decision. The doctrine of universal salvation is the expression of a boundless confidence in God: what God wants to do he can do, and will do. If he wants all human beings to be helped, he will ultimately help all human beings. The doctrine of the double outcome of Judgment is the expression of a tremendous self-confidence on the part of human beings: if the decision "faith or disbelief" has eternal significance, then eternal destiny, salvation or damnation, lies in the hands of human beings. What will happen to people in eternity really depends on their own behavior. God's function is reduced to the offer of salvation in the gospel, and to establishing acceptance or rejection at the Judgment. Christ becomes a person's Savior only when that person has "accepted" him in faith. So it is the acceptance in faith, which makes Christ the Savior of that man or that woman. But if this is so, do people not really save or damn themselves? The doctrine of the double outcome of Judgment is a relatively modern doctrine compared with the doctrine of universal salvation. It fits the modern age, in which human beings believe that they are the measure of all things, and the center of the world, and that therefore everything depends on their decision. But what human being does this mean? Can children who die young, for example, decide for faith, or can the severely handicapped? Are they saved or lost?

Who makes the decision about the salvation of lost men and women, and where is the decision made? Every Christian theologian is bound to answer: *God* decides for a person and for his or her salvation, for otherwise there is no assurance of salvation at all. "If God is for us, who can be against us . . ." (Rom. 8:31f.)—we may add: not even we ourselves! God *is* "for us": that has been decided once and for all in the self-surrender and raising of Christ. It is not just a few of the elect who have been reconciled with God, but the whole cosmos (2 Cor. 5:19). It is not just believers whom God loved, but the world (John 3:16). The great turning point from disaster to salvation took place on Golgotha; it does not just happen for the first time at the hour when we decide for faith, or are converted. Faith means experiencing and receiving this turning point personally, but faith is not the turning point itself. It is not my faith that creates salvation for me; salvation creates for me faith. If salvation and damnation were the results of human faith or unfaith, God would be dispensable. The connection between act and destiny, and the law of karma, would suffice to create the causal link. If, even where eternity is at stake, everyone were to forge their own happiness and dig their own graves, human beings would be their own God. It is only if a qualitative difference is made between God and human beings that God's decision and human decision can be valued and respected. God's decision "for us," and our decisions for faith or disbelief no more belong on the same level than do eternity and time. We should be measuring God and the human being by the same yardstick if we were to ask: What, and how much, does God do for the salvation of human beings, and what, and how much, must human beings do? To see God and a human being on the same level means humanizing God and deifying the human being. "Offer and acceptance" is a frequently used formula which brings divine grace and human decision on to the same level in just this way. The trivial slogan "the church on offer"[12] turns God into the purveyor of a cheap offer in the religious supermarket of this society of ours, which has set out on the road to "the global marketing of everything." The customer is king, says a German tag. So then the customer would be God's king too.

5. DOUBLE PREDESTINATION OR GOD'S UNIVERSAL ELECTION?

To answer questions about the end with the presuppositions of the beginning was a favorite method in theology. It is therefore not surprising that the question about a double outcome of Judgment should be discussed most fully in the doctrine of predestination as it was developed in Calvinist theology. Let us look at the different answers.

(*a*) *Particularismus verus* (true particularism): Calvinist orthodoxy as it was taught by [Theodore] Beza and [Franciscus] Gomarus, laid down in the Canons of Dort in 1618, and substantiated by the Leyden Synopsis of 1628, maintained the following doctrine: Before the creation of the world, God resolved to elect the one human being in Christ, but to reject the others because of their sins, in order to reveal in the one "vessel" his fathomless grace, in the others his righteous wrath. Both "vessels" serve the glorification of God. But because in history who the elect are, and who the rejected, is hidden from us, God has the gospel proclaimed to all. To believers their election is *historically* revealed, as is their rejection to non-believers. At the Last Judgment the elect and the rejected will *finally* be revealed, for God's grace and his wrath will then be openly manifested. *Perseverantia usque ad finem*—perseverance to the end—therefore belongs to true faith, while real disbelief manifests a corresponding hardness of heart to the end.

According to this supralapsarian doctrine of predestination, God's decision about the salvation and damnation of human beings is not already revealed in Christ, nor is it revealed in the gospel. It is revealed provisionally in history, in faith and disbelief, but finally only at the Last Judgment. "Experience teaches," Calvin had already argued, that the same gospel has a dual effect, evoking in the one faith, in the other disbelief, so that it divides human beings through the decision of faith. In this division God's eternal resolve becomes manifest and the double outcome of the Last Judgment anticipated, for—as Aristotle taught—what is last in execution is always the first in resolve. According to this doctrine of double predestination (*praedestinatio gemina*), God by no means desires that all human beings should be helped and that everything should be created anew; he created human beings only in order to have "vessels" through which to reveal his grace and his anger, and thus to glorify himself in this antithetical way.

The deeper reason for this terrible doctrine of predestination is not to be found in theology at all; its location is aesthetics. Antitheses in art make for symmetry. Antitheses enhance clarity and beauty in God and human beings. That is the Aristotelian "theorem of juxtaposition," which Augustine introduced into theology.

> Through God's decree, the beauty of the world is enhanced through
> contrasts. Truly, God would have created no human being, let alone
> an angel, whose future depravity he foresaw, had he not also known

how he would use that being for the benefit of the good, in order thus to grace the order of the world, as one embellishes a poem through antitheses. What one calls antitheses are the most delightful among the adornments of language. . . . Hence, just as such contrasts, when they are ranged against one another, make up the beauty of the style, so the beauty of the world is enriched through the contrasting of antitheses. . . . For just as a painting has dark shadows in the proper place, so the totality of things, if we know how rightly to observe them, is beautiful even with sinners, although the sinners, if we see them for themselves, disfigure the picture through their ugliness.[13]

If the aesthetic of juxtaposition is the inner motive for the doctrine of double predestination, then in actual fact this is a doctrine about the universalism of God's glorification. It then permits the following possibility of hearing in the No the divine Yes: The salvation of created beings is to be found solely in the glorification of God; if through disbelief I become the vessel of God's wrath, and through wrath God glorifies himself in me, then I too, castaway though I am, minister to his glorification and am, in a negative sense, in salvation. A truly Dostoyevsky-like, *resignatio-ad-infernum* argument![14]

(*b*) *Universalismus hypotheticus* (hypothetical universalism): This theory was developed by the Calvinist theologian Moyse Amyraut in the seventeenth century at the Huguenot Academy in Saumur. He took up Calvin's idea about the *electio generalis*, according to which God has meant the gospel for everyone—that is to say has determined that everyone shall hear his word, even though he foresees that only a few will believe, and it is only believers whom he will save. The general proclamation of the gospel is a hypothetical universalism (*universalismus hypotheticus*), because the gospel can only save conditionally—that is to say, under the condition of faith. At the Last Judgment the eternal particularism of the divine election and rejection will then be manifest. God's good intention is therefore universal, but the outcome of history is particularist, as the dual effect of the gospel on believers and non-believers shows, even in the history of the universal proclamation.

(*c*) *Universalismus verus* (true or real universalism): This theory is maintained by the Calvinist theologian Friedrich Schleiermacher. He sees the matter in exactly the opposite way: what is conditional is the particularism of the divine election of believers—what is unconditional is the universalism of salvation. The historical path to salvation proceeds by way of the divine election and rejection, but the eschatological goal is universal salvation. God *desires* to save everyone: that is the divine resolve; God *can* save everyone: that is his eternal and essential being; God will *save* everyone: that is the fulfillment of his resolve. Historical experience shows that God rejects in order to elect, that he casts into hell in order to save, that he gives people up for lost in order to gather them. He permits disbelief temporally, but his grace is in the end "irresistible." The human being cannot eternally maintain his unbelief contrary to God's love.[15]

(d) *Open universalism*: The new version of the doctrine of predestination put forward by Karl Barth led to a new eschatological prospect.[16] Before God chooses human beings or rejects them, he determines himself to be for these human beings their Creator, Reconciler, and Redeemer. Predestination is in the first place God's determination of himself, before it becomes the determination of human beings. Consequently God's "eternal resolve" is universal. It becomes manifest in Christ, in whom "God in His free grace determines Himself for sinful man and sinful man for Himself. He therefore takes upon Himself the rejection of man with all its consequences, and elects man to participation in His own glory."[17]Because this divine self-determination has taken place in eternity, this divine predestination must be understood as supralapsarian. Because in the crucified Christ God has taken upon himself the rejection of sinful men and women in order to give them his grace, this christological predestination must be understood as "double predestination." There is rejection and there is one who is rejected: Christ, who on the cross became sin for us and a curse, as Paul says, so that we might be saved. The resurrection of Christ manifests that universal rejection has been overcome by election, which applies equally universally to all human beings. Predestination does not mean a symmetry of Yes and No, electing and rejecting; it means the a-symmetry of a Yes, which proceeds out of the confuted No. Because Christ has borne "the sins of the world" and the whole of rejection on the cross, all human beings are in Christ "objectively" reconciled, whether they know it or not. Through faith they experience themselves subjectively as reconciled. It follows from this that a Christian can only view other people as those who have been reconciled in Christ. He cannot take the disbelief of others more seriously than the fact of their being reconciled with God. He can always only believe in the belief of the other person.[18]

The fundamental idea of this doctrine of universal election can already be found in Christoph Blumhardt, who strenuously resisted the compulsion towards symmetry in this question: "They say: 'If there is no everlasting torment then there is no everlasting bliss either.' As if good and evil could ever be on a par with each other! Just because good is eternal, evil cannot possibly be eternal; because God's salvation is eternal, wretchedness can never be eternal. . . .

Because salvation is God's, everything that is not salvation comes to an end."[19] This has a practical consequence: "My father once wrote to me that I should make it a rule for myself at all times to view everyone as a believer, never to doubt it, and never to talk to a person in any other way. This found an echo in my own soul. If a Mohammedan comes, I call him a believer, I never accept that anyone is an unbeliever. . . . Every human being believes, because God believes."[20]

Barth's new version of the doctrine of predestination leads to an *open universalism* of salvation. There is no particularism in principle, and there is no automatic universalism. Believers expect that there will be "an open multiplicity of the elect" and expect universal salvation for Christ's sake in "the confession of hope."[21] Their assurance of hope is no less than their assurance of faith; it is the other side of their assurance in Christ.

6. CHRIST'S DESCENT INTO HELL AND THE RESTORATION OF ALL THINGS

If we follow the method of providing christological answers for eschatological questions, then in trying to measure the breadth of the Christian hope we must not wander off into far-off realms, but must submerge ourselves in the depths of Christ's death on the cross at Golgotha. It is only there that we find the certainty of reconciliation without limits, and the true ground for the hope for "the restoration of all things," for universal salvation, and for the world newly created to become the eternal kingdom. It is only the person who understands what Christ suffered in his God-forsaken death who understands what, by virtue of his resurrection, is manifested in his present rule and in his future "to judge both the quick and the dead." In the crucified Christ we recognize *the Judge of the final Judgment*, who himself has become the one condemned for the accused, in their stead and for their benefit. So at the Last Judgment we expect on the Judgment seat the One who was crucified for the reconciliation of the world, and no other judge. The person who in the history of Christ has experienced the righteousness of God which creates justice for those who suffer injustice, and which justifies the godless, knows what the justice is which at the Last Judgment will restore this ruined world and put everything to rights again: it is not retaliatory justice, Ulpian's *suam cuique*, to each his due—the justice that gives everyone their "just deserts," which requites the wickedness of the wicked and repays the goodness of the good; it is the righteousness and justice of the God of Abraham, the Father of Jesus Christ, who creates justice, puts things to rights, and justifies.

This means that the eschatological Last Judgment is not a prototype for the courts of kingdoms or empires. This Judgment has to do with God and his creative justice, and is quite different from the forms our earthly justice takes. What we call the Last Judgment is nothing other than the universal revelation of Jesus Christ, and the consummation of his redemptive work. No expiatory penal code will be applied in the court of the crucified Christ. No punishments of eternal death will be imposed. The final spread of the divine righteousness that creates justice serves the eternal kingdom of God, not the final restoration of a divine world order that has been infringed. Judgment at the end is not an end at all; it is the beginning. Its goal is the restoration of all things for the building up of God's eternal kingdom.

The *Christian* doctrine about the restoration of all things denies neither damnation nor hell. On the contrary: it assumes that in his suffering and dying Christ suffered the true and total hell of godforsakenness for the reconciliation of the world, and experienced for us the true and total damnation of sin. It is precisely here that the divine reason for the reconciliation of the universe is to be found. It is not the optimistic dream of a purified humanity, it is Christ's descent into hell that is the ground for the confidence that nothing will be lost but that everything will be brought back again and gathered into the eternal kingdom of God. *The true Christian foundation for the hope of universal salvation is the theology of the cross, and the realistic consequence of the theology of the cross can only be the restoration of all things.*

In order to explain this thesis, let me take up Luther's teaching about Christ's descent into hell.

In his meditations, the young monk Luther exercised himself in profound trials such as Gabriel Biel had described and laid down. The first trial was the *tentatio de indignitate*: "Am I, unworthy as I am, worthy of God's grace? How shall I become righteous before God?" The second trial is the *tentatio de particularitate*: "Only a few will be chosen. Am I not one of the rejected?" In this trial, Johannes von Staupitz, the Vicar General of the Augustinian Order, to which Luther belonged, advised him that if he wished to wrestle with predestination he should begin with the wounds of Christ, after which the dispute about predestination would cease of itself. Luther followed this advice all his life. Even in 1542 he could still say: "Why tormentest thou thyself with such speculations? Look upon the wounds of Christ—there thine election is assured for thee."[22] Why? Because, according to Luther, in his forsakenness on the cross Christ suffered all the torments of hell, the rejection by God and eternal death, and did so vicariously for us, in our stead and for our benefit. The Christ dying on the cross was the most assailed and the most deeply rejected of all human beings. Because he suffered our rejection in his body, we perceive our election from his wounds.

When did Christ suffer hell for us, and what hell is it? Luther talks about Christ's descending into hell *before* his physical death on the cross, not afterwards. This is new, compared with tradition.[23] Here Calvin followed Luther.[24] The forsakenness of Christ between Gethsemane and Golgotha is the forsakenness of one who has been damned for all eternity. The prayer in Gethsemane which was not heard was the preparation for Christ's hellish torment. That is why sweat and blood fall from him on to the earth.[25] Luther says that he fell "*in gehenna et in inferno.*"[26] When he was dying on the cross, what Christ experienced was not just God's present anger over the godless world, but his "*futuram iram, künftig hölle*" too (future wrath, future hell).[27] Did Christ then descend to the realm of the dead after his death, in order to preach to the spirits in prison, as theological tradition said, following the Apostles' Creed? Luther did not believe that hell was "a special place."[28] It was not a place anywhere in the world, not even in the underworld. It was an existential experience, the experience of God's anger and curse on sin and godless being. Christ suffered this hell on the cross in order to reconcile this world, damned as it is, with God. Here Luther is following Paul, for whom Christ "was made sin" (2 Cor. 5:21) for our reconciliation, and according to Gal. 3:13 even "became a curse for us." Those are the real "pangs of death" (Acts 2:24) which God "loosed" through the raising of Christ from the dead.

In the view that hell is not some remote place, but an existential experience, modern Protestant theologians follow Luther and Calvin. For Barth, the idea of Christ's descent into hell is "the inner explanation of what happened outwardly in death and burial."[29] According to [Paul] Althaus, "in his death [Jesus] also suffered hell, that is to say the satanic temptation of God-forsakenness, and overcame it for us, in that even here he remained the Son."[30] [Wolfhart] Pannenberg thinks that Christ's "descent into hell is a way of expressing the universal significance of Jesus' accursed death, vicariously suffered."[31] I myself have said: "Only if disaster, forsakenness by God, absolute death, the infinite curse of damnation and sinking into nothingness is gathered into God himself, is community with this God eternal salvation, infinite joy, indestructible election and divine life."[32]

Christ's descent into hell therefore means: even in the experience of hell you are there (Ps. 139:8).

Christ's decent into hell means: you have suffered the experience of hell for us, so as to be beside us in our experiences of hell.

Christ's descent into hell means, finally: hell and death have been gathered up and ended in God: "Death is swallowed up in victory. O death where is thy victory? O death where is thy sting? But thanks be to God, who gives us the victory through our Lord Jesus Christ" (1 Cor. 15:54f., 57).

In his moving "Sermon on preparing for death" of 1519, Luther explains: "Thou must look upon hell and the eternity of torment, and election too, not in thyself, not in themselves, not in those who are damned, nor shouldst thou trouble thyself about the many in the whole world who are not chosen. . . . Look upon the heavenly picture of Christ who for thy sake descended into hell and was forsaken by God as one eternally damned, as he said on the cross, 'O my God, why hast thou forsaken me?' See, in that picture thy hell is conquered, and thy uncertain election made sure. . . . Seek thyself only in Christ and not in thyself, so wilt thou eternally find thyself in him."[33]

By way of a deepened doctrine of Christ's descent into hell, Hans Urs von Balthasar has tried in the spirit of Origen to mediate between the universal assurance of salvation held by the Eastern Fathers of the church and the emotional emphasis on freedom of Western theology. The godless are forsaken by God and in this sense "damned." They experience the hell they themselves have chosen. But Christ's descent into hell says that even in their hell Christ is their companion and brother. That is "the solidarity of the dead Christ with the dead." "In this way Christ disturbs the absolute solitariness for which the sinner strives; the sinner who desires to be 'damned' away from God, finds God again in his solitariness, but God in the absolute powerlessness of love, who in the Not-Time unpredictably puts himself on the side of the one who damns himself."[34] Balthasar calls this the "Easter Saturday experience" of Christ, who in his forsakenness by the Father experiences hell, because in pure obedience he seeks the Father where he is not to be found, and through his descent into hell takes hell and all those who are in it into his trinitarian fellowship with the Father.[35]

Christ gave himself up for lost in order to seek all who are lost, and to bring them home. He suffered the torments of hell, in order to throw hell open, so that these torments are no longer without hope an end. Because he suffered hell, he gives hope where otherwise "all hope must be abandoned," as Dante said. Because Christ was brought out of hell, the gates of hell are open, and its walls broken down. Through his sufferings Christ has destroyed hell.[36] Since his resurrection from his hellish death on the cross there is no longer any such thing as "being damned for all eternity."

What Christ *accomplished* in his dying and rising is *proclaimed* to all human beings through his gospel and will be *revealed* to everyone and everything at his appearance. What was suffered in the depths of the cross and overcome through suffering will be manifest through his parousia in glory. This inner connection between cross and parousia was already perceived by Johann Christoph Blumhardt when, in the Good Friday sermon he preached in Möttlingen in 1872, he proclaimed a "general pardon": "What the Lord Jesus endured there [i.e., on Golgotha] will be revealed again. For just because of this the Savior has also acquired rights over this darkness, so that just here, here on the cross, the prospect is opened up for us that one day the point will be reached when every knee must bow, in heaven and on earth and under the earth, and every tongue confess that Jesus Christ is Lord to the glory of God the Father. . . . Good Friday proclaims a general pardon to the whole world, and this general pardon is still to be revealed, for it was not for nothing that Jesus hung on the cross. . . . We are moving towards a general pardon, and it will soon come! Anyone who is unable to think this greatest thing of all knows nothing about a Good Friday."[37]

To make Christ's death on the cross the foundation for universal salvation and "the restoration of all things" is to surmount the old dispute between the universal theology of grace and the particularist theology of faith. The all-reconciling love is not what Bonhoeffer called "cheap grace." It is grace through and through, and grace is always and only free and for nothing. But it is born out of the profound suffering of God and is the costliest thing that God can give: himself in his Son, who has become our Brother, and who draws us through our hells. It is costliest grace.

The question whether at the end all human beings, and even the Devil, will then really be redeemed, can receive a sure answer in "the confession of hope":

"The confession of hope has completely slipped through the church's fingers. . . . There can be no question of God's giving up anything or anyone in the whole world, either today or in eternity. . . . The end has to be: Behold, everything is God's! Jesus comes as the one who has borne the sins of the world. Jesus can judge but not condemn. My desire is to have preached this as far as the lowest circles of hell, and I will never be confounded."[38]

The eschatological point of the proclamation of "the Last Judgment" is the redeeming kingdom of God. Judgment is the side of the eternal kingdom that is turned towards history. In that Judgment all sins, every wickedness and every act of violence, the whole injustice of this murderous and suffering world, will be condemned and annihilated, because God's verdict effects what it pronounces. In the divine Judgment all sinners, the wicked and the violent, the murderers and the children of Satan, the Devil and the fallen angels will be liberated and saved from their deadly perdition through transformation into their true, created being, because God remains true to himself, and does not give up what he has once created and affirmed, or allow it to be lost.

"The Last Judgment" is not a terror. In the truth of Christ it is the most wonderful thing that can be proclaimed to men and women. It is a source of endlessly consoling joy to know, not just that the murderers will finally fail to triumph over their victims, but that they cannot in eternity even remain the murderers of their victims. The eschatological doctrine about the restoration of all things has these two sides: *God's judgment*, which puts things to rights, and *God's kingdom*, which awakens to new life.

Notes

1. Moltmann 1995; ET 1996:xi.

2. Cf. Moltmann 1989; ET 1990/1993:334ff.: ". . . To judge both the quick and the dead" (ch. 7, §5).

3. Fidelis Rädle, "Dies irae," in Hansjakob Becker, et al., eds., *Im Angesicht des Todes. Ein interdisziplinäres Kompendium* I (St. Ottilien: EOS, 1987), 331ff.

4. Hans-Josef Klauck, introduction to idem, ed., *Weltgericht und Weltvollendung. Zukunfsbilder im Neuen Testament*, Questiones Disputatae 150 (Freiburg: Herder, 1994), 11f.

5. Paul Gerhardt's well-known Christmas hymn "Iche steh an deiner Krippen hier" ("Beside Thy Manger Here I Stand") also contains consoling lines in which Christ promises that he "will restore all things":

Lasset fahr'n,
O lieben Brüder,
was euch quält,
was euch fehlt,
ich bring' alles wieder.

For Bonhoeffer's personal and moving comment on the verse see his letter to Bethge of 18 December 1943, in *Letters and Papers from Prison,* ed. Eberhard Bethge, trans. Reginald H. Fuller, enl. ed. (London: SCM Press/New York: Macmillan, 1971).

6. This is also brought out in a well-known hymn from the same period written by Isaac Watts (1674–1748):

Jesus shall reign where e'er the sun
Doth his successive journeys run,
His kingdom stretch from shore to shore,
Till moons shall wax and wain no more.
Where he displays his healing power,
Death and the curse are known no more;
In him the tribes of Adam boast
More blessings than their father lost.

7. Karl Barth, "Vergangenheit und Zukunft. Fredrich Naumann und Christoph Blumhardt" (1919), in Jürgen Moltmann, ed., *Anfänge der dialektischen Theologie* I (Munich: Chr. Kaiser, 1962), 37–49.

8. Emil Brunner, *Dogmatik* I (Zurich: Zwingli Verlag, 1946), 359; ET: *The Christian Doctrine of God: Dogmatics,* vol. 1, trans. Olive Wyon (London: Lutterworth, 1949). The last

sentence, it must be said, is illogical, since universal reconciliation could, after all, be the result of judgment.

9. Paul Althaus, *Die letzten Dinge: Entwurf einer christlichen Eschatologie* (Gütersloh: Bertelsmann, 1926), 187, 194, 195.

10. Gerhard Ebeling, *Dogmatik des christlichen Glaubens* I (Tubingen: J. C. B. Mohr, 1979), 527f.

11. Walter Michaelis, *Die Versöhnung des Alls. Die frohe Botschaft von der Gnade Gottes* (Bern: Siloah, 1950), 151.

12. That was the motto for the Synod of the Evangelical Church in Germany (EKD) in 1993.

13. I am indebted for this reference and the quotation to Christine Janowski, *Apokatastasis panton—Allerlösung. Annäherungen an eine entdualisierte Eschatologie* (Tübingen: J. C. B. Mohr, 1993), 30; Augustine, *De Civitate Dei,* XI, 18 and 21.

14. The young Luther also drew on this mystical doctrine of the *resignatio ad infernum,* the purpose of which was to be saved through conformity with God's will to condemn; see his lectures on Romans, 1515/16. Cf. *Luthers Werke in Auswahl V* (Berlin: De Gruyter, 1933), 271–79.

15. John A. T. Robinson, *In the End, God: A Study of the Christian Doctrine* (New York: Harper & Row, 1968), ch. 11: "All in All," 119ff., sees the problem of universalism in the encounter between human freedom and divine love. For human freedom the alternative between heaven and hell continues to exist, but for divine love the universe must be won; otherwise God would not be God. "Hell, so limitless to the man who has chosen it, is still bounded by the 'nevertheless' of divine love. And that love must win" (132). He does, certainly, quote Charles Wesley's verse:

I yield, I yield,
I can hold out no more;
I sink by dying love compelled
To own thee conqueror!

But what he really finds convincing is Origen's legendary saying that Christ hangs on the cross as long as there is still a sinner in hell. God will in the end be all in all, not because God's love overcomes the very last unbeliever, but because the shadows of Christ's cross dissolve hell.

16. Karl Barth, *Christian Dogmatics* II/2.

17. Ibid., §33, 94ff.

18. Ibid., 295f.

19. Johannes Christoph Blumhardt, *Ansprachen, Predigten, Reden, Briefe: 1865–1917,* ed. Johannes Harder (Neukirchen: Neukirchener Verlag, 1978), 134f.

20. Ibid., 133.

21. Ibid., 130f.

22. Martin Luther, *Tischreden* I, 1017 (ET: *Table Talk,* London 1833, and frequently, at least in selection).

23. For the theology of Christ's descent into hell in general cf. Wilhelm Maas, *Gott und die Holle. Studien zum Descensus Christi* (Einsiedeln: Johannes Verlag, 1979); Hans Urs von Balthasar, "Abstieg zur Holle," *Theologische Quartalschrift* 150 (1970): 193–201; also his "Der Gang zu den Toten (Karsamstag)," section 4 of *Mysterium Paschale* in *Mysterium Salutis* III/2 (Einsiedeln: Benziger, 1969), 227ff.; Herbert Vorgrimler, *Geschichte der Holle* (Munich: Fink, 1993); Jerry L. Walls, *Hell: The Logic of Damnation* (Notre Dame, IN: University of Notre Dame Press, 1992).

24. Calvin, *Inst.* II, 16, 10 (ET: John T. McNeill, ed., *Institutes of the Christian Religion,* trans. F. L. Battles [London: SCM Press/Philadelphia: Westminster, 1961]).

25. Martin Luther, *Genesisvorlesung* (1544).

26. Martin Luther, *Weimar Ausgabe* [WA] 44:523.

27. Martin Luther, WA 46:312.

28. Martin Luther, WA 19:225.

29. Karl Barth, *Dogmatik im Grundriss im Anschluss an das apostolische Glaubensbekenntnis* (Stuttgart: Kohlhammer, 1947), 126ff. (ET: *Dogmatics in Outline,* trans. G. T. Thomson [London: SCM Press, 1949]).

30. Paul Althaus, *Die christliche Wahrheit: Lehrbuch der Dogmatik,* 6th ed. (Gutersloh: Bertelsmann, 1962), 485.

31. Wolfhart Pannenberg, *Jesus—God and Man,* trans. Duane Priebe and Lewis L. Wilkins (London: SCM Press/Philadelphia: Westminster, 1968), 269ff.

32. Moltmann 1972; ET 1974/1993:246 (trans. slightly altered).

33. Martin Luther, "Sermon von der Bereitung zum Sterben" (1519), in WA 2:685–97, esp. 691.

34. Hans Urs von Balthasar, "Über Stellvertretung," in *Pneuma und Institution,* Skizzen zur Theologie IV (Einsiedeln: Johannes Verlag, 1974), 408; cf. here M. Kehl, *Eschatologie,* Wiirzburg 1986, 297f.

35. Balthasar, *Mysterium Paschale,* 246ff.; see here Maas, *Gott und die Holle,* 244ff.

36. According to the Armenian view, Christ "*per suam passionem destruxit totaliter infernum.*" I believe that this is correct, although this opinion was condemned by the patristic church. Cf. Heinrich Denziger and Peter Schönmetzer, eds., *Enchiridion symbolorum definitionum et declarationum de rebus fidei et morum,* 36th ed. (Freiburg: Herder, 1965), 1011.

37. Johannes Christoph Blumhardt, *Gesammelte Werke* II (Göttingen: Vandenhoeck & Ruprecht, 1969), 190.

38. Blumhardt, *Ansprachen, Predigten, Reden, Briefe* II, 131.

8

Ethics of Hope

Although his Ethics of Hope *comes at the end of his systematic contributions to theology, the topic had been in Moltmann's mind ever since the 1970s. But for a number of reasons, at that time he did not yet feel ready. Now, following a long series of major books, he picks up this concern, making explicit and developing some of the themes touched on implicitly or in less detail in earlier books. Here again, the framework is eschatology. In the preface to his* Ethics of Hope *he writes: "The hope for God's eschatological transformation of the world leads to transformative ethics which tries to accord with this future in the inadequate material and with the feeble powers of the present, and thus anticipates it."[1] In individual sections he addresses the issues urgently confronting society—medical ethics, ecology, human rights, the criteria for a just peace, and the rest—but sets them in the context of a specifically Christian ethics. This, as the book's title says, is an ethics of hope. "An ethics of fear sees the crises; an ethics of hope perceives the chances in the crises."[2] And since, as the Greek philosophers already saw, the Good and the Beautiful belong together, the end of ethics is joy and doxology. The Sabbath joy over God's creation is followed by delight in the glory of the resurrection; and the two are caught up into hope for God's promised future.*

But, as Moltmann already makes plain in earlier books, this hope implies challenge and participation. And he quotes the message already proclaimed in 1968 at the Fourth General Assembly of the World Council of Churches in Uppsala: "Trusting in God's renewing power, we call upon you to participate in the anticipation of God's kingdom and to allow now something of the new creation to become already visible which Christ will complete on his day."[3]

Eschatology and Ethics

Source: Moltmann 2010; ET 2012:3–8.

Introduction

What Can I Hope For? What Can I Do? Free Action

In this first chapter we shall look at the theological connection between hope and action. The different answers to Kant's question: "What can I hope for?" always affect the various choices of action which are open to us in response to the question: "What should I do?" We become active insofar as we hope. We hope insofar as we can see into the sphere of future possibilities. We take in hand what we think is possible. If, for example, we hope that the world will continue to be as it is now, we shall keep things as they are. If we hope for an alternative future, we shall already change things now as far as possible in accord with that. If the future is closed, then nothing more is possible; we cannot do anything more. Unlike Kant, I am talking about an acting impelled by hope, one not in the mode of "ought" but one in the mode of "can." An action sustained by hope is a free action, not one under compulsion,

Hope is always a tense expectation and rouses the attentiveness of all our senses, so that we can grasp the chances for the things we hope for, wherever and whenever they present themselves. That distinguishes hope from mere expectation or a patient waiting. When all the senses are attentive, reason is the vehicle which conveys the knowledge of change. We then perceive things not just as they have become and now exist, but also in the different way they could be. We perceive things not only *sic stantibus* but also *sic fluentibus*, as fluid not static, and try to realize their potentialities for change in a positive direction.

Realism teaches us a sense for reality—for what is. Hope awakens our sense for potentiality—for what could be. In concrete action we always relate the potentiality to what exists, the present to the future. If our actions were directed only to the future, we should fall victim to utopias; if they were related only to the present, we should miss our chances.

In hope we link far-off goals with goals within reach. What is last of all gives meaning to the next-to-last. So in the imaginations of hope there is always a superabundance of what is hoped for. It is only when we want what is now impossible that we arrive at the limits of our possibilities. It is good to stress this added value of hope, for we generally fall short of our possibilities. Lethargy is the real enemy of every hope.

WHAT MUST I FEAR? WHAT SHOULD I DO? NECESSARY ACTION

We become aware of the future not only in our hopes for better times in the future but also, if not even for the most part, in our fears and anxieties. We are worried by the possibility of all the things that can happen. Fear and anxiety are early warning systems of possible dangers, and are necessary for living. As long as potential dangers can be discerned and named, they give rise to fears which impel us to do what is necessary in good time, and so to avert the dangers. But if discernible threats swell into insubstantial dangers, they result in diffuse anxieties in the face of nothingness or the total write-off of the world and one's own existence. These anxieties generally lead to despairing resignation and paralyzed inactivity or to over-reactions which only intensify the dangers.

As well as the fundamental question, "What can I hope for?" Immanuel Kant should have asked the reverse of this question, "What must I fear?" But Kant was an "Enlightened" optimist—theologically, as he himself said, a millennialist. Every answer to the question about our fear affects what we do. Our sense for the possible is roused at least as much by the fear as by the hope.[4] Anxiety is concerned for our lives—hope, for our fulfilled lives. Anxiety awakens all our senses, making them alive to imminent threats, and prepares our reason to recognize in the facts of the present "the signs of the end." Without these abilities we would be like the people in Pompeii who didn't notice the outbreak of Vesuvius, or couldn't accept that it was happening. We would feel as safe as the people before the Flood, who in spite of a biblical warning did not see anything coming (Matt. 24:38-39). Humanity would long since have become extinct. An ethics of fear sees the crises; an ethics of hope perceives the chances in the crises. In the exuberance of hope, the temptation is utopianism; in fear, the temptation is alarmism.

In Ernst Bloch's *Principle of Hope*, we find the foundation for an ethics of change; in *The Imperative of Responsibility*, Hans Jonas gives us an ethics of fear.[5] The hope for what can come is replaced by the fear for what will perhaps no longer be. So it becomes more important to retain what is old than to attain the new. Hans Jonas therefore maintained that the prediction of the bad takes precedence over the prediction of the good: "It is the rule, to put it in primitive terms, that the prophecy of disaster has to be listened to more attentively than the prophecy of salvation." For him, general anxiety about the continuance of humanity is the foundation for the fear of the unforeseeable consequences of human technology. He uses the alarm over humanity's threat to its own existence in order to ensure authentic human being in the present. The "heuristic of fear" awakens responsibility in the present. That is not pessimism any more than what Bloch disseminated was optimism. It is the reverse side of hope, although the two sides are not equal, since hope precedes fear: without hope there would be no fear, and without "the prophecy of salvation" there would be no "prophecy of disaster."

In Jewish and Christian apocalyptic the endtime is announced with every conceivable catastrophe scenario, but at the same time deliverance in the new divine beginning is proclaimed all the more intensively. In the catastrophes of the endtime, nothing less than God's Spirit itself will be poured out, so that everything mortal may live (Joel 2:28-32; Acts 2:16-21). With the outpouring of the divine Spirit of life, the new creation of all things begins in the downfall of the world. After "the heavens pass away" and "the earth is burnt up," on the Day of the Lord there will be "a new earth on which righteousness dwells" (2 Peter 3:13).

> Near and hard to grasp the God,
> But where there is danger deliverance also grows.

So wrote Friedrich Hölderlin in his Patmos Hymn.[6] The Christian ethics of hope is called to life through the recollection of the raising of the crucified Christ and therefore expects the dawn of God's new world in the passing away of the old one (Rev. 21:1). The endtime is simultaneously the new-time. In the perils of time it lives from hope for the coming of God. It mobilizes energies out of surmounted fears. It holds instructions for resistance against the old world in anticipation of the new one. It presupposes a transformative eschatology and, correspondingly, is itself transforming action. It is this unity of messianic awareness of the time and transformative action that is meant in Rom. 13:12:

> The night is far gone,
> the day is at hand.
> Let us then cast off the works of darkness
> and put on the armor of light.

Christian hope is founded on Christ's resurrection and opens up a life in the light of God's new world. Christian ethics anticipates the universal coming of God in the potentialities of history.

PRAYING AND WATCHING

All Christian action is embedded in a particular spirituality. In the Benedictine tradition, this spirituality is *ora et labora*, pray and work. Prayer is directed towards God, work towards the world. But through prayer work in the world is seen *sub specie aeternitatis*, in the light of eternity, and is brought before the face of God. In other words, it is answerable to God. Consequently, it is not a pious irrelevance if we begin our daily work, or any special project, with a prayer.

What does hope add to prayer? I think what it adds is "watching." In Christian life according to the New Testament, the call to prayer is always linked with the messianic wake-up call to watch. In the night of God in the Garden of Gethsemane, when the disciples are sunk into the deep sleep of hopelessness, Jesus does not ask them, "Could you not pray with me" but "Could you not watch with me one hour?" (Mark 14:37), and he warns them: "Watch and pray that you may not enter into temptation." Specifically Christian prayer is always linked with expectation for what is to come, whether it be out of fear of evil and catastrophes or out of hope for the kingdom of God. Watching awakens all our senses for what is to come. Watching and being sober, watching and expecting, watching and being open-eyed, go together in the messianic hope.[7]

In watching we open our eyes and "recognize" the hidden Christ who waits for us in the poor, the sick, the weary, and heavy-laden (Matt. 25.37). In the faces of the poor of the people we "see" the face of the crucified God. Today the messianic awakening for God's future is often translated into sensibility for the little things in everyday life. That makes it more realistic but also weaker. Attentiveness in the messianic awakening surely lies in attentiveness for the signs of the times, in which God's future is heralded, so that Christian action, inspired by hope, becomes the anticipation of the coming kingdom in which righteousness and peace kiss each other. So Christian action is accompanied by prayer and watching, by the trust of the heart, by wide-open eyes, and by attentive senses.

WAITING AND HASTENING

Out of hope for God's future, all theologians of hope from [John Amos] Comenius to [Christoph] Blumhardt have praised these two attitudes to life: Blumhardt called them *warten und pressieren*—"waiting and being in a hurry." It is the Second Letter of Peter (3:12) which tells Christians they should be "waiting for and hastening the coming of the Lord's future." By this he means the new earth "on which righteousness dwells."

Waiting and hastening: that sounds like a contradiction. If we are waiting, then what we are waiting for is not yet there. If we are hastening, then what we have waited for is already in sight. These are the two extremes between which attitudes to the future are played out. As boundary marks they do not have to be mutually contradictory. Let us translate "waiting and hastening" into our own language and experience:

Waiting: that doesn't mean a passive waiting-it-out; it means an active expectation. A passage in the prophet Isaiah offers an apt example of the difference. When they are in exile and far from home, the prisoners come to the prophet and ask: "Watchman, what of the night?"—and he replies: "Morning is coming, but it is still night. If you will inquire, come back again" (21:11-12). The apostle Paul picks up this image about the night and proclaims the dawn of God's day in the light of Christ's resurrection: "The night is far gone, the day is at hand" (Rom. 13:12). So waiting turns into expectation, and the dreams of the night become an awakening in the daybreak colors of the new day. The eclipse of God becomes the sunrise of God. As Paul, in his ethic of hope, calls for the "weapons of light," so the awakening of hope carries the promised future of righteousness into one's own life. God's coming unfolds a transforming power in the present. In our tense expectation we are prepared for God's future, and that future acquires power in our present.

The ability to wait also means not conforming to the conditions of this world of injustice and violence. People who expect God's justice and righteousness no longer accept the so-called normative force of what is fact, because they know that a better world is possible and that changes in the present are necessary. Being able to wait means resisting the threats and seductions of the present, not letting oneself be brought into line, and not conforming.

The ability to wait means not giving oneself up, not capitulating, either before the supremacy of the powers of this world or before one's own helplessness, but living with head held high. The "upright walk" Kant commends is deserving of every respect. It is the heroic stance of the unbowed back of the free. But "the head held high" is a result of the approaching redemption (Luke 21:28).

The ability to wait is faithfulness in faith. Hope does not only give faith wings, as we say; it also gives faith the power to stand firm and to endure to the end. That is the famed "perseverance of the saints" (*perservantia sanctorum*) to which Calvin and the Huguenots held fast. "O Lord our God, other lords besides thee have ruled over us, but thy name alone we acknowledge" (Isa. 26:13). For the resistance of the Confessing Church in Nazi Germany after 1933, these words were of vital importance.[8] The Huguenot Christian Marie Durand endured thirty-six years of captivity in the Tour de la constance in Aigues-Mortes and scratched her famous *resistez* on the door instead of denying her faith and so regaining her freedom.

Hastening: to hasten is really to go swiftly in space from one place to another. To hasten "towards the future" transfers this movement from space into the time of history. The present becomes the transition from what has been to what will be, to the future. To "hasten" in time means crossing the frontiers of present reality into the spheres of what is possible in the future. In crossing these frontiers we anticipate the future for which we hope. With every doing of the right we prepare the way for the "new earth" on which righteousness will "dwell." If we achieve some justice for those who are suffering violence, then God's future shines into their world. If we take up the cause of "widows and orphans," a fragment of life comes into our own life. The earth is groaning under the unjust violence with which we are exploiting its resources and energies. We are "hastening" towards the Lord's future when we anticipate the righteousness and justice out of which, on the Day of the Lord, a new and enduring earth is to come into being. Not to take things as they are but to see them as they can be in that future, and to bring about this "can be" in the present, means living up to the future. So looking forward, perceiving possibilities, and anticipating what will be tomorrow are fundamental concepts of an ethics of hope. Today "waiting and hastening towards the Lord's future" mean: *resisting and anticipating*.

An Ethics of Life: A Culture of Life

Source: Moltmann 2010; ET 2012:45–69 (ch. 5).

Terror of Death

Today human life itself is in acute danger. It is not in danger because it is threatened with death—that was always so. It is in acute danger because it is no longer loved.

After World War II Albert Camus wrote: "It is Europe's mystery that it no longer loves life."[9] It was true that at that time my generation had become so used to the killing and the being killed, to the mass deaths and the cities destroyed in the fire-storm of nights of bombing, that we no longer got excited about death. Life was for us a matter of indifference because it had been made meaningless. We had stopped loving life so as not to be so deeply touched by our own death and the death of people we loved. We wanted to make ourselves untouchable through an emotional armor of indifference. We fled into the death of the soul. It was only slowly, and years after the end of the war, that the survivors of my generation woke up out of this deadly paralysis of the soul and came back to life.

Terrorism

Today we are experiencing a new and frightening "religion of death." "Your young people love life; our young people love death," the Taliban leader Mullah Omar once said to a Western journalist. After the bomb explosions in the commuter trains in Madrid on 11 March 2004, letters claiming responsibility were found with the same tenor: "You love life, we love death." This is the expression of an Islamic terror ideology against the Western world which is spreading, but which is first of all costing the Islamic world itself unnumbered victims. Yet "this love for death" could once already be found in Europe too: "*Viva la muerte!*" cried an old Fascist general in the Spanish civil war. "Give death—accept death" was the slogan of the German SS. Its symbol was the skull and crossbones—the death's head.

Deterrence

Behind this terrorist surface lurks a greater danger still. All peace treaties, disarmament treaties, and nuclear non-proliferation treaties have one self-evident premise: they presuppose the will of all the signatories to survive. But what if someone doesn't want to survive but wants to die? What if he can perhaps drag this whole depraved world into the abyss with him at the same time? What if in their attack terrorists use biochemical methods of mass destruction against which there is no defense? Up to now we have only had to do with an international network of suicidal mass murderers. But what if a whole nation in possession of weapons of mass destruction wants not to live but to die if by so doing it can destroy this "wicked " or "unbelieving" world? A deterrent only works if the opponent wants to survive as well. The person whose own life has become a matter of indifference to him has left the terror of the deterrent behind him. He can no longer be threatened. We saw a terrible example of this in Nazi Germany, which began the Second World War in 1939. We see this attitude reflected in one of the SA's favorite songs, written by the Nazi songwriter Hans Baumann:

> The rotten bones of the world
> are trembling before the great war.
> But we have broken the terror,
> and victory beckons us on.
> So we will march onwards and forwards
> till nothing but potsherds are left.[10]

The attraction of annihilating a world viewed as "rotten," corrupt, or unbelieving can become a universal death wish for which one's own life is willingly sacrificed. "Death" becomes a fascinating and a terrible deity. This "religion of death" is the true enemy of the love for life. Necrophilia is the somber attendant of every biophilia. Every affirmation of life also implies the possibility of its negation.

THE NUCLEAR SUICIDE PROGRAMME

Behind this real deadly political danger to the shared life of the peoples of the earth is a greater danger still. When the atomic bomb was invented and was dropped on Hiroshima and Nagasaki in the August of 1945, it was not just the Second World War that was ended. The whole human race entered its endtime as well. That is meant in an entirely non-religious sense. The endtime is the age in which the end of humanity is possible at any time. Through the potentialities for a global nuclear war, the human race as a whole became mortal. No human being could survive the nuclear winter that would follow a major nuclear war. It is true that, since the end of the Cold War in 1989, a major nuclear war is for the moment not very likely, but there are still giant arsenals of atomic and nitrogen bombs in the United States, Russia, China, England, France, India, Pakistan, and Israel, ready for "the final solution" of the question about humanity. "The one who shoots first dies second." That is humanity's latent but always present suicide program. Today it has been forgotten and suppressed, pushed out of public awareness. But it hangs over humanity as a somber fate.

THE DECLINE INTO SOCIAL DESTITUTION

For more than forty years we have been continually hearing on every side the lament that the gap between rich and poor is getting wider and wider. A small, wealthy upper class dominates the masses of impoverished people, and not just in the poor countries of the Third World (I am still deliberately using this term even today). In the democracies of the First World too the gap between the top executives with their millions and the people living on social security benefits is becoming grotesque. But democracy does not depend merely on liberty. It also rests on a balance felt to be equitable. Without social justice with regard to chances in life and living conditions, the common good dies—that is to say the good of the whole community and with it the bonds that hold a society together. The liberty enjoyed by individuals and the wealthy classes becomes a public danger if "privatize profits, socialize losses" becomes the ruling motto. Ever since the deregulation of the economy and the financial world in the great economic nations of the earth, the imbalance for many people between liberty and equality has become life-threatening, because the outcome is their impoverishment. A political capitalism—a capitalism no longer controlled by the common good—is the enemy of democracy, because it destroys a society's sense of community. We are on a downward path, socially speaking.

Where do we find the destructive drive behind this decline into poverty in modern societies? Let us pick out here only the social and psychological perspective. "There is not enough for everyone": this impression, deliberately disseminated, postulates a general state of emergency which plunges many people into existential anxiety. The pointer to deficits in every sector of life justifies an ideology of growth as being the motor for the modern belief in progress. The general struggle for jobs, earnings, and profits is supposed to mobilize the energies of the general public. "Every man for himself" is the slogan, and solidarity gets left behind. In modern societies the community falls apart into winners and losers, "the winner takes all" and the devil takes the losers. The existential fear of "not making it" leads to a boundless greed for life and an insatiable hunger for power. "It's cool"—"it's a must-have"—is already dinned into the ears of the young so as to make them buy designer clothes. Competition in modern societies has nothing to do with satisfying the basic needs of life. It has to do with social prestige, recognition in one's own social class. Modern existential anxiety tells people: "You're nothing if you haven't anything—make something of yourself. If you don't you will be despised and looked down on"; and so the social struggles begin. Everyone competes against everyone else. It is a fight of each against all. This greed for life and this hunger for recognition are the reverse of the suppressed fears of dropping down the social ladder and of death. "You only live once." "Look out for yourself." "You might miss out on something." These deadly games with fear are really at the bottom of the modern competitive society. If solidarity gets left behind, if concern about the general good gets lost, if what belongs to everyone is viewed only as unclaimed property which can be grabbed without punishment—the result is a socially frigid world. In this dog-eats-dog society, everyone's neighbor is himself.

Once public spirit disappears from a society, trust disappears too. Conviction is no longer needed, only control. "Trust is good, control is better," said Lenin, and most capitalists today still believe him. But "who controls the controllers?" Even Karl Marx couldn't find an answer to this age-old question posed by the Roman poet Juvenal, for answers to it reach, practically speaking, into infinity. So the modern controlled economies and surveillance states come up against a dead end and spread mistrust.

It is the loss of solidarity and commitment to the common good, together with the loss of trust, which brings about society's divisions into poor and rich, the differences between the present and the future generation, the impoverishment of people in the countries of the Third World. These consequences are not a matter of fate, and are not inevitable; they are the sicknesses which the modern world has brought on itself. They can be healed. "Another world is possible," as the international organization ATTAC[11] critically and rightly proclaims.

THE ECOLOGICAL ANNIHILATION TRAP

Unlike the nuclear catastrophe, the climate catastrophe—and together with it a general ecological catastrophe—is no longer merely latent, nor can it be pushed out of public awareness any longer. It has come about exactly as Donella Meadows and the Club of Rome's study *The Limits of Growth* already in 1972 said that it would.[12] Nevertheless, public awareness lags behind the true development. Some people don't know what they are doing and others are not doing what they know they should. Although we know better, little has been done up to now because—in spite of the limits that have been demonstrated—the ideology of quantitative "growth" reigns unbroken, and to this ideology human beings, animals, plants, and the earth are being sacrificed.

Growth is a "must." If there is no growth, that is called "zero growth," because growth is hope, and recession is depression. The greed for growth and enrichment cannot be halted. That is why today hardly anyone still talks publicly about the natural limits of growth. Yet the biosphere of the blue planet earth is *our limited space for living*. A human civilization that spans the world and is based on growth and consumption has long since arrived at these limits and is beginning permanently to destroy the living conditions of this living space in the earth's organism. Year after year, animal and plant species are becoming extinct; atmospheric pollution is destroying the ozone layer and raising the climatic temperature; the polar ice caps are melting; the water level of the oceans is rising; the deserts are spreading, and storms and hurricanes are on the increase. We know all this, or we can know it, but it is as if we were paralyzed, changing neither our economic growth ideology nor our private and public way of life. *We are not acting on what we know.*

If we were to recognize the natural limits of growth, we would have to overthrow the idols of growth and learn to be moderate ourselves. But we are like smokers—who know that smoking can damage your health and is deadly—but we still cannot stop believing that growth is a good thing. We are publicly showing ourselves to be suicide-prone, because ecologically we are living on the brink.

But there is another side to this growth crisis, although it is not much talked about. That is the *overpopulation* in countries in the Third World, which to an astonishingly degree corresponds proportionally to the aging of the population in the First World. This overpopulation destroys living spaces and triggers the migrations of millions of people. It is the poor, the neglected, and the people who expect to die young who react to their situation with an immoderate population increase. Proportionately, the highest fertility rate is to be found in the poorest and most dangerous city on earth: Gaza City. A population bomb is developing in the Third World which threatens the wealth of the less-fertile population of the West. In the long run, the fortresses of the more prosperous countries will not be able to barricade themselves against mass immigration.

But population growth can be encouraged and deliberately used to advance a particular aim or viewpoint. By rejecting birth control, popes want to increase the number of Catholics in the world and, with the same policy, the mullahs the number of Muslims. Ironically, this used to be called "bedroom mission." But to reject and resist responsible birth control is irresponsible. The resulting overpopulation has a catastrophic effect—and for many people even a deadly one. Whole regions become poverty-stricken, children die, and young people have to leave the region where they belong. "Poverty is the worst pollution," said Indira Gandhi rightly. No animal species destroys its habitat through overpopulation; it is only the human being who possesses no ecological wisdom. Even the dinosaurs were wiser and will probably have lived longer on earth than the human species if human beings go on as they have up to now.

We don't know whether humanity will survive its self-made fate and whether it can free itself from this suicide trap. And that is just as well: for if we knew that we were not going to survive, we would not do anything more to ward off our annihilation—while if we knew that we were going to survive in any case, we would do nothing to practice new ways of dealing with our habitat, the earth. It is only when the future is open for both possibilities that we are compelled to do what is necessary, here and now, to avert the crash. Because we cannot know if humanity will survive, we have to act now as if its future depended on us today.

HUMANITY'S EXISTENTIAL QUESTION: IS THERE AN "ANTHROPIC PRINCIPLE" IN THE COSMOS?

That brings us finally up against humanity's existential question in general. Today there are more than six billion human beings on this earth. But the earth could also be uninhabited by humans. It existed for millions of years without them and probably would go on for millions more if the human race disappeared from the earth. So if there were an "anthropic principle" in nature—that is, if the development of intelligent life in nature had a certain inevitability—then humanity could feel "at home in the universe," as the American biologist Stuart Kauffman suggests in the title of his book.[13] However, the difference between a strong and a weak "anthropic principle" diminishes this assurance.

As far as the development of intelligent human life is concerned, there are only three possible perspectives:

Human life is a fortuitous product of nature, perhaps even a malformation of life.

In human life the universe reveals the plan of its creator: in human knowledge nature comes to the awareness of itself. That would be the "strong anthropic principle."

Human life is the result of a self-organization on the part of life. That would be the "weak anthropic principle."[14]

I assume that the phenomenon of life in all the wealth of its forms and in the build-up of its complexities did not inevitably follow from the "Big Bang," nor did it come about entirely fortuitously, but that it is an emergent phenomenon, that is to say, a wholly new thing in the history of the universe and of nature on the earth. This phenomenon cannot be reduced to something different, nor can it be viewed in isolation; but it can be interpreted as an anticipation of a new future for the universe.

The universe provides no answer to the question whether there should be a human race or not, nor does it tell us whether the human race can survive or whether it is going to perish. In view of what human beings are doing today to the earth they live in, it is hard to give self-evident reasons for their survival. As the German philosopher Hans Jonas recognized, the survival of the human race is a matter of belief, the answer to which precedes all worldly reasoning.[15] He answers the question: "Ought the human being to exist?" by saying that existence is an obligation.

If we search for an answer in the universe, we shall arrive at the American physicist's Steven Weinberg's sad assessment: "The more the universe seems comprehensible, the more it also seems pointless."[16] Even the Catholic philosopher Romano Guardini was reduced to "the innermost core of melancholy" by the silence, the coldness, and the indifference of the universe to human beings.[17]

THE TERRORIZED CONSCIOUSNESS

Let us look finally at the mental and spiritual effects of the threatening scenarios of the present as we have described them. I am talking only about public awareness, not about the diversity of individual consciousness. Yet all individuals participate in the public awareness and relate to it either positively or critically.

We said that some people do not know what they are doing and are not concerned about its effect on others and the consequences for succeeding generations, while the others do not act on what they know; so they do not do the good they want, but the evil they do not want is what they do. If this analysis is correct, then public awareness is profoundly confused and the result is a general lack of orientation. People feel that they have no overview, and the result is stress. This stressful situation evokes contrary reactions. On the one hand there are *panic* attacks—on the other, people sink into apathy; on the one hand the public scene is stirred up by an alarmism which at every piece of bad news sees the end of the world on the way, and pop-apocalyptic books are in vogue—on the other hand fatalism spreads and people sink into social frigidity and a creeping lack of feeling called "psychic numbing."

The threats of universal death exist, and are felt, but the reactions to the threats are themselves life-threatening, because they do not ward off the threats but bring about the very thing that is threatened. It is like a kidnapping in which the victim does not defend himself but cooperates and gives himself up. A typical reaction of this kind is to enjoy life in the present at the cost of those who come later. "Let us eat, drink, and be merry, for tomorrow we die"—though then, of course, our children too! To run up unlimited debts means living at the cost of coming generations. Since they are unable to protest, it is easy to thrust the burden on them. So it is best to stay single, let alone to burden oneself with children. This hedonistic attitude is in actual fact the expression of an extremely nihilistic apocalypticism: we celebrate the end and bring it about—today! The banking crisis of 2008 was brought about by the greed for life in the here and now.

Another evading reaction is *escapism*. If a threat emerges, one ducks down and plays dead, hoping that one won't be affected or at least won't feel the blow. One resigns oneself, becomes indifferent. Nothing much matters if one no longer loves life, and then death no longer touches one either. One becomes apathetic, anticipating death in mind and heart, and then one no longer feels it physically when it comes. With an attitude like this, we no longer withstand the threats either; we surrender ourselves to them, and by doing so actually make what is threatened happen.

Here a *religious* escapism is coming to the fore especially in the present spread of a vague Gnostic religiosity of redemption. The person who surrenders himself to this religiosity feels at home in "the world beyond" and on earth sees himself merely as a guest. So it is only by the way he is concerned about the fate of life on this earth. His soul is going to heaven, that is the main thing. In the body and on this earth, it was no more than a guest, so the fate of this hostelry really has nothing to do with him. Religious practices lauding an indifference to life are on offer under many high-sounding names. A Western form of Buddhism has many adherents but has little to do with original Indian Buddhism. American pop-apocalyptic offers an especially dramatic escapism. Before the great afflictions at the end of the world, true believers will be "raptured"—snatched away to heaven, so that they can then build the new world with Christ at his Second Coming. All unbelievers unfortunately belong to the "Left Behind," the people who are not "caught up" and who will perish in the downfall of the world ("Left Behind" is the title of an American book series read by millions).[18] Whether people throw themselves into the pleasures of the present or flee into the next world because they either cannot or will not withstand the threats, they destroy the love for life and put themselves at the service of terror and the annihilation of the world. Today life itself is in acute danger because in one way or the other it is no longer loved but is delivered over to the forces of destruction.

THE GOSPEL OF LIFE

According to the Synoptic Gospels, salvation is the kingdom of God which Jesus anticipated, proclaimed, and practiced. According to Paul, it is to be found in the conversion to righteousness which God brings about. In the Gospel of John and in the Johannine epistles, it is the fullness of life, which has appeared in Christ. In this sequence we can detect an intensification of salvation and a heightened perception of it.

THE SYNOPTIC GOSPELS

Everything which Jesus proclaims according to the Synoptic Gospels derives from the conceptual material of the Judaism of the time. Nevertheless, while some people welcomed it, for the others it was annoyingly new. Although what Jesus preaches and does is not new in detail, it is nonetheless new in the form of its totality, as one must put it in the terms of todays's emergence theories. What is new in Jesus is identified by the name "gospel."

What kind of life is manifested through the earthly Jesus, the Son of God? Luke 4 sums up Jesus' divine mission in words taken from the prophet Isaiah:

> The Spirit of the Lord is upon me,
> because he has anointed me
> to preach good news to the poor.
> He has sent me to proclaim release to the captives
> and recovery of sight to the blind,
> to set at liberty those who are oppressed,
> to proclaim the acceptable year of the Lord. (Luke 4:18-19)

In Isaiah 61 this is followed by the words: "and the day of vengeance of our God." Luke leaves this out. The gospel to the poor says that it is to the poor that the kingdom of God belongs. "The acceptable year of the Lord" is the messianic Sabbath, in which debts are forgiven and prisoners are set free. When the Messiah comes, the demons disappear from the earth and the sick are healed. When the blind see, the lame walk, lepers become clean, and the poor hear their gospel about the kingdom—then the Messiah has come, and with his coming the messianic era dawns. The miracles of healing Jesus performs, or which take place in his proximity, are not intended to present him as a divine exceptional human being; they are miracles of the kingdom and signs of the messianic future which, with Jesus, breaks into the present in its sickness. They are "miracles" only in an unchanged world. If the kingdom of God becomes powerful in the present, healings and liberations are not "miracles" at all; they are a matter of course. The kingdom of the living God is health and life, and the fullness of life. The kingdom of God embraces the whole creation and is as protean and multicolored as creation itself. This kingdom is not merely an ethical ideal of righteousness and justice and peace. It is that too, but in its fullness it is earthly and bodily and is experienced with the senses, just as the sick experience their healing and just as people who have been imprisoned outwardly and inwardly experience their liberty with all their senses. Everything that lives and has to die longs for the fullness of life of God's kingdom. That is why the kingdom of glory on earth will fulfill the longings of the whole earthly creation. For human beings, this bodily dimension of the kingdom is especially important, because men and women are inclined to flee from the mortality of the body into a dreamed-of immortality of the soul and to leave earthly life with its infirmities and frailties to itself. But the life Jesus brings and makes a truly living life is the harbinger and beginning of the bodily life of the new creation.

Mark sums up Jesus' message by saying: "The time is fulfilled, and the kingdom of God is at hand; repent, and believe in the gospel" (1:15). At the center of his message is the kingdom of God. The phrase "at hand" does not mean that this is chronological information. What is meant is the presence of his future here and now. People who are reached by this message are freed from the existing world and the fabric of its life, and are brought by it to the beginning of a life that is new. "Repent and believe" is the call. Conversion means turning away from the old world and turning towards the new one; it is a turn to the future. This turn comprehends the entire life of the people addressed. What is being talked about is not a freedom they already have. Conversion is the new birth of a freedom that overcomes the world, a freedom capable of future. The kingdom of God which is "at hand" opens up for these people the liberty to begin a new life. Conversion is the anticipation of life in the kingdom of God in the conditions of the old world. It is the new way of living of people who do not "conform" to this world and do not allow themselves be brought into line. They have this world's possessions "as if they did not have them."

Resistance against the forces of death and unconditional love for life are characteristics of this new, free way of living. Faith is the trusting self-surrender to the coming kingdom and an experience of freedom in its proximity. The apocalyptic aeon doctrine which lies behind Jesus' message about the kingdom of God makes it clear that this is not a matter of improvements to the old system; it has to do with a fundamental alternative. In Christian terms this is no longer meant apocalyptically: in Christ the kingdom has already come so close—it is actually "at hand"—that people no longer have just to expect it, but in community with it can also already actively "seek" it, and should and can make its righteousness and beauty the goal of the way they shape the world and life. That does not mean that the kingdom of God is in their hands, but their hands are supposed to prepare the way for God's coming, and should open closed doors and lethargic hearts in expectation of his coming.

PAUL

For Paul, salvation is concentrated in the righteousness of God which is manifested in the self-giving and raising of Jesus, "who was put to death for our trespasses, and raised for our justification" (Rom. 4:25). It is the *transition* from death on the cross to the raising from the dead which in the light of the resurrection reveals the death of Jesus to be a self-giving for godless and godforsaken sinners, and which allows the Jesus who appears in the light of the resurrection to be recognized as the one crucified. It is this *turn* from self-giving to raising, from humiliation to exaltation, from death to life, which is decisive, because with this turn in Christ *the eschatological turn of the world* begins, from transience to non-transience, from the night of the world to the morning of God's new day and to the new creation of all things.[19]

It is therefore mistaken to reduce the justification of sinners to the forgiveness of their sins. We become just only in the power of the Spirit of Christ's resurrection. But it is of course also mistaken to celebrate the resurrection only on Easter morning. Without liberation from the burden of the sins of the past, there is no future for a just life.

In his Christ mysticism, Paul perceives a mutual indwelling between Christ and believers: we in Christ—Christ in us.[20] Believers become "like in form" to the crucified and risen Christ "always carrying in the body the death of Jesus, so that the life of Jesus may also be manifested in our bodies" (2 Cor. 4:10). The sufferings of Christ and the resurrection life of Christ mark the existence of believers simultaneously, and do so paradoxically "as dying, and behold we live" (2 Cor. 6:9).

Because Paul starts from the raising of Christ *from the dead*, he reaches out beyond Israel's expectation of the messianic future to the promise of creation, and sees in Christ not only Israel's messiah but also the head of the new humanity. "The first man Adam became a living being but the last (new) man became a life-giving spirit" (1 Cor. 15:45). "For as in Adam *all* die, so in Christ shall *all* be made alive" (15:22). According to Jewish Wisdom teaching, God has created human beings for eternal life. So when mortality is overcome in the raising of Christ, that begins the fulfillment of the creation promise: eternal life in the new creation, which will be without the possibilities of sinning and of death, because the living God is present in all things.

JOHN

In the Gospel of John, salvation is fully understood for the first time as life and is identified with Christ himself. The eternal God has the fullness of life in himself, and is therefore rightly called "the living God." In the same way, the Son of God also has life in himself and through his coming into this world becomes the source of the world's life, and life-giving life for others (John 5:26). "In him was life, and the life was the light of people," says the prologue to John's Gospel (1:4), and in the same Gospel Jesus says about himself "I am the bread of life; I am the light of the world; I am the resurrection and the life" (6:35; 8:12; 11:25). This makes clear which life of Jesus is meant here; it is the eternal life in which the risen Christ appeared to the disciples and which they perceived with all their senses:

> That which was from the beginning,
> which we have heard,
> which we have seen with our eyes,
> which we have looked upon
> and touched with our hands,
> concerning the word of life—
> the life was made manifest,
> and we saw it, and testify to it, and
> proclaim to you the life which is eternal. (1 John 1:1-2)

That is the fullness of life, the life that is wholly and entirely filled with livingness. It is a life which by virtue of the risen Christ, the Christ who is present in the presence of God, is liberated from terror, from death, and from anxiety. It is an entirely and wholly human life participating wholly and entirely in the divine life. It is a human life which God indwells and which, for its part, dwells in God. Where do we find a life like this?

The answer given in John's Gospel is clear: it has appeared in Jesus Christ, is experienced in the life-giving Spirit, and will one day become the life of the whole future world.

This eternal life is synonymous with *the love of God* the Synoptic Gospels, Paul, and the Gospel of John talk about. For the eternal life which God has within himself presses in love beyond him to the creation of a beloved world, to the redemption of this world from terror and death, and to the perfecting of this creation. Love is the self-communication of life. So in this way eternal life becomes loving and loved life. In the sending of the Son into this world, which is not merely threatened by powers hostile to life but is actually dominated by them, the love of God appears, and with that love true life (Rom. 8:38-39; 1 John 4:9). And in that way, this loved and loving life becomes a possibility for human beings:

> God is *love*, and he who abides in love
> abides *in God*
> and God abides *in him*. (1 John 4:16)

In the Synoptic Gospels the ethos of hope is conversion in faith to the gospel of the kingdom of God. In Paul it is the effect of the raising of the crucified Christ in the justification of the godless. In John it is eternal life in love. The turn to the future, resurrection into life, and the life lived in love: these things constitute the Christian ethos of hope.

WHAT FOLLOWS FROM THIS FOR A THEOLOGY OF LIFE?

What follows from this for a theology of life relevant for a culture of life today? We ask first of all: In what way is eternal life eternal? As the word "eternal" is used in the Old and New Testament, it does not define the quantity of life but its quality. Eternal life is not an endless life; it is a life full-filled by God. So eternal life has nothing to do with life-prolonging projects and tedious longevity. Nor is eternal life timeless life. According to Plato indeed (whose belief in immortality is followed by many Christians and theologians) we experience time as a sequence of fleeting moments in life which cannot be brought back. That is the time signified by the Greek word *chronos*. According to the Greek interpretation, *chronos* is the brother of death, *thanatos*. Time is transitory, and transience is the time of death. If time is the quintessence of the transitory, then eternity must, in contrast, be what abides, what is timeless and non-transient. If we apply this antithesis between time and eternity to life, we can conceive of timelessness, but not of a timeless life. Applied to God, the idea of a timeless eternity makes God a non-living being without relation. But the God of the biblical traditions is the "living" God, who has a living relationship to his temporal creatures. His eternal life is the wellspring of the livingness of all temporal living things. So we have to measure eternity against the concept of life, not life against the concept of eternity. Over against Plato, Boethius proposed a different concept of eternity: *Aeternitas est interminabilis vitae tota simul et perfecta possessio*[21]—"Eternity is the unlimited, complete, simultaneous, and perfect enjoyment of life." Applied to God, God's eternity then means his unrestricted and perfect livingness in his inexhaustibly creative fullness of life. Applied to human beings, eternal life means the perfect fullness of life in unhindered participation in the life of God.

Eternal life is life filled by God's presence in the risen Christ and in the vital powers of his Spirit. That is the lived experience of God in the full-filled moment. Every moment of life full-filled in this way is "an atom of eternity," as [Søren] Kierkegaard said,[22] and a promise of the coming consummation.

The corresponding experience of time is not transience; it is futurity. The essence of this is not the experience of time in the evening, but time as it is experienced at daybreak. What is important is not the time of death but the time of birth. *Chronos* disappears, its place being taken by *kairos*, for *kairos* is a brother of life, *zoe*. Empty, transitory time is transformed into fulfilled time, and every full-filled moment becomes the foretaste of the eternal and perfect enjoyment of life.

We go on to ask: In what way is eternal life living? What belongs to the livingness of life?

Human life lives from being *affirmed*, since it can also be denied. For human life to be destined for eternal life means its unequivocal and unconditional affirmation by the living God. If God himself becomes a human being, and if in Christ eternal life appears among mortal men and women on this earth, then the human race is wanted by God, and every individual person can have confidence in his own existence. Every woman, every man, and every child is desired and wanted and expected. The creation of human beings in the earth's community of creation, the taking flesh of the eternal Word among us, and the outpouring on "all flesh" of the life-creating Spirit are an affirmation of humanity within the community of all the living in the living space of the earth. Humanity is affirmed like this by God not just for itself, and not for heaven, but in the community of life, and for this earth.

The only answer to the question "Why are you alive?" is, as Meister Eckhart said, "I live because I live." "The rose blooms, it blooms without a why, it blooms because it blooms," says Angelus Silesius in a poem. Life is an end in itself—that it to say, it is beyond utility or uselessness. It has its meaning in itself. So it must be lived. It has no "value," so it cannot be "utilized." There is no "valueless life" which can be destroyed, neither the life of others nor one's own. Every life holds within itself the spark of eternal life. "The right to life" is an uninfringeable human right, and its dignity must be protected against commercialization through patents and licenses.

In spite of the evil which people suffer and inflict on each other and on life itself, people become "good, whole, and beautiful"[23] through the righteousness of God which rectifies and justifies. God even affirms the human life which has destroyed itself and other life, in order to put it right and to heal it. That is the meaning of the Pauline doctrine of justification. Solely out of grace and solely through grace the victims and the perpetrators of sin are made just. Through the divine righteousness they are delivered from evil and liberated from "the body of sin," as Paul describes in Romans 7. God's righteousness is not a righteousness that pins people down to what they have done, and retaliates; it is the healing "sun of righteousness" which puts things to rights and awakens everything to life. Once the compulsion of evil is broken, death too will lose its power. Right through the night of terror, the terror of evil, God's affirmation of life becomes visible. There is no reason to deny life, to despair of this world, or to give up on oneself. Even the life burdened with sin and given over to death will be accepted by God and recognized and loved as the life he has created. So the most succinct definition of being human is that the human being is justified by God.[24] It follows from this that human life is aligned towards *acceptance* as well as affirmation, for in this world it is often rejected and handicapped. The fear of guilt, on the other hand, condemns it to meaninglessness.

The gospel of life is God's Yes to loved and loving life, to personal life and to a life of fellowship, to human and natural life on God's beloved earth. At the same time it is God's No to terror and death, to injustice and violence against life, to resignation, apathy, and the death wish.

If we really want to live life, we must fight against the forces of death in the very midst of life. We must not surrender to lethargy of heart. We must not withdraw into private or churchly life. The resurrection hope of Christ encourages us to commit ourselves to a love for life everywhere and at all times, because it allows us to look for the universal victory of life beyond death. The love for life against death *here* is a wonderful resonance of the future of eternal life *there*. The resurrection hope reveals humanity's destiny to survive. It justifies life against the claims of death. But that already brings us to the heart of the question about a "culture of life."

LOVE FOR LIFE

BUT WHAT IS LIFE? WHAT IS HUMAN LIFE? IN WHAT DOES THE HUMANITY OF LIFE CONSIST?

The concept of life must include all the knowledge collected by biology. But this is hardly possible, because there are transitional fields, and through a concept we would limit the creative future of life itself. It is easier to draw up some boundaries that mark the negation of life: life as a state of being is contrasted with death and with things that are dead; life as a process of activity and movement is contrasted with inactive and immobile life; life as being that is limited in time between beginning and end is contrasted with unlimited being; organic life is differentiated from inorganic matter. But here too there are so many transitional fields that a definition of life as distinct from its negation can only be provisional and heuristic. Nor must we forget that "life" is not merely a biological concept; in general use it has so many connotations and evokes so many expectations that its reduction to biology would abbreviate and impoverish the understanding of what life is. For a full understanding of life, the biological concept of life has to be integrated into the social, political, philosophical, and theological concepts of what life is. It is only the observation of its interacting relations that makes a life-furthering understanding of life possible.

Human life is life that is engendered and given birth to by human beings. It has a livingness specific to its own species, is bracketed by birth and death, and is closely connected with organic stages. It is numbered among the self-referential forms of life; it is lived socially in the spaces of human communities and in the times of human generations; it exists in an exchange of energy with the atmosphere and in exchange of the means of life with the biosphere, and in its body-soul totality it is part of the earth's organism; not least, it is aligned towards transcendence, and as long as it is alive it is involved in the process of transcending. It is being and ability-to-be, it is at once the reality and the potentiality of itself.

Modern anthropology has with particular interest stressed the special position of the human being in the cosmos of living things, and has judged that what is specifically human is what differentiates human beings from animals, the purpose here being to justify the human being's dominant role.[25] This is the origin of the view that human existence is hostile to nature, the view that characterizes modern human beings: the animal is tied to its environment, the human being is open to the world; the animal has no spirit, the human being is a spiritual being; the animal is soulless, the human being is ensouled. Behind this stand the great disjunctions which legitimate human domination in the bourgeois and industrial age: subject—object; history—nature; spirit—matter; necessity—freedom; civilization—nature. The new psychosomatic view of the human being, and the ecological viewpoint which stresses the community between nature and civilization, are steps with which to surmount these divisions, which are deadly for both sides.

We ask about a human life which corresponds to the life which has appeared in Christ.

According to the biblical interpretation, human life is only experienced and lived in a warp and weft with all the living, with animals and plants; for human beings are earthly beings (Genesis 2), and it was together with the animals that they were saved from the Flood. The covenant with Noah is a covenant of life made with human beings and "every living creature" (Gen. 9:9-10). The biblical word "flesh" (*kol' basar*) means "all the living," and embraces human life together with all the living on earth. The "becoming flesh of the Word" (John 1:14) and the outpouring of God's Spirit "on all flesh" are not meant anthropocentrically.

The new psychosomatic, ecological, and theological anthropologies are orientated towards a comprehensive concept of life, and are well suited to overcome Western anthropocentrism. It is not the human being that is at the center of the earth; it is life. Human life is part of universal life, even if a special part. Human beings will only fulfill their special task as "the image of God" if they recognize the community of creation in which and from which and with which they live.

Human life is not as yet identical with the *humanity of life*, as a task for living. Every man or woman is a human being, but he or she has also *to be* a human being. Human beings are intended to live and act as such, for they can also live and act inhumanly. We may gather together some factors which are indispensible for the humanity of human life:

1. *The affirmation of life*: Human life must be affirmed, for it can also be denied. Even before it is born, a child must already be affirmed in its mother's womb, for it can only grow, develop, and live healthily in an atmosphere of affirmation. If it lives in an atmosphere of rejection, as an "unwanted child," it withers spiritually and deteriorates physically. It is only when a child feels that its life is affirmed that it can learn to affirm itself, and that is essential for living.

2. The same is true for the conscious *acceptance of life*. Human life must be affirmed and actively accepted. Only then will it become a life that is lived and experienced. It is only positive acceptance and esteem which activates the motivation system in body and soul. If a child feels that its existence is rejected,

it becomes ill, and withers away in its innermost being. If a grown-up feels rejected and despised, that person withdraws into himself, becomes defensive, or begins to despise himself and lose his vitality. Unless he experiences confidence, he never learns self-confidence. But if a life can no longer be experienced as a human life, it grows numb and turns to stone. This used to be called "the death of the soul."

3. Human life is *participation and sympathy*. Life comes alive when it finds that other people enter into it, and when it can enter into other life. Again we can easily make the cross-check: lack of sym-pathy leads to a-pathy, and that is a symptom of illness. Complete lack of sympathy is unlived life, "death in life." Human existence is social existence. To be humanly present means to be interested. As long as you are interested you are alive. Human life is alive as long as it exists in relationships. The loss of relationships which play an important part in a person's life leads to "social death," which is generally a preliminary stage to the real death of the human being as a whole.

4. Human life is marked by a *striving for fulfillment*. It is this striving that lends it its dynamic. The striving for fulfillment is part of "the struggle for existence." It is what the American Constitution when it is talking about human rights calls "the pursuit of happiness." We also talk about the "fulfilled life," the "good life," the "successful life," or the "meaningful life." But what we mean is nearly always the same: the potential of human life is supposed to be fulfilled in such a way that life can be completely affirmed, and that the person can feel satisfied. Two ways of leading a meaningful life have developed—either through participation in human responsibility for the world, or through self-fulfillment. But at bottom the two belong together and cannot be separated, because the human self belongs within the world, and the world belongs to the human self.

To sum up: *Human life is affirmed, accepted, interested, and fulfilled life.* It has to be lived and experienced, accepted and loved.

From this the second principle follows: *Consciously lived life is therefore a life which holds the contradictions within itself and finds the strength to endure and surmount them.* "The life of the Spirit is not the life that is afraid of death and keeps itself untouched by devastation but the life that endures death and maintains itself in it."[26]

Can the *eternal* life we talked about in the previous section be experienced in this life and on earth? Or can we expect it only in the life beyond death? The answer is that in the loved and loving life, eternal life can be experienced in every moment with the senses, for love—Hegel calls it "spirit"—is as strong as death and is the real beginning of a life which overcomes death.

PRELIMINARY ORIENTATIONS: POLITICS FOR THE WHOLE OF LIFE

1. When the atomic bomb was dropped on Hiroshima in 1945, the quality of human history was fundamentally changed: our time has become time with a time limit. The dream about "a world without nuclear weapons" is certainly a beautiful dream, but it is only wishful thinking. Nobody seriously expects that one day people will again stop being able to do what they can do now. Anyone who has once learnt the formula can never again forget it. Ever since Hiroshima, humanity has lost its "nuclear innocence" and will never get it back again.

If the nuclear age is humanity's final age, this means that today the fight for human survival is the fight for time. The fight for life is the fight against the nuclear end. If this is our endtime, we try to make it as endless as possible by continually giving threatened life on earth new time limits. This fight to postpone the end is a permanent fight for survival. It is a fight without victory, a fight without an end—and that at best. We can extend this nuclear endtime, but we and all the generations that follow us must eke out life in this endtime under the Damoclean sword of the bomb. The lifetime of the human race is no longer guaranteed by nature as it has been up to now; it must be ensured by human beings by way of deliberate policies of survival. Up to now nature has regenerated the human race after epidemics and world wars. Up to now nature has protected the human race from annihilation by individuals. From now on this will no longer be the case. Ever since Hiroshima life has irrefutably become the primary task for human culture, for political culture too. This means that all our decisions today must be considered in the light of the life of coming generations. That is the new, hitherto unknown responsibility of all human beings.

2. The nuclear age is the first age shared by all nations and all human beings. Ever since Hiroshima, the many different histories of the peoples on earth have become the shared world history of the one, single humanity—but initially only in a negative sense, in the mutual threat and the shared danger of annihilation.

Today the nations have entered the first common age of humanity, because they have all become the potential common object of nuclear annihilation. In this situation the survival of the human race is only conceivable if the peoples organize themselves into becoming the collective determining subject of action on behalf of survival. Ever since Hiroshima, the survival of humanity has become indissolubly linked with the uniting of the peoples for the purpose of together averting these deadly dangers. Only the unity of humanity will guarantee survival, and the premise for the survival of every individual is the unity of humanity. The life-saving unification of humanity in the age of nuclear threat demands the relativization of national interests, the democratization of the conflict-laden ideologies, the recognition and acceptance of different religions, and the general subordination of the peoples as a whole to their common concern for life.

JUSTICE—NOT SECURITY—CREATES PEACE

Today deterrents no longer safeguard peace, because suicide assassins can no longer be deterred, and because there is hardly any protection against attacks with biological weapons. The biblical traditions and the Christian experience of faith tell us that it is only righteousness and justice which create lasting peace (*shalom*). So there is no road to peace other than just action and concern for worldwide righteousness and justice. All Christian memoranda have correctly maintained this thesis. But what is righteousness and justice?

If Jews and Christians want to bring righteousness into the world, they will start from their experience of God's righteousness. They experience his righteousness as a creative righteousness and justice that makes people just and creates justice. God is just and righteous because he creates justice for people who are without rights and puts to rights the unjust. His righteousness is a saving righteousness, through which he creates the peace which endures: *shalom*.

From this it follows that there is no peace where injustice and violence prevail, even if "law and order" are enforced. It is not security and deterrents that bring peace; it is righteousness and justice. Injustice always creates inequalities and destroys just balances. Unjust systems can only be kept alive with the help of violence. There is no peace where violence prevails, for where violence prevails it is death, not life, that rules.

The biblical traditions and the Jewish and Christian experience of faith talk about an all-embracing peace because they talk about God's peace. Shalom means the sanctification of the whole of life God has created, in all its relationships. It is life blessed in fellowship with the life-giving God, with other people, and with all other created being: peace with God, peace among human beings, peace with nature. For God's sake, it is impossible to restrict shalom religiously or individually. Shalom is in tendency universal and enduring. What Jews and Christians experience of this peace in history is, as they see it, also the beginning and anticipation of the peace of God which will one day bring all created being to eternal life. Judaism and Christianity at their best are movements of practical hope for peace for all peoples and all creatures.

It follows from this that in history peace is a process not a state, a shared path not an individual possession. Peace is not the absence of violence; it is the presence of righteousness and justice.

In history, lasting peace is never there only for a particular generation alone, but also springs from responsibility for justice between the generations. Humanity has been created as a sequence of generations. Consequently, every generation is indebted to the generations that have gone before, and consequently, every generation bears responsibility for the life of the generations to come. Only justice in this unwritten human generation contract contributes to a lasting peace. Peace in history is not a condition in which one could sit back and rest on one's oars; it is always a way forward which has to be pursued, so as to create time for humanity, and so as to make life for coming generations possible.

FROM POWERLESSNESS TO COMMUNITY

The qualitative alternative to poverty and wealth is *community*. In a community determined by solidarity, all its members become rich in relationships, in brothers and sisters, friends and neighbors, comrades and colleagues, rich in trust. In communities like this, in most cases we can help ourselves. Men and women are there for each other, so their ideas, their abilities, and the means at their disposal are available for all of them. In communities united in solidarity we take our lives into our own hands, and out of the hands of the people who dominate us and want to exploit us. Helpful initiatives are not ordered from above but come into being at the grass roots. Kindergartens, neighborly help, co-operatives, trade unions, and many citizens' action groups originated when men and women combined spontaneously in manageable groups. It was only as they developed that these groups became professionalized and bureaucratically organized. In society's great bureaucratic institutions, there are always deficits which have to be administered. When people join forces for the purpose of mutual help, the richness of life emerges. When people find the courage to say "we are the people," dictatorships collapse, as they did in 1989 in East Germany, in what was then the GDR. When Christian congregations say "We are the church," they come of age.

The stress on individualization rather than community makes people in modern societies powerless and open to manipulation, in accordance with the old Roman motto *divide et impera*, divide and rule. On the other hand amalgamations at the grass roots for the purpose of a shared life call up the power of the people, and a community for the common good is created in which everyone can acquire a just share. This is also true on the level of the world market: if the nations take the liberty to provide for themselves first of all, before they produce for the world market, there will be enough for everyone. For this to be possible they must demand their right to their own land, which is taken from them by alien forces and global concerns.

It is quite possible to live in poverty if the poverty is borne by everyone together, and is justly distributed. Only injustice makes poverty a torment. Only the dissolution of community kindles just anger. If everyone is in the same boat, people help one another. Once there ceases to be equality, the mutual help often stops too. We shall come back later to forms of the common life.

THE TURN FROM DOMINATION TO COMMUNITY

If in a biosystem where human society is linked with nature there is a crisis in which nature dies, this logically becomes a crisis in the system as a whole—in the attitude to life, in the conduct of life, and not least in fundamental values and convictions. The dying of the forests finds its correspondence in the spread of mental and spiritual neuroses, the pollution of the seas and rivers is paralleled by the nihilist feeling about life which is prevalent among many people who live in the mega cities. The crisis we are experiencing is not just an ecological crisis, nor can it be solved merely technologically. A reversal in convictions and basic values is necessary as well as a reversal in the attitude to life and in the conduct of life. What are the interests and values which govern our scientific and technological civilization? To put it simply: the main concern is the boundless will for domination which has driven men and women to seize power over nature, and continues to do so. It is the modern Western civilizations which for the first time have been programmed with a bias towards growth, expansion, and conquest. To gain power and to secure power are the fundamental values which are virtually in force, regulating everything in our society. Why has this come about?

Its deepest reason is probably to be found in the religion of modern men and women. In Western Europe, ever since the Renaissance, God has always been interpreted in an increasingly one-sided way as "the Almighty." Omnipotence has counted as the preeminent attribute of his divinity. God is the Lord, the world is his property, and God can do with it what he likes. He is the absolute determining subject, and the world is the passive object of his rule. In Western tradition, God moved more and more into the sphere of transcendence, and the world came to be seen as purely immanent and earthly. God was thought of as world-less and so the world could be conceived of as god-less. It lost its divine creative mystery and through science could be stripped of its magic, as Max Weber aptly described this process. The strict monotheism of modern Western Christianity has become a decisive reason for the secularization of the world and nature.

As God's image on earth, the human being was obliged to see himself quite correspondingly as lord and master, as the determining subject of knowledge and will, and had to stand over against his world, which was his passive object, and to subjugate it. For it is only through his rule over the earth that he can correspond to God, the Lord of the world. God is the Lord and possessor of the whole world, so the human being must endeavor to become the lord and possessor of the earth, in order to prove that he is the image of his God. It is not through goodness and truth, not through patience and love, that the human being will come to resemble his God; it is through power and domination.

In order to experience that our place is within nature and that we belong to the same family as all other living things, we must undergo a reversal. This must begin with the picture of God from which we take our bearings. The consequence will be a turn away from one-sided domination, and a turn to mutual community.

The triune God—the very name makes this clear—is not a solitary, apathetic ruler in heaven who subjugates everything; he is a God rich in relationships and able to enter into relationships, a fellowship God: "God is love." The ancient doctrine of the Trinity was an interpretation of this experience. If this is true, then human beings can correspond to this triune God not through domination and subjugation but only through fellowship and life-furthering reciprocity. It is not the human being as a solitary determining subject who is God's image on earth; it is the true human community. It is not individual parts of creation which reflect his wisdom and his beauty; it is the community of creation as a whole.

The perception of the divine Spirit in all things engenders a new view of the world. If God's Spirit has been poured out on the whole creation, then the divine Spirit effects the unity and the community of all created beings with each other and with God. Life is communication. The life of creation is the communicating fellowship of creation. This warp and weft of mutual relationships in life is brought about by the divine Spirit, who in this respect can also be called the "cosmic Spirit."

The perception of the divine Spirit in the community of creation corresponds to the new ecological understanding of nature which we are seeking. The era of the mechanistic world picture was also the era of subjectivity and of the sovereignty of human beings over against nature. The subjectivity of human existence and the reification of natural being conditioned each other mutually. If this bifurcation of the world we share is not to lead to the destruction both of nature and human beings, we must replace it by a new paradigm of a communicative community of culture and nature resting on reciprocity.

WE ARE STARDUST

If the cosmos does not show any "strong anthropic principle," why should this recognition cast us into melancholy? Does the silence of the universe offend us, as an insult to our narcissism? Are we then the "crown" of the universe, or at least the summit in the development of matter and the organic stages? Or have we asked the wrong question? Even if there is no anthropic principle in the cosmos, is there not at least a *cosmic principle in anthropology*? The cosmos does not have to be aligned towards the appearance of the human race on the planet earth, but we human beings are aligned towards the cosmos and dependent on it. We are "stardust." The fundamental molecules which make up human life derive from the explosions of supernovae and are distributed throughout the universe. The elements of the cosmos are present in our physical constitution. We are a part of the cosmos. The consequence of this fact is a *cosmic anthropology* in which the human microcosm corresponds to the universal macrocosm. It is an ancient and fascinating idea that the cosmos arrives at consciousness of itself in the human perception of it, and in the human consciousness in general. However fragmentary our cosmological knowledge may be, when we do not merely ask what something means for us, but also what it means for the cosmos, what emerges is an anthropological cosmology in correspondence to a cosmological anthropology. For it could well be that the future of human consciousness converges with the future of the cosmos. In a Christian eschatology of the cosmos, a cosmological Christology such as we find in the Epistles to the Ephesians and the Colossians will bind together the fate of humanity with the fate of the cosmos in the vision of the new creation. However speculations about the possible death of the universe through heat-death or the Big Freeze may frighten us with the senselessness of the universe, we believe for Christ's sake in the deification of the universe through the coming indwelling of the eternally living God in all things.

An Ethics of Life: Medical Ethics

Source: Moltmann 2010; ET 2012:71–75.

Some Benchmarks for a Judgment

Before we come to some problematical areas of modern bioethics, we have to clarify a few essential benchmarks if we are to form a judgment.

1. The greater the scientific and technological power over the vital processes becomes, the more far-reaching is the responsibility of everyone concerned.[27] Earlier, birth and death, health and sickness were largely regulated by nature and personal fate. People came to terms with the fact that here nothing much could be changed. They accepted the natural processes in their own bodies as being God's will, or surrendered themselves to their fate. The Hippocratic oath enjoined that life should be protected and furthered, but this meant life within the limits laid down by nature and personal destiny. The splendid advances in biogenetic research and reproductive medicine are continually pushing back human dependence on nature and progressively extending the area of what was humanly possible. Nothing is a matter of fate any more—everything is possible: that seems to be the goal. The human being is to become the master of his own constitution and his own potentiality. But we do not have to do everything we can do. In order to handle the power that has been gained wisely and in a way that furthers life, society must set up ethical principles and rules, to which scientists and doctors have to conform. The Hippocratic oath applies not only to medical practice but already to the sciences themselves. It is foolish to develop more power than can be responsibly used ethically and controlled by law, the consequences of which cannot be foreseen. The natural regulating systems which have hitherto obtained are being replaced by imposed social systems. So we talk about health "policies," population "policies," and scientific "policies." We have to ask about ethical rules precisely at the points where nature and fate once reigned supreme. The powers of nature and fate were blind, as chance and fate are always portrayed as being. But the power of human beings must be clear-eyed if it is to protect and further human life, and the humane quality of that life. Today, instead of accepting nature and fate as "God's will," we have to inquire about God's will in human ethics.

2. Human nature is a free nature. Of course every person's particular freedom is conditioned by his physical and mental constitution. Nor has he any control over the place and time of his birth, and hence initially his life. Yet his nature and his fate provide no directions for the way he should act. I am unable to understand why the demand to be "true to nature" has to be an

uninfringeable doctrine of the Catholic church, since the human being has an "ex-centric" position to his own nature. He *is* bodily and *has* a body, so at the same time he is nature and has nature. The freedom of his nature is shown in the ambivalence of being and having. An ethics of life will try to find tenable balances between being and having. Human beings must take responsibility for what they do and leave undone. They cannot push off that responsibility on to "nature." Birth control, with all the methods which do not endanger life, is part of responsible parenthood. The ethical question is not whether the pill or condoms are used but *how* they are used. The Knaus-Ogino method of abstinence during periods of ovulation leaves more to nature but it is no better ethically. The biological concept of nature alone (for nature is more than biology) does not tally with the responsibility of human beings for the birth of human life. It seems to me more important to stress the fact that every fusion between sperm and ovum brings about not just a new human life but also a mother and a father who must stand up to their responsibility. And what we discuss in the sector of birth control cannot be silenced when it is a matter of the control over dying. Here too a purely biological concept of nature fails to take account of the dignity of dying, and its human quality.

3. According to the Christian view, every human life is created to be the image of God on earth, and must be respected as such. This fact has two dimensions: It means first of all God's relation to the human being, and secondly the human being's relation to God. God puts himself into a relationship to human life which reflects his divinity in the way a mirror does. God's relationship to the human being is universal, indestructible, and inalienable. The human being's relationship to God, on the other hand, is potential: it can be realized through a life which corresponds to God and is responsible, or—running counter to this—it can fail to be so realized. The human being's relationship to God is visibly portrayed and given concrete form in God's incarnation. This incarnation, or becoming human, in Jesus Christ is also the incarnation or becoming human of God's eternal Word. "All the works of God end in bodiliness," said Friedrich Oetinger in the eighteenth century, in opposition to [Julien Offray de La] Mettrie's book *Man a Machine*. Today, to see divinity in human bodiliness is a necessary contrast program to the modern computerization of human bodiliness. That is "the profound this-worldliness of Christianity" which Dietrich Bonhoeffer talked about, which "includes the ever-present knowledge of death and resurrection."[28] Love for life ensouls life's bodiliness and its sensory nature, and the resurrection hope gives the readiness to accept its mortality.

4. In order to arrive at exact scientific findings, we have to objectify the object to be investigated. It must be isolated from other contexts and reduced to one moment in its development so that it can be subjected to the interests of research. "Reason has insights only into that which it produces after a plan of its own," said Kant. "It must not allow itself to be kept, as it were, in nature's leading-strings, but must itself show the way with principles of judgment based upon fixed laws, constraining nature to give answer to questions of reason's own determining."[29]

The "plan" establishes the question which nature is constrained to answer, and eliminates other questions as being irrelevant. It establishes the dimensions of meaning within which the nature so questioned has to be understood. Perception and judgment are dependent on the perspective from which nature is seen. In the experiment, only the aspect is put forward in any given case in which nature is constrained to answer the question put to it. These are artificial situations made abstract through exclusion. The criterion for the correctness of the results is their repeatability.

Objectifications, isolations, and reductions of this kind are methodologically necessary if scientific verifiable results are to be arrived at. But if we wish not merely to establish them but to understand them as well, we must integrate them once more into the wider contexts out of which they have been extracted. The investigation of the parts does not as yet lead to an understanding of the whole. The scientific methods must not lead to an ideological reductionism. If we want to avoid this reductionism, we shall gather specialist sciences together and build up integrative sciences, as in the geosciences, for example, and in researches into the brain. To put it rather more generally, we shall integrate anthropologically the parts of the body analyzed in the specialist sciences into the total organism of the human body, and integrate the total organism of the body into the life history of the persons concerned, the persons into their societies, these societies into the community of humanity, and ecologically into the community of life on earth; and shall integrate all together into the systems of values and certainties in which we live and judge. We can make this clear to ourselves from our own experience of illness. Illnesses are objectified by the sick person. In severe cases he will be taken out of the world he lives in and put into hospital, possibly in an isolation ward. Once he is healed, the reverse process takes place: he is moved to the normal ward, is discharged, and returns to his own world. The reintegration process corresponds to the isolation process and is just as necessary—and occasionally even more difficult. What does this mean for ethics? We must not view the individual parts each for itself, but must comprehend their significance for their own relative totalities.

5. *Ultra posse nemo tenetur*: "No one is obliged to do more than he can." A Christian ethics must be neither abstract nor rigorous, but must take into consideration what the person can do "as far as he can," and what is objectively possible for him. Immanuel Kant's motto, "You ought, therefore you can," is an illusion, for the obligation does not provide the energies for an enabling. It is law without gospel. Anyone who sets up demands in God's name which people cannot fulfill is blaspheming God. Anyone who sets up demands which cannot be fulfilled does not want what he demands to be done; he is generally only ministering to his own self-righteousness and to the humiliation of other people. Excessive and impracticable demands are just as irresponsible as moral indifference. The medieval principle we quoted at the beginning of this section describes very well the limits of ethical demands and of human self-reproaches. We should do what we can and what it is possible for us to do, but should also recognize our limitations. No one is obliged to abrogate himself completely, because by doing so he would destroy himself as the determining ethical subject. What is impossible cannot be demanded or expected. An ethics of life is intended to serve life, the life of the acting person too. One should love one's neighbor as oneself, and that presupposes a healthy self-love. The person who despises himself will not be able to love his neighbor either. Someone who is uncertain in himself will make his neighbor uncertain too. The self-love which is presupposed has nothing to do with the egoism which seeks itself because it has lost itself or wants to fulfill itself but does not know itself. To accept oneself because one has been accepted by God purely out of love liberates us from the condition which Kierkegaard described as despairing at being oneself or despairing at not being oneself.[30]

6. The more perfect therapeutic methods become, the more doctors find themselves in borderline situations in which they have to decide over life and death, and are faced with an ethical dilemma: Should they determine the "value" of a patient according to external criteria? In that case the person must survive who clinically speaking has the greatest chances to live. Or should it be the person who has the greater social "value"? Does a positive judgment about the survivor imply a negative judgment about the one who cannot be helped? Can one weigh up people against one another in the way one weighs up commodities? Is one not destroying one's own integrity by making judgments of this kind? In borderline cases like this there are no simple solutions. Every decision in favor of one life at the expense of another leaves behind a feeling which I should like to describe as metaphysical sadness. It is not a feeling of moral guilt, for there are no alternatives, but it is certainly a feeling for the tragedy of history. It is good to be aware of this tragedy, for the awareness

makes us immune against the tempting notion that the life that has been saved was after all of more value than the life that could not be saved. It is only if we remain aware that unavoidable decisions of this kind are not good decisions that we cease to be content with them. The medical decisions in borderline cases of life and death resemble political decisions in critical situations. One has to do the better under poor conditions and yet be aware that it is not good. In history, tragic action of this kind is aligned in a trans-moral sense towards reconciliation. This awareness keeps the ethos healthy, because it is a preservation against the temptation of rigorous ethics which lead to inactivity, and permits no one to play God over the life or death of other people.

Is there an ethical rule of thumb for a decision at the borderline between life and death? In a seminar meeting about medical ethics an experienced doctor said to me *in dubio pro vita*—in case of doubt, decide for life. If there is still the faintest hope of saving life, try your utmost; if there is no longer any hope, accept the unavoidable.

EARTH ETHICS

Source: Moltmann 2010; ET 2012:147–48.

BENCHMARKS FOR FORMING A JUDGMENT

"THE PRESERVATION OF CREATION"?

The conciliar process for "Justice, Peace and the Integrity of Creation" was set on foot at the General Assembly of the World Council of Churches in Vancouver in 1983. What is at stake in the "preservation of creation"? The ecological theme was not new in the ecumenical movement. As early as 1961 the American Lutheran theologian Joseph Sittler demanded a new "Christology of nature" for the redemption of creation, on the basis of Colossians 1:20. In early Christianity the salient point of concern was Christ and the powers of nature, to which human beings felt they were delivered up. Today it is Christ and the human beings to whom nature is delivered up. In the ecumenical community, Orthodox theologians have always maintained a sacramental view of nature, because they hope for the eschatological deification of the cosmos. At the General Assembly of the WCC in Nairobi in 1975, in which I participated, the close connection between the social exploitation of human labor and the exploitation of the resources of nature was recognized and criticized. Because social and ecological justice correspond, "a just, participatory, and sustainable society" was formulated as model for an ecumenical ethics.

Some people criticized the concept of "the preservation of creation" because only God can preserve his creation; others rejected it because "preservation" has a very conservative flavor and fails to indicate innovative connotations. The original English phrase was "the integrity of creation"; but this is equally open to misunderstanding, because creation in its present condition is not "integer" or untouched. It is not complete and intact. It is imperfect, in need of redemption, and open to the future. According to Gen. 3:17, a curse lies over the earth. So the earth together with human beings waits for its redeeming integrity.

If we take as formula "the preservation of creation," and if we look at it more closely, this can mean only the part of creation that is at the disposal of the human being, not the universe and not heaven. The earth is to be preserved from depredations by human beings. Is that "conservative"? No, if progress leads to the annihilation of life on this earth, hope for the future of life lies in the preservation of the earth's sustainability. But this preservation has its own progress into the future of life, for it will further the earth's sustainability in order to anticipate the future of "the new earth on which righteousness dwells."

In this sense "the preservation of creation" must be called innovative through and through.

Economic growth and industrial development are thought of in terms of the linear temporal scheme of progress. There, past and future are in imbalance. But continuance can only be acquired if more and more equilibriums and cycles are introduced into the growth and development, in order to give them stability. It is only that which can be "recycled" which does not disappear, and serves "the preservation" of the earth's organism, the structure of which is itself cyclic and rhythmical. In order to further the earth's sustainability we have first to accept the divine promises which indwell the earth. The consequence is acceptance of the life-furthering patience of the earth, with which down to the present day it endures the human race and its civilizations—and this acceptance must precede definition of the role of human beings as protectors and stewards of the earth. Not least, it means acting in harmony with the spirit of the earth, so that "the wilderness will become a fruitful field, and the fruitful field is deemed a forest. Then justice will dwell in the wilderness, and righteousness will abide in the fruitful field" (Isa. 32:15-16).

I would formulate the motto for ecumenical ethics as follows: "For freedom and justice; for freedom and the future of the earth."

ETHICS OF JUST PEACE

Source: Moltmann 2010; ET 2012:165–67.

CRITERIA FOR FORMING A JUDGMENT

We shall begin with the introductory question about the criteria for forming a political judgment in questions about a just peace.

RIGHTEOUSNESS, JUSTICE, AND EQUALITY

The first question in political decisions is whether they serve social equality in a society or promote the inequality of its citizens politically, socially, and economically. The foundation of every democracy is the equality of it citizens. According to the tradition of democratic constitutions equality comes before liberty, for there is only liberty on the basis of equality—only social equality can secure a society's internal peace.

Between the nations too it is only justice which secures peace, not the supremacy of a nation or an imperium. The military, ecological, and terrorist perils have already become so great that if the human race is to survive, the concern for its survival must be given absolute precedence over and above the particular interests of nations, classes, and races. Egoistic, particularist interests will bring about the world's downfall. It is only in a community of human beings that it can survive. Human rights are an initial outline for a universal basic law or constitution for humanity.

THE DEFICITS OF POLITICS IN THE FACE OF GLOBAL PROBLEMS

Every political decision and every political demand is made in the face of the fact that the problems of the modern world are becoming global, whereas the political institutions have remained local. The peoples of the earth are increasingly becoming the objects of man-made crises, but they must become the subjects of their own history if they wish to overcome these crises. New nuclear powers are emerging which do not feel bound to any treaties about the non-proliferation or non-distribution of nuclear weapons. The financial markets have been deregulated and are leading the worldwide economy into catastrophes under which the poor countries have to suffer most. The ecological disasters do not come to a halt at national frontiers. The growth of the world population is uncontrollable. The nation states of the nineteenth century and the empires of the twentieth are becoming increasingly helpless. Out of their own self-interest, they are furthering the dangers instead of preventing them. Consequently, people are losing interest in their powerless policies and prefer to engage in citizens' initiatives locally and in global movements and non-governmental organizations (NGOs). These non-parliamentary global movements are driving beyond nationally limited policies. Greenpeace and the European Social Forum are the best examples. So the first task in the face of the global problems will be to overcome this deficit in politics.

ARE ETHICS ALWAYS TOO LATE ON THE SCENE?

If we ask about ways out of the present worldwide dangers, we are always already too late. Politics then become a matter of crisis management, and ethics turn into damage limitation. What is ethically required is demanded only in case of need, and after it has become the subject of general agreement. But what we need is crisis prevention and we must first surmount the ethics which are the cause of the crisis. We are not just looking for ways out of the dangers, but also for ways of preventing them. That is why it is important to look beyond the dangers themselves, and to anticipate a future in which all human beings will be able to live. Since the dangers are becoming global, what is required are not just system repairs but also a restructuring of the chaotic foundations of the world's previous political world systems. It is only if we believe that "another world is possible," as ATTAC says, and only if we hope that it will be better than the present one, that we can do what is necessary today. Erich Fried wrote forty years ago that:

> The man who wants the world to stay
> just as it is,
> doesn't want it to stay at all.

This is even more apt today than it was then.

IS TRUST THE SUBSTANCE OF DEMOCRATIC POLITICS?

Trust is the substance of democratic politics, said Konrad Adenauer, the first chancellor of the German Federal Republic (although his relationship to truth was very much his own)—not power, not even the sovereignty of a government. Democratic politics is essentially speaking the self-government of the people, which means that it is peace politics, not power politics. Politics, as Althusius said long ago, is *ars consociandi*—the art of consociation. For a democratically elected government trust is the greatest good because, unlike authoritarian and autocratic forms of government, it has to be trustworthy. Everyone must deal circumspectly with this general good and must not put it at risk through lies. People must do what they say they are going to do, and must say what they are doing. Anyone who replaces trust by controls sows mistrust and destroys his own basis. Without trust nothing works in a democracy. Trust is won through truthfulness and is strengthened by honesty. Mistrust evokes fear, and leads to the struggle of each against all.

JOY IN GOD: AESTHETIC COUNTERPOINTS

Source: Moltmann 2010; ET 2012:229–39.

Ever since the time of classic Greek philosophy, the Good and the Beautiful have belonged together and cannot be separated. Whatever is ugly cannot be good; whatever is evil has no beauty. Consequently, aesthetics is the reverse side of ethics, and every ethics of the Good issues from the aesthetics of the Beautiful, and leads to these aesthetics. Christian ethics is the human reaction to the coming of Christ into this world, and is an anticipation of his future in the new world.[31] That is why every good Christian ethics ends in doxology, so as with the praise of God to intensify the cry of hope, "Amen, come Lord Jesus" (Rev. 22:20). For in Christian ethics it must be clear that we do not make use of God in order to change the world, but we change the world in order to enjoy God, as Augustine said.

In ethics too, God and faith in God cannot be measured by their utility. That would deprive both God and faith of their dignity. But the world is there so that we may use it and sanctify it for God's sake, and so that we may glorify God and enjoy his presence.

But how can I sing when I am in a strange land?[32] How can I laugh where it is grief and tears that reign? How can I praise the beauty when I am surrounded by hate and by so much that is hateful?

Is there really freedom in the midst of slavery? Is there a home in what is so alien? Is there "joy in every sorrow," as Paul Gerhardt says in one of his hymns—hope where fear overwhelms us, and praise of the Creator even in the sighs of those he has created?

I believe that there is already a true life in the midst of false life, otherwise we should not feel the falsity of life at all. How could we feel the humiliations of captivity if we knew nothing about freedom? How could our suffering become conscious pain if there were nothing in which to rejoice? And why should we sigh over our own fragility and the transitoriness of our fellow creatures if we did not already have the praise of the Creator in our ears?

WHERE FREEDOM IS NEAR, THE CHAINS BEGIN TO CHAFE

It is only when the kingdom of God "is near" that we make an about turn. In the dawn of the day we sense the darkness of the night and get up. It is only when we experience the nearness of God with all our senses that we come alive and resist the powers of death. The people who are oppressed politically and socially do not surrender to their oppressors, but mock them, unmasking them in jokes about their miserably pompous rulers, and "the laughter of the oppressed"[33] echoes the laughter of God. "He who sits in the heaven laughs; the Lord has them in derision" (Ps. 2:4). The revolt of the humiliated begins with the mocking exposure of the powerful: "Let us tear their bonds asunder and cast away their ropes."

Every ethics of being-able-to-act and of having-to-act needs counterpoints of this kind. According to the Chinese Tao te Ching, this is the "wuwei," the not-doing in doing; according to Israel's Torah this is the Sabbath rest; this, according to the gospel, is the Easter jubilation of Christ's raising into the kingdom of God. The peace of God is not an ideal—beautiful, but for us mortal and fallible human beings unfortunately unattainable. Nor is it some far-off future at the end of our laborious days on earth. It is the immediate present in our hearts and in the mystery of the world, and we discover, as Friedrich Hölderlin's "Hyperion" says, that "All that is sundered finds back to itself / And there is peace in the midst of strife."

In this final chapter of the *Ethics of Hope* let us find a taste for peace, and think about:

1. God's Sabbath rest,
2. The Easter jubilation over the raising of Christ,
3. The "peace in the midst of strife."

SABBATH—THE FEAST OF CREATION

According to the first creation account in the Bible, the creation of the world *ends* on the sixth day: "And God looked at everything that he had made, and behold, it was very good" (Gen. 1:31). And yet "on the seventh day God *finished* his work which he had done" (Gen. 2.2).[34] What did he add to his finished creation on the seventh day? What was still lacking in his creation? What did its completion consist of?

The answer is a surprising one: the completion of the creation consists of the coming to rest of its Creator, and from the Creator's rest spring the blessing and sanctification of the seventh day of creation. According to Exod. 31:17, God "was refreshed"—he "heaved a sigh of satisfaction." The Creator withdraws himself and frees himself from his work, he detaches himself from what he has made and leaves what he has created in peace. The first step in this detachment is that "God looked at everything he had made" (Gen. 1:31). In order to look at it he needed space, for seeing is a remote sense. The second step in the detachment was that "God rested on the seventh day from all his work which he had done" (2:2). This resting in himself brings peace to what he has created.

This is a strange way of "completing" his works. Today, when we retire, start drawing a pension, and have to leave our job or professional life, we ask: Are we still of any use? What will I do now? We talk about "active retirement" or "happy non-retirement." One surely can't just stop going! One surely doesn't just belong on the scrap heap of aging, passive, useless senior citizens! Christians especially feel that they are "always at the service" of an unceasingly active God. *Deus non est otiosus*, ran a medieval saying—"God is never unoccupied." So we have become what [J. W.] Goethe describes Faust as being, "a monster without rest and peace." To go faster is not a problem, but to leave everything aside certainly is, and to reduce our speed is almost impossible. Yet "power lies only in rest."

On the seventh day of creation God encounters us in a very different way: he is at leisure, so to speak. God comes to rest. God detaches himself from his works. God puts aside his Being as Creator. God comes to himself again, after he had creatively gone out of himself. As their Creator, God is wholly with those he has created, but now he detaches himself from them and becomes free from his works and withdraws into himself. God comes to rest in the face of all those he has created, and with his being, resting within itself, is wholly present among them. His pleasure in his creation becomes the joy of those he has created. God is not just active, he is passive too; not only creative but also at rest; not just speaking but also listening; not merely giving but also receiving. In the beginning God created, and at the end God rests: that is the marvelous divine dialectic.

Perhaps artists can best understand how one can "complete" a creation by coming to rest. A painter puts his whole soul into his painting. When it is finished, he stands back in order to come to himself again and to let his work of art make its own way. Without this withdrawal, no work of art is ever "completed."

Only in one respect was the physico-theology of the eighteenth-century Enlightenment (Deism) represented by the notion of God as the "watchmaker" behind the machinery of the world who became "unemployed" after the creation of this law-regulated world because he had arranged everything splendidly and no longer could intervene without contradicting himself. In another respect, this was part of the baroque "theology of glory," which perceives and extols the Creator of the world in his Sabbath rest.[35] The much-abused Deism was also *Sabbath theology*.

"So God blessed the seventh day and hallowed it." What he blesses, he endorses. His blessing gives self-confidence and strength. So God blesses his living things with fertility (Gen. 1:22, 28). But on the Sabbath what he blesses is not any living thing; he blesses a time, the seventh day of creation. This is remarkable, because time is not an object. Time is invisible and flowing; we cannot hold time fast. How ought we to understand this divine blessing of a time for all God's creatures? God blesses this day not through an action but through his rest, not through something he does but through his being. He blesses those he has created through this day of his resting presence on which they too are supposed to arrive at their rest.

"Thou hast made us for thyself and our hearts are restless within us until they find rest in Thee," wrote Augustine.[36] This restlessness is not limited to human beings; it torments all living things which want to live and have to die. Where is the harbor of happiness, the home of identity, the place of rest? It is not far off in "the seventh heaven"; nor is it in the innermost part of the human being—in the seventh chamber of "the castle of his soul," as the mystics Teresa of Avila and Thomas Merton have described. It is on earth and easy to find in time: on the Sabbath day the eternal one is present in his rest, and those he has created can find him if they themselves come to rest.

God's first blessing was not conferred on his chosen people, nor on the promised land, but on the universal Sabbath day of creation. This was the way Israel understood the Sabbath from the time of the Babylonian exile. God dwells in time. The Sabbath is the Jewish cathedral.[37] On the Sabbath, time and eternity touch. The Sabbath is the mystical moment, the "present" of eternity.

That means that the weekly day of rest is not merely a making-present of creation in the beginning; it is also a making-present of redemption at the end, a time of remembrance and a time of hope. Beginning and end are present on this day, on which time and eternity touch. On the Sabbath, transitory time is abolished, the time of death is forgotten, and the time of eternal life is perceived. It is the liberating interruption of transient time through eternity.[38] And if we then look at the weekly succession of Sabbath days, we perceive a rhythm that belongs to eternity: the times oscillate in the dance of eternity. On every Sabbath, time is born anew.

The Sabbath is not only the day of rest, but also the day of no longer intervening in nature. In the Sabbath stillness, people no longer intervene in the natural environment through their work. With this the view of the world changes: things are no longer valued for their utility and practical value. They are perceived with astonishment in their value as being. Things appear as they are in themselves. With this, the environment as it is related to human beings becomes the world as it proceeded from God's creation. There is no proper understanding of the world as God's creation without this way of perceiving it in the Sabbath stillness.[39] In pure pleasure, without reason or purpose, things display their creaturely beauty. The world becomes more lovable when we no longer weigh it up according to the criteria of utility and practical value. We shall then also become aware of ourselves—body and soul—as God's creations and as his image on earth. We are then entirely without utility—we are quite useless—but we are wholly there, and know ourselves in the splendor of the shining face of God. The fearful questions about the meaning of life and our usefulness vanish: existence itself is good, and to be here is glorious. On the feast day of creation we come to ourselves and to God, who surrounds us from every side; but we cannot purchase the peace of this day; it cannot be earned. We must seek this leisure; and then it will suddenly find us.

The Jewish Sabbath corresponds to God's creation Sabbath and as the "seventh day" is a day of ending and completing. It is the day of rest after six working days. It is like the quiet evening after a laborious day. When "Queen Sabbath" enters Jewish houses, a completed week is crowned. The Jewish Sabbath with its rituals teaches us joy in existence and the wisdom of age.

Consequently, this celebration is full of gratitude for the works of creation and for safe-keeping in the history of the world and is an echo of the Creator's judgment: "And God saw that it was good." And yet, or just because of that, hidden in the Sabbath lies a hope that embraces the world. All the days of creation have an evening, when night falls, but the seventh day knows no night. It is like a day without end, and because of that it points beyond itself to the day of God's coming, the day when he will come to dwell eternally in his creation. That is why the rabbis often said, "If Israel were only to keep one single Sabbath, the Messiah would come immediately." The experiences of the Sabbath were always used as a way of describing the happiness of the messianic time.

The Jewish wisdom of the Sabbath is the completing: "All's well that ends well." That is why the origin of the world is not celebrated on the first day of creation, as it is in the creation myths of the different peoples, but on the last.[40]

The Christian churches, on the other hand, moved the weekly feast day from the seventh day to the first. That has a profound symbolic meaning. It celebrates the feast of Christ's resurrection on "the eighth day," as it was called in the patristic church—that is to say, on the day following the Jewish Sabbath. The Jewish Sabbath passes over into the Christian Sunday: out of the resting comes the resurrection jubilation; out of the end, the new beginning. The Christian Sunday too is a feast of creation. It is with Christ's resurrection the beginning of the new creation of all things. It is the consummation towards which creation at the beginning points. That is why the first creation account is read as part of the Catholic liturgy for the Easter vigil. The whole creation is drawn into the happening of the resurrection, which begins with Christ. With this the Christian Sunday becomes entirely "the feast of the beginning." Franz Rosenzweig characterized the Christian very well, from Jewish eyes: "The Christian is the eternal beginner; the completing is not for him: all's well that begins well. That is the eternal youth of the Christian; every Christian really lives his Christianity every day as if this day were the first."[41]

THE JUBILATION OF CHRIST'S RESURRECTION

Sunday as an officially decreed day of rest is not really a Christian feast day at all. The birth of Sunday can be viewed as being 3 March 312: "The Emperor Constantine to A. Helpidius: 'All judges, the people of the cities, and all forms of trading are to be free to rest on the worshipful day of the sun.'"[42] What has the day of the Roman sun god, *sol invictus optimus*, got to do with the Christian feast day?

The Christian feast day was celebrated by the Jewish Christians on what according to the Jewish calendar was "the first day of the week" (Acts 20:7; 1 Cor. 16:2). The expression "the Lord's day" (Rev. 1:10) was then added, being taken from Syria. In the second century, the curious phrase about "the eighth day" came into use. These terms presuppose the Jewish Sabbath, and do not replace it. The Christian feast day is not the Christian Sabbath. Consequently, Sabbath laws cannot be applied to the Christian feast day either, although all the Christian catechisms do so. When we look at the events that are celebrated, we find rather that there is a close *factual* connection between the celebration of the Jewish Sabbath and the Christian feast day.[43] On the Christian feast day, Christians celebrate the raising of Christ from the dead into eternal life and with that the annihilation of death through the beginning of a new creation in which death will be no more. They celebrate God's uprising against the powers of destruction in order to complete and perfect of his creation. Historically speaking, this goes back to the first appearances of the risen Christ at the empty tomb, without which we should know nothing at all about Jesus. But in the content of its truth, it is of the most tremendous explosive power, so that men and women break out into terror and jubilation.

On the day of the resurrection Christians perceive the beginning of the new creation of all things into their true and abiding form. Whereas Israel's Sabbath lets us look back to creation in the beginning, the Christian feast day points forward to creation's future. Whereas the Sabbath lets men and women share in God's rest, the feast of the resurrection confers a share in God's life-awakening power. The Sabbath holds within itself the wisdom of the ending—the Christian feast, the joy of the beginning. Remembering and thanking on the one hand, and hoping and beginning on the other, belong substantially together. It is necessary to be clear once more about the connection between the Sabbath and the Christian feast day, because the Christian feast became pagan when it coincided with the Roman day of the sun. In actual fact the Christian "first day of the week" is already hidden in the Jewish Sabbath, since although for God the creation Sabbath is certainly "the seventh day," for the human beings created on the sixth day it was the first day they experienced.

Among the Christian churches, one has radically detached itself from the Sunday of the Constantinian Christian imperium and celebrates the Jewish Sabbath in a Christian way—the Seventh-Day Adventist Church. For the post-Constantinian church this is an important signal, but does it not mean surrendering the special Christian day of resurrection?

My own suggestion, which I try to live by, is this: Why don't we on Saturday evening let the week merge into the Sabbath stillness and begin the new week on the following day with the feast of the resurrection and the new beginning? Why don't we celebrate from Saturday midday until Sunday midday? The "Sunday" will again become the authentic day of the Christian resurrection if we succeed in celebrating a Sabbath the evening before. From Saturday midday onwards, I should like to let the week draw to a close, finish work, or lay the work aside, and love and marvel over the created things round about me, then on "Sunday" morning begin afresh with Christ's resurrection and anticipate the new creation. In the creation story too we read that from the evening and the morning came the new day. The modern, worldwide way of counting time, which counts from Monday ("1") to Sunday ("7"), is not Christian. It was established by the churches without its being noticed. Anyone who has flexible working hours is forced to see his days of rest as movable holidays and has to incorporate them deliberately into his timetable. These days do not just contribute to one's health, as people say today; they are holy too, as used to be said.

The piety and devotion of the Western churches stresses Christ's resurrection from the dead and the assurance of eternal life;[44] in the Orthodox church, on the other hand, emphasis lies on the annihilation of death and the new creation of all things. In the West, stress lies on redemption from sin through Christ's giving of himself and the vanquishing of death through his resurrection; but in the East, the transformation of creation is emphasized. In the Lutheran church, Good Friday counts as the greatest of the feast days; if we want to encounter the original Christian Easter jubilation, we must go into an Orthodox church, for the Eastern churches are churches of the resurrection. All things are caught up in the resurrection joy, so that the Easter jubilation of us human beings embraces the whole cosmos. In order to draw this ecological dimension once more into the Christian feast day, and especially into the Easter festival, we can pick up thoughts from the "Sacred Hymns of the Eastern Church" and follow the canon of John Damascene for the feast of Easter.[45]

Rejoice ye heavens in worthy wise!
Earth too shout for joy!
Exult greatly, O cosmos,
the visible and the invisible both.
Christ has awoken, He the joy of the aeons.

Therefore we celebrate the slaying of death
and the binding of Hades—
the beginning of a new life
which will endure eternally.

Day of resurrection,
Yes, let us be light on the people's feast,
we will embrace one another!
We shall call brothers those who hate us!
And the resurrection lets us forgive all things.
So we shall cry:
Christ has risen from the dead,
defeating death through death,
and giving life to those who lie in graves.

It is good to react with such cosmic resurrection jubilation to the catastrophes in the human world, and to the terrors of the coming climate changes and to natural disasters. The ethics of life, of the earth, and of righteousness and justice follow from this jubilation. The exuberance of the Easter joy carries over into the continuing hope for God's future. This answer to the question, "What may we hope for?" makes the hope greater than anything we have to fear, for it takes our fear away.

"AND PEACE IN THE MIDST OF STRIFE"

On the Sabbath, a peace becomes possible in the unrest of transitory time. The nearness of God resting in himself radiates an atmosphere of tranquility. In the festival of Christ's resurrection, we too experience resurrection into life, in spite of all the violence of death. In the presence of the risen one, we are seized by the fullness of life in many dimensions, and an atmosphere of hilarity spreads abroad which I should like to call Easter jubilation compared with the Sabbath stillness. In addition to tranquility and to jubilation, we may add as third gift *peace*—not already the peace which ends all strife but as yet only the peace which makes it possible for us, in the midst of strife, to bring the conflict to a just end. Theologically, this is called "reconciliation"; this ends the enmity and is the beginning of a peaceful community.

According to Ephesians 2 and Colossians 1, through Christ's giving of himself God has created "peace" between Gentiles and Jews, since he "brings the hostility to an end" through himself (Eph. 2:16) and proclaims peace to those who were near and those who were far off. In the Epistle to the Colossians, the cosmic dimension is added to this concrete peace between Jews and Gentiles, since through Christ God "has reconciled to himself all things, whether on earth or in heaven, making peace by the blood of his cross" (1:20). In the human dimension as well as in this cosmic one, it is important to perceive that peace has already been made by God; so for human beings the one thing necessary is to perceive and accept what is objectively already existent *sub specie aeternitatis*, whether in human conflicts or in the cosmos. "God was in Christ and reconciled the cosmos with himself" (2 Cor. 5:19).

This is the "peace in the midst of strife." In the depths of the paralyzing and often deadly conflicts between the peoples, this *divine peace* already reigns. In the divine depths of the universe, everything is already reconciled. The person who perceives this views his enemies as "already reconciled" and will try to turn the conflict into just community with them. The universe, which to some scientists seems so meaningless and pointless, holds in its transcendent depths this divine peace and appears meaningful in itself. The person who perceives this will not fear the universe as silently alien but will know himself to be reconciled with all things. These two things may seem contrary to appearances, but the certainty of human and cosmic peace transcends the visible contradiction; "peace in the midst of strife" goes beyond the strife.

Just as the peace of God already dwells in the midst of the world, it is already present in the depths of human existence as well. "Contemplation in a world of action" is the way Thomas Merton described the spirituality in which we find this peace in the resting point of one's own soul. On the one hand this peace of God is "above" all understanding, and yet on the other hand it "keeps our hearts and minds" and senses within us. Why? The reason which Paul gives in Philippians 4:5 is that "the Lord is near." How near? As near as

Christ is in us. According to Augustine, God is closer to us than we can be to ourselves. According to the Qur'an, God is closer to us than our jugular vein. Consequently, Augustine told us to "withdraw into yourself. Truth dwells in the inner man."[46]

We "withdraw into ourselves" when in a quiet hour, or in conscious meditation, or in a momentary insight, we let all actions, interests, burdens, and projects fall away and ourselves become calm. We do not then fall into vacancy but are gathered up by the divine peace which dwells in us in the depths of our being. We then attain to the soul's hidden resting point, where we can gain a foothold and stand. In Christian contemplation we call this mystery: God, who dwells within us, Christ who lives in us, the divine Spirit, out of whom we are born anew. This hidden resting point of the soul is also the point from which our livingness springs. The closer we come to this point the more the peace within us grows, and, more than that, an immeasurable joy lays hold of us.

It is not only our "restless heart" that will be "kept" but our five senses too: feeling, tasting, smelling, hearing, and seeing. If through Christ in the peace of God they are preserved within us, they become aware, attentive, and curious for God's future. Ancient Christian mysticism turned away from the world and told us: "Close the gateway of thy senses and seek God deep within" ([Gerhard] Tersteegen). The new Christian mysticism is turned towards the future, and with its hope for God awakens all the senses for the future of God's world. Those who have found God in their innermost being can forget themselves, go out of themselves, and do their utmost without losing themselves. The person who senses in himself the nearness of the risen Christ will be filled with a joy that embraces the world. He sees this disputed and suffering world as already in the daybreak glory of its eternal beauty.

Notes

1. Moltmann 2010; ET 2012:xiii.

2. Ibid., 4.

3. Ibid., xii.

4. Søren Kierkegaard, *The Concept of Anxiety: A Simple Psychologically Orienting Deliberation on the Dogmatic Issue of Hereditary Sin*, Kierkegaard's Writings VIII, ed. Reidar Thomto and Albert B. Anderson (Princeton: Princeton University Press, 1981).

5. Hans Jonas, *The Imperative of Responsibility: In Search of an Ethics for the Technological Age*, trans. Hans Jonas and David Herr (Chicago: University of Chicago Press, 1984).

6. Friedrich Hölderlin, *Werke*, vol. 1, ed. Emil Staiger (Zurich: Atlantis, 1944), 334.

7. Jürgen Moltmann, "The Spirituality of the Wakeful Senses," in *In the End—the Beginning: The Life of Hope*, trans. Margaret Kohl (Minneapolis: Fortress Press/London: SCM Press, 2004), 79–86.

8. Cf. Ernst Käsemann, "Theologischer Rückblick," in Jens Adam, Hans-Joachim Eckstein, and Hermann Lichtenberger, *Dienst in Freiheit. Ernst Käsemann zum 100. Geburtstag* (Neukirchen: Neukirchener, 2008), 101.

9. Albert Camus, *The Rebel: An Essay on Man in Revolt* (New York: Knopf, 1961), 305.

10. "Es zittern die morschen Knochen / der Welt vor dem großen Krieg.Wir haben den Schrecken gebrochen, / für uns war's ein großer Sieg.Wir werden weiter marschieren, / bis alles in Scherben zerfällt."

11. Association for the Taxation of Financial Transactions and for Citizens'Action.

12. Donella H. Meadows, et al., *The Limits of Growth: A Report for the Club of Rome's Project on the Predicament of Mankind* (New York: Signet, 1972).

13. Stuart Kauffman, *At Home in the Universe: The Search for the Laws of Self-Organization and Complexity* (New York: Oxford University Press, 1995).

14. Paul C. W. Davies, *Cosmic Jackpot: Why Our Universe Is Just Right for Life* (New York: Houghton Mifflin, 2007).

15. Jonas, *The Imperative of Responsibility*.

16. Steven L. Weinberg, *The First Three Minutes—A Modern View of the Origin of the Universe* (New York: Basic, 1994).

17. Romano Guardini, *Freedom, Grace, and Destiny: Three Chapters in the Interpretation of Existence,* trans. John Murray (London: Harvill, 1961).

18. Tim LaHaye and Jerry B. Jenkins, T*he Glorious Appearing: The End of Days* (Carol Stream, IL: Tyndale, 2004), is the last volume in this latest pop-apocalyptic "Left Behind" series of Christian endtime stories, which created a stir in America but did not sell at all in Europe. See here Barbara R. Rossing, "Prophecy, End-Times, and American Apocalypse: Reclaiming Hope for Our World," *The Anglican Theological Review* 89, no. 4 (Fall 2007): 549–64. There is evidently a correspondence to Christian fundamentalist apocalyptic in the Islamic Hakkani movement and its spiritual mentor Ayatollah Mohammed Mesbah Jasdi in Ghom, Iran. These are "Mahdists" who believe that the "Twelfth Imam" "disappeared" in the ninth century and will return at the end of the world, in order, after a catharsis of the world through a catastrophe, to carry off believers to paradise and unbelievers to damnation. Iran's president Ahmadinejad belongs to this movement (*Der Spiegel* 26 [2009]: 104–107).

19. Ernst Käsemann, *Perspectives on Paul,* trans. Margaret Kohl (London: SCM Press/ Philadelphia: Fortress Press, 1971), 24-25.

20. Albert Schweitzer, *The Mysticism of Paul the Apostle,* trans. William Montgomery (Baltimore: Johns Hopkins University Press, 1998 [1931]) is still the only book on Paul's Christ mysticism.

21. Boethius, *The Consolations of Philosophy*, Book V.1.

22. Kierkegaard, *The Concept of Anxiety*.

23. Elisabeth Moltmann-Wendel, *Gib die Dinge der Jugend mit Grazie auf. Texte zur Lebenskunst* (Stuttgart: Radius, 2008), 51–60.

24. Martin Luther, "hominem justificari fide" in *Disputatio de homine* (1536), *Weimar Ausgabe* 39.1, 175ff.

25. Max Scheler, *Die Stellung des Menschen im Kosmos* (Munich: Nymphenburger, 1947 [1927]), 41: "to become human is to be elevated to openness to the world by virtue of the spirit."

26. G. W. F. Hegel, *Phenomenology of Spirit*, trans. J. Michael Steward, in *G. W. F. Hegel: Theologian of the Spirit*, ed. Peter C. Hodgson, Makers of Modern Theology (Minneapolis: Fortress Press, 1997), 101.

27. Jürgen Moltmann, *Science and Wisdom*, trans. Margaret Kohl (Minneapolis: Fortress Press/London: SCM Press, 2003).

28. Dietrich Bonhoeffer, *Letters and Papers from Prison,* trans. Isabel Best, et al., Dietrich Bonhoeffer Works, vol. 8, ed. John DeGruchy (Minneapolis: Fortress Press, 2009), 541.

29. Immanuel Kant, *Critique of Pure Reason*, Preface to the Second Edition, trans. Norman Kemp Smith (London: MacMillan, 1929), 20.

30. Søren Kierkegaard, preface to *Sickness unto Death*, 1849.

31. When after the unrest of 1968 the necessary political and social-ethical emphasis of my political theology became too strong, I freed myself in 1971 from the total claim of the law in the little book *The Theology of Play*, trans. Reinhard Ulrich (New York: Harper & Row, 1972), published as *Theology of Joy* (London: SCM Press, 1973), in order once again to give weight to the joy in aesthetics.

32. One of the spirituals begins: "How can I sing the Lord's song in an alien land?" Cf. James H. Cone, *The Spirituals and the Blues: An Interpretation* (New York: Seabury, 1972).

33. Jacqueline Aileen Bussie, *The Laughter of the Oppressed: Ethical and Theological Resistance in Wiesel, Morrison, and Endo* (New York: T&T Clark, 2007).

34. I am gratefully drawing on Abraham Heschel, *The Sabbath: Its Meaning for Modern Man* (New York: Farrar, Straus and Giroux, 1951); and Franz Rosenzweig, *The Star of Redemption*, trans. W. W. Hallo (New York: Holt, Rinehart and Winston, 1971).

35. Cf. Wolfgang Philipp, *Das Werden der Aufklärung in theologiegeschicht-licher Sicht* (Göttingen: Vandenhoeck & Ruprecht, 1957).

36. Martin Grabmann, *Die Grundgedanken des heiligen Augustinus über Seele und Gott* (Darmstadt: Wissenschaftlich, 1957). For the discussion about the restriction to the soul, cf. ch. 7, "Life's New Spirituality," in Jürgen Moltmann, *The Source of Life: The Holy Spirit and the Theology of Life*, trans. Margaret Kohl (London: SCM Press/Minneapolis: Fortress Press, 1997), 70–88.

37. Heschel, *The Sabbath*, 8.

38. Jürgen Moltmann, "What Is Time? And How Do We Experience It?" in *Dialogue: A Journal of Theology* 39, no. 1 (2000): 27–35.

39. Today some people associate this way of looking at things with meditative contemplation, but as Plato said, it is the view which comes from astonishment. In pure theory we perceive in order to participate, not in order to dominate, exploit, or utilize. We perceive things with our eyes, not with our grasping hand. We let things be what they are, and do not claim them for ourselves.

40. Rosenzweig, *Star of Redemption*, part 3, book 1.

41. Ibid., 359.

42. For more detail, see Moltmann 1985; ET 1985/1993: 292–96.

43. Franz Rosenzweig has remarked on this connection. See *Star of Redemption*, 358–59.

44. A typical documentation of this is Benedict XVI's encyclical *Salvi Spes*, which is concerned with the soul and its future in eternal life. The proximity to Gnostic redemption religion cannot be overlooked.

45. Cf. Ernst Benz, Hans Thurn, and Constantin Floros, *Das Buch der Heiligen Gesänge der Ostkirche* (Hamburg: Furche, 1962), 102, 103, 107, 114.

46. Grabmann, *Die Grundgedanken*, 11.

Bibliography

Theology of Hope: On the Ground and the Implications of a Christian Eschatology. 1964. Trans. James W. Leitch. London: SCM Press/New York: Harper & Row, 1967. Reprint: Minneapolis: Fortress Press, 1993.

The Crucified God: The Cross of Christ as the Foundation and Criticism of Christian Theology. 1972. Trans. R. W. Wilson and John Bowden. London: SCM Press/New York: Harper & Row, 1974. Reprint: Minneapolis: Fortress Press, 1993.

The Future of Creation: Collected Essays. 1977. Trans. Margaret Kohl. London: SCM Press/Philadelphia: Fortress Press, 1979. Reprint: Minneapolis: Fortress Press, 2007 (Ex Libris Ed.).

The Trinity and the Kingdom: The Doctrine of God. 1980. Trans. Margaret Kohl. London: SCM Press/San Francisco: Harper & Row, 1981. Reprint: Minneapolis: Fortress Press, 1993.

God in Creation: A New Theology of Creation and the Spirit of God. 1985. The Gifford Lectures, 1984–85. Trans. Margaret Kohl. London: SCM Press/San Francisco: Harper & Row, 1985. Reprint: Minneapolis: Fortress Press, 1993.

The Way of Jesus Christ: Christology in Messianic Dimensions. 1989. Trans. Margaret Kohl. London: SCM Press/San Francisco: Harper & Row, 1990. Reprint: Minneapolis: Fortress Press, 1993.

The Spirit of Life: A Universal Affirmation. 1991. Trans. Margaret Kohl. London: SCM Press/Minneapolis: Fortress Press, 1992.

The Coming of God: Christian Eschatology. 1995. Trans. Margaret Kohl. London: SCM Press/Minneapolis: Fortress Press, 1996.

Ethics of Hope. 2010. Trans. Margaret Kohl. Minneapolis: Fortress Press, 2012.

Also:

A Broad Place: An Autobiography. 2006. Trans. Margaret Kohl. Minneapolis: Fortress Press/London: SCM Press, 2008.

Index

123, 125–29, 131, 135, 138, 140,
142, 146, 151, 153–54, ch. 6
(passim), 202, 205, 209, 211, 230,
242, 244–45, 247, 250–51, 256, 275.
See also God, Spirit of; Jesus/Christ,
Spirit of.
and baptism, 131, 135
of the church, 164
of creation, 118, 125–28, 164–65
as divine person, 166–69, 171–96
of faith, 164
"forgetfulness of," 158
formative metaphors of (energy,
space, Gestalt), 166, 172, 176–79,
190, 194
of hope, 51
human, 161–62
kenotic forms of, 167
of life, 5–6, 50, 173–75, 184, 230
of the Lord, 173–74, 242
movement metaphors of (tempest,
fire, love), 172, 179–82
mystical metaphors of (light, water,
fertility), 182–85
personal metaphors of (lord, mother,
judge), 172–75, 186–87
of promise, 163, 205
of redemption, 164–65
of the resurrection, 146, 165, 173
of truth, 174
of the universe, 128
and Word, 158–60
The Spirit of Life, 5, ch. 6 (passim), 202
von Staupitz, Johannes, 220
Steffen, Bernhard, 46
Stirner, Max, 188
subordination/-ism, 85, 87, 89, 96, 129,
161, 166, 192, 195, 253
substance, divine/supreme, 49, 73, 74,
75, 76, 78, 79–82, 85–86, 88–92, 171
suffering, 11, 13, 33, 35, 39, 48–54,
56–62, 68–69, 99, 109–111, 116,
127–28, 132, 134–36, 149, 162,

167–68, 179, 187, 220, 222–23, 233,
244, 266, 276

Teresa of Avila, 269
terror(s), 24, 63, 75, 200, 206, 224, 233,
235, 240–41, 245–46, 248, 272, 274
terrorism/-ist, 134, 234–35, 264
Tersteegen, Gerhard, 276
Tertullian, 79, 87, 89–90, 92, 166, 171
theology, 1–6, 9–10, 19–20, 22–23, 25,
30, 31, 36–39, 41, 43–44, 46, 48,
52–54, 57–61, 65–66, 69, 71–74,
78–79, 83, 88, 92, 94, 98, 100, 104,
106–107, 112, 116, 118, 120, 122,
134, 142, 150, 158, 161–62, 170,
171, 201, 203, 207, 209–10, 215–16,
222–23, 246, 269
"after Auschwitz," 3, 59–60, 63
apathetic, 53, 55–58, 60. *See also*
apatheia; God, apathetic
as communal, 202–203
dialectical, 38–39, 161
doxological, 72, 94–95
ecological, 5, 82, 118–21, 126–27,
129, 165
ethical, 3, 6, 71, 78
Jewish, 4, 53, 57, 124, 202, 230, 253,
270–72. *See also* Judaism/Jewish
tradition.
liberation, 71–72
natural, 44, 79–80
political, 5, 66, 71, 84, 98
Protestant, 41, 78, 158, 164
of revelation, 79–80
Roman Catholic, 74, 164, 169
dogmatic/systematic, 3, 48, 65, 67,
131, 199, 202, 227
trinitarian, 3, 4, 41–56, 60, 62, 66–82,
83–96, 98–101, 118, 120, 125,
127, 161, 167–71, 189–96. *See also*
trinitarian thought/understanding;
Trinity; tritheism; unity, tri-.